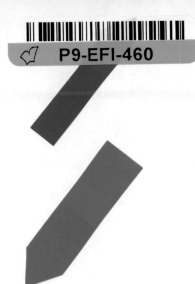

Also by Deborah Tannen

YOU'RE WEARING *THAT*?
Understanding Mothers and Daughters
in Conversation

I ONLY SAY THIS BECAUSE I LOVE YOU
Talking to Your Parents, Partner, Sibs, and Kids
When You're All Adults

THE ARGUMENT CULTURE
Stopping America's War of Words

TALKING FROM 9 TO 5
Women and Men at Work

YOU JUST DON'T UNDERSTAND
Women and Men in Conversation

THAT'S NOT WHAT I MEANT!
How Conversational Style
Makes or Breaks Relationships

You Were Always Mom's Favorite!

Deborah Tannen

You Were Always Mom's Favorite!

Sisters in Conversation Throughout Their Lives

RANDOM HOUSE  NEW YORK

*ELKHART IN
Goodwill
2024
.99*

Published in the United States by Random House, an imprint of
The Random House Publishing Group, a division of Random House, Inc., New York.

RANDOM HOUSE and colophon are registered trademarks of Random House, Inc.

Grateful acknowledgment is made to the following for permission to reprint previously
published material:

ABRAMS ARTISTS AGENCY: Excerpt from *Crimes of the Heart: A Play* by Beth Henley,
copyright © 1982 by Beth Henley. Reprinted by permission of Abrams Artists Agency.

DOUBLEDAY, AN IMPRINT OF THE KNOPF DOUBLEDAY PUBLISHING GROUP: Excerpt from
"White Horse" from *Moral Disorder and Other Stories* by Margaret Atwood, copyright © 2006
by O. W. Toad, Ltd. Rights in Canada are controlled by McClelland & Stewart Ltd.
Reprinted by permission of Doubleday, an imprint of The Knopf Doubleday Publishing Group
and McClelland & Stewart Ltd. Used with permission of the publisher.

FRANCES GOLDIN AGENCY: Excerpt from "I Stand Here Ironing" from *Tell Me a Riddle* by
Tillie Olsen, copyright © 1956, 1957, 1960, 1961 by Tillie Olsen. Reprinted by permission
of Frances Goldin Agency.

HARPERCOLLINS PUBLISHERS: Excerpt from "Rain in Summer" from *The Seven Ages* by
Louise Glück, copyright © 2001 by Louise Glück. Reprinted by permission of
HarperCollins Publishers.

Library of Congress Cataloging-in-Publication Data
Tannen, Deborah.
Your were always mom's favorite!: sisters in conversation
throughout their lives / Deborah Tannen.
p.   cm.
Includes bibliographical references.
ISBN 978-1-4000-6632-2
eBook ISBN 978-1-5883-6913-0
1. Sisters.   2. Communication in the family.
3. Interpersonal communication.   I. Title.
BF723.S43T36   2009   306.875'4—dc22   2009019713

Printed in the United States of America on acid-free paper

www.atrandom.com

2 4 6 8 9 7 5 3 1

First Edition

Book design by Liz Cosgrove

To my sisters

Mimi Tannen
and
Naomi Tannen

Contents

You Were Always Mom's Favorite!

Preface

Visitors to my home always notice the framed black-and-white photograph of my family. Pointing to the two seated little girls identically dressed, they ask, "Which one is you?" I always respond, "Guess!" They guess right about half the time: I'm on the right, my sister Mimi on the left. I love that people can't tell us apart, because in the photo I'm six and she's eight. Then they usually ask about the three adults standing behind us. I explain, "That's my parents and my sister Naomi. She's eight years older than I am." When they look more closely they see how much younger one of the standing women is than the other.

The question, "Which one is you?" is telling. Many sisters ask it of themselves. They can hardly think about who they are without thinking about how they are like or unlike their sisters. A sister is the person you might have been but aren't, by choice or by chance.

The photo also dramatizes the enormous difference that a difference in age makes. A sister close in age is the one you played and fought with; an older sister can be much like a mother. And as with mothers, conversations with sisters can be some of the best and the worst conversations you ever have.

A word from a sister can make you laugh your head off, or giggle and be silly like when you were kids.

A word from a sister can send you into a tailspin because, as one woman put it, "She's part of my being, she's part of the fabric of who I am.

So when there's disapproval, you *feel* it in a place that you don't feel it with other people."

Sisters don't even need words to feel it in that place; sometimes a look is enough.

"You know Sadie doesn't approve of me sometimes," said Bessie Delany of her older sister. "She frowns at me in her big-sister sort of way." When she said this, Bessie Delany was 101 while Sadie was 103. And Sadie said, "I told Bessie that if she lives to 120, then I'll just have to live to 122 so I can take care of her." Sadie explained: "The reason I am living is to keep *her* living."

The Delany sisters' comments encapsulate the way sisters combine, in a uniquely intense way, two dynamics that drive all conversations and all relationships: connection and hierarchy. No one is closer than a sister who shares your family, your past, your memories. That connection is always there, whether you live together your whole lives, as the Delanys did, or see each other rarely or not at all—even if one has passed away. And sisters are also immutably arrayed by age, with resulting differences in influence and power that also endure, in obvious or subtle ways, throughout their lives. Those two dynamics, power and connection, work together and can't be pulled apart: The Delany sisters' lifelong devotion was inseparable from the fact that one was younger and the other older—and therefore protective, and maybe a tad judgmental.

Sisters are inevitably compared to each other, because they are often together and, in any case, are thought of together. Each one's character or personality tends to be described in contrast to the other's: the outgoing one and the shy one; the artist and the athlete; the smart one and the pretty one. And comparison is never far from competition. That too is built into the relationship, because sisters seek support and approval from the same adults, and it can often seem, whether it's true or not, that love and attention given to one depletes what's available for the other. The same is true of brothers, and of sisters and brothers. Indeed, much of what I say about sisters applies to brothers too. I am certain that examples I give of sister conversations will remind many readers of their brothers and of other relationships.

Yet there is a particular texture and special complexity of conversations among sisters, because they are women. Women typically talk to their sisters more often than they talk to their brothers or than brothers talk to one another. Women's conversation is more likely to be about personal topics—either emotionally intense concerns or seemingly trivial details of their day-to-day lives. And talk itself typically plays a greater role in girls' and women's relationships than it does in boys' and men's. Because many women regard the sharing of personal information as a requirement of closeness, sisters often feel left out when they learn of secrets they were not told. But complications and hurt feelings can also result when secrets are revealed.

For all these reasons, conversation is an apt starting point to understand—and improve—relationships among sisters. And understanding conversations among sisters is a window into dynamics that drive all conversations and, hence, all relationships.

The language of conversation has been the focus of my research in linguistics, the study of language. For this book, in addition to analyzing transcripts of recorded conversations, I interviewed well over a hundred women about their sisters—women whose ages spanned late teens to early nineties, and who came from a wide range of ethnic, regional, and cultural backgrounds. Most were American, but some were from other countries. Americans included Asian-Americans, African-Americans, Indian-, Italian-, Irish-, German-, and East-European-Jewish-Americans, and so on. They were straight, gay, Deaf, hearing, married, and single. I made a point of including women of these many backgrounds in order to hear a range of experiences. I did not attempt to compare one group with another or to generalize about any group. Readers should not assume that the women I refer to are white and European-American simply because I haven't identified them otherwise. The chances are excellent that they're not.

A woman told me that a friend, a guy, to whom she frequently talked about her sister, remarked, "Gee, it's like having a serious romantic relationship." He was right; it is. In the same spirit, a woman told me she has a good relationship with her sister but commented, "We work on our relationship, like a marriage." She also said, in exasperation, "Shouldn't there be some relationship in my life that's just *easy*?"

There should be, yes. But there rarely is. A lucky few have relationships with their sisters that are just easy: They enjoy and appreciate each other, no stresses or strains. But the vast majority of sister relationships are like marriages—the source of great solace but also occasional or frequent frustration, irritation, or outright pain. As with marriage, some sisters grow apart or sever ties. But most continue to have contact—and conversations—throughout their lives. And whereas marriages may end in divorce, sisters are sisters forever.

My expertise and my passion are aimed at understanding and explaining how the language of conversation affects and reflects relationships. That understanding in turn yields ways to change and improve them. Many women I interviewed thanked me afterward, saying that our conversation helped them figure out what was going on with their sisters or inspired them to talk to their sisters more often and in new ways. I hope this book will likewise provide readers with insight, and start as well as enhance conversations among sisters.

My own two sisters have always been a cherished part of my life—my whole life, since I'm the youngest. I dedicated my first book to them. The dedication read: "To Naomi and Mimi, my sisters in every sense of the word." Fifteen years later I used the same dedication (with the order of the names reversed). Dedicating a third book to my sisters might seem redundant, but there is no other way this book can be dedicated. And having written it, I understand even more deeply how many senses of the word there are, and how fortunate I am to have these two magnificent women, Mimi Tannen and Naomi Tannen, as my sisters.

CHAPTER ONE

Sisters in Lifelong Conversation

"I love her to death. I can't imagine life without her," a woman says of her sister. Another says of hers, "I want to be around her all the time. She's the only one who knows all kinds of stuff from the past. All we have to do is say one word, and we know when the other one will start laughing." I heard many comments like these from women who told me that their relationships with their sisters are among the most precious aspects of their lives.

I also heard comments like this one: "I don't want anyone to kill my sister because I want to have the privilege of doing that myself."

Though they sound so different, these remarks have something in common: the intensity of feelings behind them. Sister relationships are among the most passionate of our lives. One woman explained, "My relationship with my sister is more deeply emotional than any other." Yet another, after telling me ways her sister had hurt her—tales of betrayal that made me wonder why she still talks to the perpetrator at all—said, "No matter how difficult my sister is, she is still part of me, part of my past, my present, and my future." Then she added, echoing the comment I quoted at the start: "Love her or hate her, I can't imagine life without her."

Conversations with sisters can spark extremes of anger or extremes of love. Everything said between sisters carries meaning not only from what was just said but from all the conversations that came before—and "before" can span a lifetime. The layers of meaning combine profound connection with equally profound competition. Both the competition and the connection are complicated by inevitable comparison with someone whose life has been so similar to yours and yet so different—and always in your view.

What's Ideal, What's Real?

I was chatting with four women at a party. As we talked, we gradually sat down, then drew our chairs into a circle. The other party guests looked on with curiosity or envy as our tight little group erupted in laughter or rippled with a wave of knowing nods. I had brought up the topic of sisters. Laxmi, a woman visiting from India, was extolling hers. "When we meet we can't get enough of each other," she said. "When we ride in a car together, my husband threatens, 'I'm taking another car! You two never stop talking and laughing!' She's my lifeline. I'm her lifeline. If I say one word, she knows what I'm going to say. We've made a pact that we'll take a vacation together at least once a year." Another woman in our group remarked sadly, "That's why I always wished I had a sister." I wanted to learn more about this wonderful sister relationship, so before the party ended I arranged to interview Laxmi one on one.

The following week, Laxmi and I sat down in private. The first thing she told me was that she had recently gone through a year during which she refused to speak to her sister. When their parents died, she explained, she and her sister had together inherited a building composed of two apartments; each sister owned one. Laxmi wanted to sell her apartment, but she realized that the value of her sister's would go down if she sold hers separately; they would both get a better price if they put the entire building on the market. But her sister wasn't ready to sell, so Laxmi tabled the idea and went away for an extended visit to her daughter, who lived abroad. When she returned, she discovered that her sister had changed her mind about selling her apartment—and had gone ahead and sold it. Now it was Laxmi whose apartment had plummeted in value. As difficult as this financial loss was for her, what Laxmi couldn't forgive was that her sister had robbed Laxmi's children of part of their inheritance, since the profit from selling Laxmi's apartment would eventually go to them. Her anger and hurt were so great, she could not bear to speak to her sister. But after a year she decided to let it go. She had only one sister and did not want to lose her.

Hearing this story, I wished I could go back to the party and tell the woman who longed for a sister that the ideal she'd heard Laxmi describe—someone to talk to and laugh with, who knows exactly what you mean and what you are going to say, a lifeline—was real, but it wasn't the whole story. A sister is someone who owns part of what you own: a house, perhaps, or a less tangible legacy, like memories of your childhood and the experience of your family. The way she manages that shared inheritance can either raise or lower its value for you—or call its value into question.

Sisterspeak

The word "sister" evokes an ideal of connection and support, like the friendships that made Rebecca Wells's *Divine Secrets of the Ya-Ya Sisterhood* and Ann Brashares's *The Sisterhood of the Traveling Pants* into bestselling novels and successful films. The friendships referred to in these titles are called "sisterhood" because the friends stuck together through thick and thin, understood each other when no one else did, and supported one another while marching arm in arm to the same music. Part of the reason these books and movies were so popular is that we all yearn to belong to a group with a bond like that. As one woman put it, "Friends are the sisters we were meant to have." Many women told me they have friends who are "sister surrogates" or "sister equivalents." They used the word "sister" to characterize what they prize in those friends.

Even the sound of the word "sister" is comforting, with its soothing s's. (The *b* of "brother" sounds more abrupt.) We have sister cities, sister universities, and, in biology, sister cells. Sister cities and universities establish mutually enriching associations based on shared characteristics like similar size. Sister cells are identical because they have split from the same "mother" cell. Sister cities are not at each other's throats; sister universities are not so named because they know exactly how to get the other's goat; sister cells don't fight over who gets the slice of cake with the buttercream rose. But these less-appealing traits can also be aspects of real-life sisterhood.

At a group gathered to talk with me, a woman said she and her sister use the term "sisterspeak" for the kind of talk they treasure and trust from each other: talk that sets the other straight. Another woman who was present chimed in: "Yeah yeah! Your sister will tell you in a way a friend can't and even a mother can't." The first continued: A sister can ask, "What were you thinking?" and force you to answer, to yourself as well as to her, "I wasn't!"

But in another setting I heard a different view: A woman commented that sisters should be called "the liars' club" because they tell each other only a version of the truth. She explained why she can't tell her sister the whole truth: "I have to be cautious about sharing my feelings, hopes, and dreams because they invariably get translated into something that will come back to hurt me. When I have met people who know about me through my sister, they are often surprised and tell me that I'm nothing like the person she described."

These two views—someone who sets you straight or someone who twists your words so they boomerang back and hurt you—represent the potential best and worst of sister conversations. And it's not always clear which type of sisterspeak your sister is speaking.

Talking Straight—or Bent?

Natalie was thrilled; she had joined Weight Watchers and stuck with it. The extra pounds she'd put on were finally falling away. Each week when she weighed in, her spirits soared as the numbers on the scale went down. Everyone told her how great she looked—except her sister Alex. "You're losing too much weight," Alex said. "You don't look healthy. Look at how your collarbones stick out." Alex's observation was accurate. When Natalie looked in the mirror, she did see her collarbones clearly defined. It was one of the changes that had given her pleasure. But now she wasn't sure if she should be pleased or not. Was Alex giving her the gift of sisterspeak: telling her the truth when no one else would? Or was it sisterspeak of another sort: tinged with envy, eager to slow her down when she got too far ahead?

A sister is the one person you can brag to—or the one you'll never tell about your triumphs because she'd be jealous. She's the one you can call in the middle of the night when you can't sleep, or the one who doesn't want to hear about your problems unless you're ready to *do* something about them. She's the one who's there when you need her, or the one whose absence in a crisis hurts most. A sister is the person who knows exactly what it was like to grow up in the home you grew up in, with the parents you knew as your own. But she can also be the one who tells you that what you recall is all in your head; she was there and she doesn't remember it that way.

In telling me how her sister frustrates her, Doris remarked, "She accuses me of having said things I never said." Later Doris commented, "She denies having said things that I know she said." Her sister, I surmise, would have the same two complaints about Doris, with the examples reversed. Reality denied for one is false accusation for the other. When memories differ about minor events, small details, it's no big deal. You may shrug your shoulders or even laugh. But if the differing recollections are facts of your life that cut to the core of who you think you are, a sister's insistence that you've got it wrong can make you feel as if the ground on which you stand is shaking. And when you make a good-natured joke and your sister takes offense, or accuses you of bad intentions when you know you meant well, it hurts more than when a stranger or even a friend misinterprets your meaning. It's a violation of the very definition of sister; it's not the way the world—and your family—is supposed to be.

We'll Be There

Every day we face challenges, some large, some tiny. It helps to have someone we can turn to for advice or reassurance—or just to say she understands and cares. Talking to women about their sisters, and reading about sisters, was inspiring, as I heard innumerable accounts of sisters supporting each other in words, in deeds, or just by being there.

I read accounts of dire circumstances where sisters literally kept each other alive by their mutual presence. A Dutch woman who was with Anne Frank and her sister Margot in a concentration camp provides two examples, her own and Anne Frank's, with starkly different endings. Janny Brandes-Brilleslijper became gravely ill with typhus, but she survived because she kept herself going in order to keep her sister, who was even sicker, alive. "Anne was sick, too," she recalls, "but she stayed on her feet until Margot died; only then did she give in to her illness."

Few of us confront circumstances this desperate, but I heard many moving accounts of sisters coming through in times of crisis. Joy, for example, drew courage from her sisters' presence when she underwent emergency surgery to save her life. It had happened suddenly: One moment Joy was walking down the street, the next thing she knew she was regaining consciousness in a hospital bed. "When I woke up," Joy recalls, "my three sisters were standing there, side by side, like linebackers." Joy knew instantly that something serious had happened to her, because none of her sisters lived in the same city she did; one had come from Boston, one from Kansas City, one all the way from Africa. And they stayed with Joy until she was out of danger. Having them there gave her courage to endure grueling medical procedures. "My temperature went up and they couldn't get it down," Joy said, "so they put me in an ice cube. It was the most miserable I've ever been, a plastic tube that has ice in it; they pump cold water into it. I thought, I can't go through this. They said, 'We'll spend the night with you. If you wake up, we'll be there.' And that made me feel, Hey, I can get through this."

Joy also described ways that she and her sisters help each other out that are not emergencies. Joy's field is education. She encouraged her youngest sister, to whom academic work didn't come naturally, not only to go to college but eventually to get a master's degree. Joy found the right program and invited her sister to stay with her while pursuing it. For her part, Joy was able to do the research required for her own academic career because her sisters helped care for her children during summers while she did her own work. And here's a final image I love: Joy has neither time nor talent to shop for clothes, so once each year she travels to Boston and stays with the sister who has an eye for fashion and knows all the outlet stores. Together they spend two days outfitting Joy for the year, while a third sister watches their children.

When women told me they'd always wished they had a sister, they were thinking of this ideal of mutual encouragement and support. Many of those who have sisters also yearn for this ideal, because their relationships with their sisters don't always live up to it. Idealized images make it harder to accept—and find ways to address—the frustrations that are as common among sisters as in any close relationship. The ideal is the connection that links Joy and her sisters. But there is another dynamic between sisters that is equally fundamental: competition.

Cinderella's Sisters

If "sister" is code for close and supportive, it can also be code for the opposite. James Reason and Deborah Lucas, psychologists who study memory, coined the term "ugly sisters" to refer to the wrong words or names that come to mind when you're trying to find the right ones. For example, in trying to recall the film title *Deliverance,* James Reason kept coming up with "intemperance" and "intolerance." The term "ugly sisters" invokes the metaphor of Cinderella's stepsisters trying to squeeze their too-large feet into Cinderella's glass slipper, thereby delaying the heroine's reunion with her prince, just as a wrong word or name interferes with your search for the word you want. The researchers find the term apt because her stepsisters share a familial connection with Cinderella, much as the wrong word that annoyingly intrudes usually bears a family resemblance in structure, meaning, or sound to the word you wanted to say.

In choosing the metaphor "ugly sisters," the authors assumed that sisters are rivals locked in bitter competition if not outright enemies. That assumption is common across cultures and time. Folklorist Maria Tatar notes that nearly every known culture has tales in which one sister treats another like a servant, tries to get what is hers, or even kills her. (In the Grimms' version we know, Cinderella's tormentors are her stepsisters, daughters of her father's second wife. But in folklore as in the memory researchers' metaphor, they are often referred to simply as "sisters." Tatar points out that folktales typically used step relations as a more acceptable way to portray "the animosity sometimes felt for biological parents and siblings.") According to Tatar, the first known Cinderella figure was Yeh-hsien, the heroine of a tale recorded in China around A.D. 850. Like Cinderella, Yeh-hsien was subjugated, mistreated, and forced to do household drudgery by her stepsisters. She too is rescued by a magic creature, in her case a ten-foot-long fish, while her stepsisters are killed by flying stones. Though the specifics of this tale are foreign to us, the sisterly rivalry is familiar.

It's revealing that Reason and Lucas added the adjective "ugly" to their metaphoric term. In the Grimms' tale, Cinderella's sisters are not ugly. *The Annotated Brothers Grimm* describes them as having "beautiful faces and fair skin." After all, only beautiful ladies were invited to the palace as potential brides for the prince. Recasting the evil sisters as ugly brings the Cinderella story in line with many other legends and tales in which undesirable women are physically unattractive, while desirable women are beautiful. In the biblical story of Rachel and Leah, Jacob falls in love with Rachel, the younger sister, because she is "beautiful and well favoured," though her father tricks him into marrying her older sister, Leah. There is also a folk song, "The Two Sisters," with a long history and a strikingly similar theme. Folksinger Peggy Seeger found four U.S. versions, and she traces the song to an old folk story found throughout the world. Though the details differ, the story is constant: A knight "loved the youngest" but "courted the eldest" who "much envied her sister fair"—and expressed that envy by drowning her. The archetypal female competition to marry the prince represents a fundamental aspect of sisters.

In the Bible story and the folk song—and in many other tales from legend and popular culture—the preferred sister is not only prettier but also younger. A contemporary example is Laura Esquivel's novel and the film based on it, *Like Water for Chocolate,* a tragic love story in which a man marries a woman only to get closer to her younger sister, the one he truly loves. In all these stories, it isn't her absolute age that makes one sister more desirable, but her age relative to her sister's.

These stories from literature and lore underscore that sisters' inevitable differences in appearance and age can contribute to rivalry and competition. In another sense, though, they are using sisters symbolically to represent the universal human dynamic, competition. Both connection and competition are forces that drive all relationships, but they are especially intense—and easy to see—among sisters, where proximity, shared history, and the built-in hierarchy of age set these dynamics in stark relief. In Chapter Two I delve more deeply into connection and comparison, while in Chapter Three I explore competition and the hierarchy of relative age. But these two dynamics are not separate; they work together in every interaction—and every conversation—between sisters.

Who's Counting?

Sisters are inescapably in competition even as they are companions traveling down the same road. I used to say to my parents, with a glimmer of humor, that they obviously meant more to me than I did to them because they had three daughters, but I had only one mother and one father. Though I said this with a smile, it was true: All my filial devotion and love went to them, whereas their parental care had to be distributed among three children. In families with more than one child, each additional child necessarily limits the available resources—time and attention as well as money. Limited resources make competition inevitable, and whenever there is competition it makes sense to try to weaken or even eliminate rivals.

There are nonhuman species for whom destructive impulses toward siblings are instinctive—and deadly. Among some bird species, second eggs are laid as backups, needed only if the first hatchling dies. If the first-hatched chick is healthy and hale, one of its jobs when the second egg hatches is to push the newcomer out of the nest. The second chick's death is necessary to ensure the first chick's survival. Some tadpoles eat their siblings when food is scarce; sand tiger shark embryos eat their siblings in the womb; and twin spotted hyena cubs, if they're the same sex, fight furiously while still in the burrow where they were born until one submits to the other—and may die from malnourishment or inflicted wounds. Competition among human siblings rarely takes such extreme forms, but it is unavoidable—and may show itself in subtle as well as obvious ways.

As a gift for their parents, Meghan and June hired a professional photographer to take pictures of themselves and their families. When the proofs arrived, Meghan lamented that she looked dreadful in every one. June assured her that she looked just fine, and the sisters framed one of the photos and presented it to their parents. But for years after, when June visited their parents and saw the photograph displayed, she felt a guilty satisfaction: satisfaction because Meghan really did look bad while she herself looked great, guilty because she should have acknowledged this at the time and insisted they retake the photos.

Photographs are a frequent focus of competition, because they seem to represent—in a tangible way—attention and even love. The number of photographs of each child tends to descend with the child's position in the family: the younger the child, the fewer the photographs—till the youngest finds that photos of her siblings far outnumber those of herself. And the pattern can continue into adulthood. Tamara was happy for her two older siblings when they got married and had beautiful weddings. But she was less happy with the aftermath: Wedding photographs featuring her sister and brother sprouted on every surface of her parents' home like weeds in an untended garden.

Tamara is not unusual in feeling slighted by this imbalance. Sisters often scrutinize and compare photographs in their parents' home: How many are there of each one, how big are they, how prominently are they displayed? Sisters who have children of their own are likewise aware of how many photos their parents have of each sister's kids. In earnest or in jest, they may shift photos around. A picture of you got pushed to the back, while one of your sister crept forward. And in the photo montage adorning the refrigerator, the photo of your kids that used to be at eye level has mysteriously moved to the bottom or somehow got covered by a photo of your sister's children. The photo contest is an expression of competition but also of connection: it's tempting to compare pictures because they're arrayed together in the same place, just as siblings are compared because they're grouped in the same family.

It Begins at the Beginning

The ties that link sisters—ties of connection and also of competition—are rooted in their shared past. When we're children, our parents and siblings make up our worlds. Though our worlds ostensibly widen when we're adults, on some level we still live in our childhoods and our childhoods live on in us.

"When I'm around my sister I feel like a child again," many women told me, "and I act like one too!" Feeling like a child again can be a joy. It's a delight to be called by your childhood nickname, to crack up over nothing, to be silly together just like when you were kids, because that kid is who you still are inside. The physical signs of adulthood—and later the wrinkles, graying hair, and extra weight of advancing age—are nothing but a mask hiding who you really are. It's a relief to let your childhood self— your real self—show and to live in it again.

My student Hannah Yates sees this happen right before her eyes when her mother gets together with her three sisters, Hannah's aunts:

When my mom is around her sisters, she seems so much younger (and happier): she gets defensive and excited about things she is usually calm about, she gets teased (and puts up with it!), she gives them birthday cards that are incredibly immature, and occasionally I'll even catch her making a mischievous look—the kind I make when I'm preparing to push my brother's buttons.

Because her mother has sisters, Hannah gets a glimpse of what she was like as a girl.

On the other hand, there may be aspects of your childhood that you'd as soon not experience again. Just *talking* about her sisters, one woman said, made her feel like a kid again—in a way she didn't like. It can hurt to be hurled back to a time when you felt incompetent or believed you were required to be supercompetent; when you felt invisible around your sister because she was older and more capable or younger and more adorable; because she was always perfect or always in trouble; because she was smarter or prettier or more outgoing or had a disability. For any of a myriad reasons, many women felt that beside a sister, they got smaller and weaker or disappeared.

"I'm Here Too!"

We all want to be listened to, to be seen for who we really are—by the world but especially by our families. That's why the comments "She gets me" and "She knows what I'm going to say when I say just one word" capture what many women cherish in their sisters. But the opposite experience is also common. It's painful when your sister doesn't listen or listens but misunderstands, when she doesn't look at you or looks but doesn't see the person you believe yourself to be.

Marge has a successful career, a happy marriage, and grown children she gets along with well. But when she is with her sister, she feels like an awkward adolescent again. Despite the reinforcement she derives from her work, her family, and her friends, being around her sister makes her feel that she needs one last stamp of approval—a stamp she never gets. To her own puzzlement as well as frustration, she keeps striving for it. For example, when a book she wrote was published, she eagerly showed it to her sister, who remarked, "Gee, I've never heard of that press. How will anyone find it?" Marge wondered why she reacted so strongly to this small comment. Her reaction drew intensity from her childhood, when her sister's accomplishments always seemed more impressive than hers. She felt like a little girl stamping her foot and demanding, "Me too! I matter! Look at me!"

Irene had a similar experience. She was excited because she was interviewed on a local television station when an after-school program she'd been working to establish was about to begin. She told everyone close to her when and where the show would air, so they could watch. Her friends called or texted to say she'd been great, to congratulate her on the project, and to compliment her on how she looked on TV. But her sister Rae didn't call, so Irene called her. "Rae," she began in anticipation, "what did you think?" "About what?" Rae asked. "About my TV interview," Irene said. "Oh," Rae replied. "I forgot to watch." Irene's heart sank. It felt as if Rae had forgotten on purpose, so she wouldn't have to witness Irene's success. And if her sister didn't see it, somehow the recognition meant less.

Perhaps Marge's sister is inclined to minimize Marge's accomplishments, and Irene's sister resists being a bystander to Irene's, to protect themselves from the stab of jealousy that one woman admitted—with chagrin—she feels when her sisters are successful (even though she would do anything for them). And this impulse may spring from their shared history. When they were children, attention paid to one really did mean less available for the other. The inclination to downplay a sister's achievements may be a leftover of childhood reality. Competition can be habit-forming.

On the other hand, their shared past adds meaning and satisfaction when sisters acknowledge and celebrate one another's success, as they often do. And after parents are gone, sisters can embody their parents' approval. When a woman was appointed to a prestigious position, her sister gave her as a gift an antique bowl that had been passed down from their grandmother to their mother to her. In a note she explained that she was giving the bowl to her sister because their mother and grandmother would have been so proud of her. Because they shared those forebears, her sister had the power to bring them—and their pride and approval—with her into the room.

Same Family—or Is It?

For many sisters, competition is muted or was never significant. But just about all sisters experience competition's cousin: comparison. Each person is an individual, each person's life unique. Yet given the connection of shared family and history, it's impossible not to think of your life in comparison to your sister's. A sister is like yourself in a different movie, a movie that stars you in a different life.

We all feel wistfulness or real regret about roads not taken—choices we made or choices we didn't have. We may think of them often or from time to time. But if a sister took the road we rejected, or a road we never had the chance to take, we are continually reminded of the landscape those roads traversed and the destinations to which they led. That repeated reminder of what we missed may cause us to feel more deprived (or gleeful) than we otherwise would. Differences in where we ended up or in the opportunities we had may seem unfair, because we were born into the same family. But in a way that's an illusion: It was a different family when each of us was born.

There are innumerable ways that families change with time. Parents change: their ages, their jobs, their relationships to each other, their states of mind. Financial conditions change: There's more money or less because of personal factors or economic developments in the world at large. Locations change: Families move to a bigger or smaller house, a different town, across the country or the ocean. And the arrival of a new child in itself transforms the circumstances of and dynamics among family members. For these and many other reasons, different choices are available to each child, and the same choice has difference consequences.

I was talking to two sisters together. As they told me about their lives, it emerged that Renee, the older, had attended Spelman College in Atlanta, whereas Jill, the younger, had attended Howard University. Because Howard is in their native Washington, D.C., Jill continued living at home through her college years. After telling me this, Jill said, "That's the only thing I regret, not going away to college." She then explained how it came about. Though her older sister and an older brother had gone to college out of town, when her turn came, their mother lamented, "All my children are leaving. I'm not going to have anybody here!" She told Jill that if she stayed home and attended Howard, she'd give her a new car. This was an offer an eighteen-year-old couldn't refuse. Though Howard University was fine, Jill said, she envied her sister and brother because "they got to go away." Then she added, "But I could have gone away. I could have stood my ground. I could have said, 'No, Mom. I don't want a car. I want to go away.'" Her sister Renee agreed: "Yeah, you could have." But Renee also pointed out that their mother had made it easy for her to leave: "My mother was the one who told me about Spelman. She said, 'Why don't you try Spelman?'"

Jill and Renee had the same mother, but in a way they had different mothers: They had mothers who guided them in different directions. When Renee attended college in a distant city, she was following rather than going against her mother's wishes. Jill could have rejected the car and attended Spelman or another out-of-town college, but had she done so, she would have been disappointing her mother. It's not that their mother capriciously encouraged one and discouraged the other from the same path. The order of their birth was an immutable circumstance that made leaving home a different act for each of them. Home was a different place when each one's high school years came to an end.

Here's Looking at You

I have no doubt that Jill decided to attend Howard not only because she was bribed by the offer of a car but also because she wanted to avoid causing her mother pain. I am certain of this, because Jill's experience reminded me of my own. After graduating from college, I worked long enough to save money to travel to Europe and ended up teaching English in Greece. I returned briefly to the United States but soon decided that Greece was where I wanted to be. I headed back for an indefinite stay, traveling by ship so I could take more belongings with me than an airplane would allow. I can remember waking up of a morning in Athens, wondering for a moment where I was and feeling elated when I realized I had done it. I was living in Greece.

But there is also another image I associate with that period of my life, an image that is still painful to recall. My mother had tried everything she could think of to dissuade me from returning to Greece. So it was a cruel irony that she, and only she, accompanied me to the Manhattan pier from which my ship would depart. Once aboard the ship, I stood at the railing and waved goodbye. The sight of my mother standing alone on the shore as she waved back tore at my heart; even now, it hurts to describe this scene. I felt as if my Greek adventure, exciting as it was for me, was purchased at the cost of my mother's happiness. And to make my leaving her even crueler, I was setting sail on her birthday.

There was a sense in which I truly was abandoning my mother by moving abroad, as Jill would have been abandoning hers had she gone to college out of town. By the time I traveled to Greece, my two sisters were married and had long since left home. When they left, I was still there, so their departures did not empty the nest. Only mine did that. In some cultures, it is assumed that the youngest daughter will remain unmarried so she can stay with her parents and care for them as they age. That was the reason the heroine in *Like Water for Chocolate,* set in early-twentieth-century Mexico, could not marry the man she loved. Few Americans expect such a sacrifice, but there is no way to escape the difference between moving out when younger siblings still live at home and being the last to leave. The image of sailing off as my mother stood alone on the shore could stand for what happens whenever the last child (or an only child) grows up and leaves home. It's a poignant example of how the same family is different for each sister, and what seems like the same choice is really a very different one.

We all make decisions we later regret. But it's likely that Jill thought about her college choice more often because Renee had made a different one. In my family too, the choice of college became a source of lingering regret, though the role played by age was reversed. My oldest sister, Naomi, often says she envies me one thing: I went away to college while she didn't. When Naomi graduated from high school, she had no option other than attending one of the free New York City colleges and continuing to live with our parents. By the time I graduated, our family's financial situation had improved. A scholarship paid my tuition, and I worked in the cafeteria to earn spending money, but my parents paid $1,000 each year for my room and board. That was $1,000 more than had been available eight years earlier. I have no doubt that Naomi would have regretted missing out on the opportunity to attend an out-of-town college in any case.

But surely her college experience came to appear more disappointing in comparison to mine.

Comparison is an unavoidable consequence of the connection between sisters. There is no equal protection clause in the family constitution.

It's My Life—and Yours

Comparison isn't the only reason that sisters have strong feelings about each other's choices. Because of the connection between them, the decisions one makes can affect or even transform the other's life. A common and striking example is the decision to move out of the family home or to move far away temporarily or permanently.

Many of us harbor two opposite impulses. One is to stay put, rooted in the place where we were born and raised, close to the people we knew as children: parents, other relatives, and friends. The other impulse is to leave: uproot ourselves from all that's familiar, discover other worlds, escape what we don't like about the place where we grew up or the people we grew up with. One urge calls us to follow an unfamiliar path; the other pulls us home. If you stayed close to home and your sister traveled far, or if you made the break while your sister stayed, she is a constant reminder of the lure of the life you didn't live. She's the side of yourself that may have been tempted—or frightened—by that other life. The way you respond to her—any combination of emotions including admiration, envy, disapproval, and disdain—can reflect how you regard the life she chose and you didn't. And, most important, the choice she makes changes your life too.

When siblings leave home for any reason—to attend school, marry, take a job, or just live on their own—the worlds of those left behind are transformed. Sometimes a sister left alone with her parents is thrilled: no more teasing, fights over nothing, sharing parents' attention. Maybe she finally gets her own room. Or maybe she at last gets heard. A mother told me that when her older child left for college, she discovered that the younger one could talk. Often, though, the one left behind feels bereft, as I did when my sister Mimi married. In some cases, the effect of an older sister's departure on a younger one can be devastating, as when a parent is abusive and a child is left to absorb a double dose of abuse. Whatever the circumstances, when older sisters leave because they made a decision about their own lives, their younger siblings' lives change utterly.

Resentment toward a sister who moved out or moved away can linger and leak out in unexpected ways. Bernice was reminded of this when she was talking to her sister about their parents, who had passed away many years before. At one point their recollections differed. Because the conversation had been casual, Bernice was caught off guard by the hint of accusation when her sister said, "You left." Bernice was surprised by that resentment, because more than four decades had passed since she'd married and "left." But there's a fundamental difference that might explain why her sister remembers more keenly than she does. She made the decision to marry; her sister had no choice in being left behind.

The impact of one sister's departure on the life of another is particularly significant as their parents or other relatives get older and need more help. The one who lives nearest usually gets the lion's share of responsibility for providing that help. Since she did not choose that distinction, her resentment might seep out in seemingly unrelated conversation—to the surprise and dismay of the one who went away.

Lillian and Vera are sisters who are also best friends. But when they talk on the phone, Vera, who still lives near their parents, sometimes makes barbed comments about Lillian's decision to live in a distant city. Vera said, for example, "You're away. We don't know what you're doing there. You could be doing anything." Lillian was hurt, not because she thought her sister was accusing her of doing something unsavory, but becasue she felt sideswiped when she thought they were merrily driving along on parallel tracks. And when Vera said, "We don't know," she was merging herself with their parents, as if the three of them are a unit while Lillian stands alone, like the cheese in the children's game. Lillian feels closely connected to Vera. That connection is what gives Vera's words the power to wound. At the same time, Vera also is gaining points in the competition for closeness to their parents. A layer of competition can be superimposed on a bedrock of sisterly connection.

You Did It on Purpose

The balance between rivalry and connection varies from one sister pair to another, and from one time to another between the same pair. Rivalry *is* a kind of connection, and it can rear its head on occasions when sister-support dominates.

Shirley is waiting for Mona to call and tell her what time they will meet. Her frustration is mounting; she has been trying to pin her sister down for days, but Mona wasn't sure when she'd be able to get out, didn't know if she'd need to drop her son off at soccer practice, didn't know what traffic would be like. Mona did finally call. They met up and had a terrific day together. Shirley's irritation dissipated as soon as she saw and embraced her sister. But this is the kind of frustration, especially if it's habitual, that can cause someone to say, "I love her to death but she drives me crazy." And either Shirley or Mona might say this. Shirley likes to know in advance exactly what's in store on a given day, but Mona prefers to make decisions at the last possible moment. One feels like she's being jerked around, the other feels subject to unreasonable demands.

Any two people who have these divergent styles will frustrate each other. But with friends it's easier to dismiss the inconvenience: "Oh, Meryl's always late" or "You know Chloe; she'll be there half an hour early." With a sister it's harder, because it's been going on forever. Your paths—and your styles—cross more often, so each new instance reminds you of the irritation you felt so many times before. And closeness itself breeds discontent. A sister's quirks can get on your nerves much like a spouse's or lover's—not only the habit of being early or late but insignificant aspects of style, like a tendency to lecture or pile on details, to use fancy words or use words incorrectly. Because a sister is family, it feels as if she represents you to the world; anything she does or is reflects back on you.

There's also another reason that a sister's clashing style can be more rather than less annoying than the same inconvenience caused by a friend. With sisters it's hard not to suspect that causing you frustration might not be an unintended consequence of different styles but an intended one. For your part, you may be aware that frustrating your sister causes you less concern than frustrating a friend, because you know your sister will forgive you no matter what. A friend might stop being your friend, but a sister can't stop being your sister. And if you dig down even deeper, you might find a tiny impulse—or a not-so-tiny one—urging you to frustrate your sister because of all the times she frustrated you.

Laurie was driving to meet a friend at a restaurant she hadn't been to before, and she was lost. It wasn't that she had failed to follow the directions she'd been given. She was lost because she *was* following them, and they were leading her astray. Her sister had given her the directions, and, though she knew it was irrational, Laurie felt as if her sister had done this on purpose! Even after she found the restaurant, her anger continued to simmer. No matter how hard she tried to reason with herself, she couldn't shake the feeling that sending her on a wild goose chase was exactly what her sister had wanted to do. This feeling didn't negate or lessen the love she felt for her sister, nor did it make them any less close. It was just a part of being sisters. Sister-suspicion can coexist with sister-support.

Who Cares?

Knowing that there can be competition as well as deep connection and love, sisters may suspect slights when none exist. Separating messages from metamessages in conversation can help dispel unnecessary hurts.

We sometimes tell each other directly how much we care. Many sisters routinely end phone conversations by saying "I love you." But whether or not those words are spoken, we gauge how much others care not through messages but through metamessages. Messages are meanings of the words spoken; anyone with a dictionary and grammar book can decipher them. Metamessages are meanings we glean from the way things are said, the fact that they're said, or what is not said. Every word spoken has meaning on both levels. Whenever we talk to someone we're close to, we're listening for and sending metamessages about the relationship. But we don't always agree on what they are, and the metamessages heard are not always the ones intended. This was the case with Janet and her sister Noreen.

Noreen told Janet that something was bothering her. Janet was surprised because she hadn't noticed anything wrong. Noreen explained: Janet frequently attends formal events and owns quite a few evening gowns; she has remarked to her sister more than once that she probably will never wear most of them again. Noreen had never attended such events, so she had no gown to wear to her first and probably her last gala. Yet Janet never offered to lend her sister a gown, so Noreen had to buy one in a secondhand store. Janet was speechless. She had no idea that Noreen had wanted to borrow a gown. "Of course you could have borrowed one of my gowns," Janet assured her. "I'd have been more than happy to lend you one. But you never asked." Noreen responded, "I was waiting for you to offer."

Janet felt as if she'd failed a test she hadn't known she was taking. Even worse, it felt like she'd been set up to fail, because there was no way she could have known what her sister wanted. There was no doubt in her mind that Noreen's complaint was unreasonable. But was it? Yes, if you think only of messages: the loan of an evening gown. But if you think about metamessages, Noreen's view makes sense. Offering to lend a gown would provide Noreen not only something to wear but also evidence that her sister is thinking about her welfare. If Noreen asked to borrow one, she would get the gown but not the metamessage. In fact, she'd get the opposite metamessage: Her sister isn't watching out for her so she has to look out for herself.

Some people think it's manipulative to expect others to know what you want if you don't tell them. To others, it's rude—and unnecessary—to state what you want; anyone who cares about you will put herself in your place and know automatically what you need or want. Both assumptions send the metamessage "I love you," but they do it in different—and mutually exclusive—ways. One assumes, "We're family; you'll ask." The other assumes, "We're family; you'll know." When sisters make these contrasting assumptions, each hears a metamessage that wasn't sent. If being family means asking outright, then waiting for an offer pushes you away. If being family means not having to ask, then waiting for a direct request pushes you away.

Metamessages account for why a remark that would roll off your back if someone else made it sets you off when it comes from your sister—or sets her off when it comes from you. You think you're having a fine conversation; then all of a sudden you're having an argument. I've heard this puzzlement from both sides. One whose anger is often sparked said of her sister, "She's the only person who knows the one thing to say that will push my buttons. I get this automatic reaction; I don't even know why." Equally puzzled is the sister who says that "one thing."

A woman told me she's baffled and hurt because her sister gets so angry when she makes jokes or remarks. It's the level of anger that catches her off guard. She admitted that her remarks sometimes have "an edge" but, she said, "not *that* much of an edge." There's the crux. It doesn't take much of an edge to upset a sister who is listening for metamessages of approval from someone whose opinion of her counts so much. Any metamessage of criticism—real or perceived, major or tiny—cuts to the core. A sister can crave approval as the forest craves rain, so even a hint of disapproval may start a conflagration like the tiniest spark in a parched forest. That's why a sister's anger may be disproportionate in response to a comment that has "not *that* much of an edge."

The disproportionate anger is sending a metamessage too. If you think of the question "Do you care?" the metamessage of her anger is the answer: "I care very much, very much indeed."

Not Who Does It but Who Decides

The overarching question "Do you care?" directly addresses the connection between sisters. Another question that is hovering over everything said in any relationship, but especially between sisters, is "Who's in charge?" This question addresses the hierarchy that comes with differences in age. Here, too, listening for metamessages is key.

"Mom's got an appointment to see the eye doctor Thursday afternoon," Loretta tells her sister Mara on the phone. "I thought maybe you could take her." Mara replies, "I'm sorry, I can't. I have a commitment I can't get out of." So Loretta takes their mother to the doctor. Though she loves her mother and is generally happy to help her as needed, she also feels angry at her sister. How come Loretta can rearrange her schedule for their mother's appointments, but Mara never can? Loretta also pays their mother's bills and makes sure that items she needs are in her refrigerator and items that have spoiled are not. She's glad to do these things, but sometimes she's exasperated that her sister doesn't do more. Surely taking their mother to the doctor is the least Mara can do.

At first glance, Loretta is clearly right. But if we move up a level, from the message to the metamessage, things look different. The doctor visit is the message. But there is also a metamessage: Loretta was operating like a boss assigning tasks to an underling. She decided that doctor visits are what Mara should take on. And she made the appointment, which means more work for her but also that she chose the time. This metamessage could explain, at least in part, why Mara resists doing it.

How else could Loretta have handled this situation? One possibility would be to sit down with Mara, together list the tasks their mother's care entails, and then have each one identify those she feels she can do. If doctor visits are among the tasks Mara chooses, she should also make the appointments. That way, she can choose times that fit her schedule or decide which commitments she's willing to break. The message would be the same: taking her mother to the doctor, but the metamessage would be different: "I'm a good daughter" instead of "I drop everything and hop to when my sister calls." Thinking about metamessages rather than messages makes Mara's response easier to understand. That understanding in turn gives Loretta more control: She can prompt a different response in her sister by talking differently herself.

I Can't Believe She Said That!

Taking metamessages into account makes it possible to see how something your sister says may be in part a response to what you said to her. This gives you the power to change how she talks to you by altering the way you talk to her. Even if that's not possible, understanding metamessages can shed light on what previously seemed inexplicable, dispelling the puzzlement if not the dismay.

Let's look closely at a conversation between two sisters and trace the source of a comment that seems to come out of nowhere. The example comes from a conversation recorded and transcribed by Leslie Cochrane in connection with a graduate seminar I taught.

Shannon lives several hours' drive from the city where she grew up, and where her sister Carrie and their parents still live. Shannon visits as often as she can, but she would visit more often if she could stay overnight, which she'd do if there were a way to put her small daughter safely to bed. Their mother told Shannon that Carrie would bring over a crib she no longer needed, to be kept in the guest room for Shannon to use when she visits. But Carrie kept putting off delivering the crib: She didn't have time; it was hard to fit the crib in her car; she'd have to wait until her husband could help get it up the stairs. One day during a phone conversation Shannon asked Carrie why she wasn't complying with their mother's request to bring over the crib. Her sister's response caught Shannon off guard: "Mom doesn't want a crib in her house. She's only telling you that because she doesn't want to hurt your feelings." Later in the conversation, Carrie pulled out the old, sharp arrow in her quiver: "You're the one who *chose* to leave home and move away, so you *deal* with it."

When Carrie told Shannon that their mother just pretended to want the crib, it was not only hurtful but puzzling. Was Carrie telling the truth, stretching it, or out-and-out making things up? I can't know the answer, but it's interesting to trace how the comment grew out of the preceding conversation. So long as the struggle was about delivering a crib for Shannon to use when she visited, it was between the sisters. Sister-support should have encouraged Carrie to come through. But Shannon raised the stakes—and the specter of competition—by accusing her sister not only of failing to help her out but of a much graver offense: failing to carry out their mother's wishes. Carrie's claim that their mother didn't really want the crib in her house was a defense against this accusation as well as a counteraccusation that raised the stakes yet higher: Their mother had told Carrie, but not Shannon, how she really felt.

The hurtful claim to know their mother's true feelings while Shannon did not is directly relevant to the dispute about the crib. But dragging in Shannon's decision to leave her hometown years before seems to come out of left field. So it's important to ask how this comment grew out of what came before. The request that Carrie transport a piece of furniture may well have reminded her of other jobs that fall to her because her sister is not in town—an example of how one sister's decision about her own life transforms the other's life as well. Carrie's remark seems out of place in this conversation, but anything said or done by a sister can tap into wellsprings that were long since thought buried.

There is another aspect to this interchange that is emblematic of sister-speak. We are creatures of conversation. By this I mean two things. First, our lives are lived as a series of conversations. Second, we are creatures created in conversation—others' as well as our own. When we think about people we know, we often recall things they said. And when we tell others about those people, and about our relationships with them, we often convey who they are by repeating things they said. Just so, Sharon recounted her sister's comments in the course of a conversation with two other women about sisters. We all sometimes say to others, and to ourselves, "Can you believe she said this to me?" We preserve recollected comments like photographs in a scrapbook, preserved because they bring back the feelings those people evoked in us. But, like photographs, recollected words lift a moment out of the context that produced them. Comments made in conversation don't appear suddenly, fully formed, from the mouth of the speaker, like Athena from the head of Zeus. Each utterance is in part a response to what was said before; that's why together they make a conversation. And often the remark we hold up to convey something about another person—"Imagine, that she said this thing to me!"—would not have been uttered had we not said what we did immediately before.

Carrie's accusation comes across as spiteful and petty. But she was reacting to Sharon's implication that she should provide the crib because Mom wants her to. In that context, it's not surprising that Carrie would counterclaim that Mom doesn't really want it. How else could she defend herself? But this defense puts her in a difficult position, because their mother did say she wants it. That leaves Carrie only one way out: "Yes, Mom said it, but she didn't mean it." And why would Mom say something she doesn't mean? "She just didn't want to hurt your feelings."

Whether or not my interpretation of this conversation is accurate (I can't be sure because I didn't speak directly with either sister), it illustrates the importance of considering the context in which a remark is made. And, regardless of the speakers' motives, it is clear that each successive move upped the ante of metamessage: from You're not a good sister because you won't do this for me, to You're not a good daughter because you won't do this for Mom, to Mom tells the truth to me but not to you. This last implies "I win, you lose," in one of the most fundamental sister competitions: Who is closer to Mom and Dad?

Like Hugging a Cat

Many of the examples I've given of sisters frustrating each other come from women who told me they are very close to, and adore, their sisters.

Competition between sisters doesn't nullify connection. It grows out of and contributes to connection, just as connection results in part from the competition and age differences that are inescapable among siblings. Because sisters remain sisters their entire lives, whether they see each other often, rarely, or not at all—even after one has passed away—the apportionment of connection and competition evolves and changes over time.

Cecile was on the phone with her sister. They weren't talking; they had run out of things to say. But they both kept their phones off the hook so the line between them was still open. They were just hanging out. They do this, Cecile told me, because knowing the other is there is a source of comfort, "like hugging a cat." She added, "When one of us has to go I always feel kind of lonely." Several months after Cecile told me this, I asked her about her sister. To my surprise and disappointment, she replied that she wasn't speaking to her. I shouldn't have been surprised: I know that sister relationships aren't always consistent and aren't always easy.

I was prepared to conclude the anecdote with that insight: Few sisters are exactly the way you'd like them to be, certainly not all the time. After all, a cat doesn't always want to be hugged. But the example won't end that way. As I was making final revisions to this chapter, I got a call from Cecile. She wanted me to know that, after more than a year, she was speaking to her sister again and they were again hanging out together with the phone line open. The year during which they didn't speak had not severed the connection between them. Quite the opposite, it was because of the strength of their connection, the depth of her feelings for her sister, that Cecile could have been so hurt that she cut off communication. Yet she must have known, even when the phone line between them was temporarily disconnected, that her sister was still there. No less than the solace of keeping each other company across an open phone line, that year of silence was an eloquent testament to the sisters' enduring connection.

CHAPTER TWO

"We're Close but We're Different"
Compare and Contrast

When does a high school student who is in all honors classes and graduates number ten in a class of two hundred believe she's not smart? When her sister graduated number two. When does a girl of 5'3" feel like a "hulking giant"? When her sisters are 5'1". And when does a woman who went to Italy on her own and lived there for fifteen years feel like she's not adventurous? When her sister is known in the family as the adventurous one.

We tend to see patterns in the people and things around us, so the world seems less chaotic and more manageable. Families too perceive patterns, to make sense of behavior and find order in the family world. Sometimes this means pigeonholing each other, settling upon labels that define who each person is—and fixing them there like bugs in amber. And often the labels come in opposing pairs.

Without prompting from me, just about everyone I spoke to described herself and her sister in terms of dualities: "My side of our bedroom was neat; hers was a mess." "She was a Goody Two-Shoes; I was rebellious." "I was a reader; she was a jock." "I was a tomboy; she loved makeup and boys." "She stayed close to home; I couldn't wait to get away." The categories by which sisters differentiate themselves are limitless. Sometimes it's physical characteristics: Who's tall, who's short? Whose hair is dark or light, curly or straight? And comparisons continue no matter how old sisters are; I heard, "I've been in therapy my whole life; she's allergic to psychology" and "I have grandchildren and she doesn't."

When there were more than two sisters in a family, I expected to hear more varied descriptions, not just two opposites. But women who have more than one sister typically compared themselves to one at a time or grouped two or more together, so they still described characteristics as dualities. For example, in an article in the *Washington Post*, six sisters explained that they think of themselves as two sets of three, the sets varying by binary characteristics. "Everything is three and three with us," one of them said. "Blood type, those who use ice and those who don't, those who choose paper bags over plastic in the grocery store and those who don't, who has a college education and who drinks with a straw and who doesn't." It doesn't matter whether a category is important or not—a college education or drinking with a straw. Anything that can be noticed can be placed in a pattern of similarity and difference.

She Got the Looks, I Got the Brains

Among the many categories by which sisters sort themselves—and others sort them—most regrettable is "the pretty one" and "the smart one." As evidence that this says more about our need to assign these labels than about genetic reality, in two cases the sisters who were distinguished in this way were identical twins!

From the moment they're born, girls are judged by appearance. The question, How pretty is she? (and in our own heads, How pretty am I?) sometimes seems to trump all others. In film, on television, in fairy tales and songs, the hero falls in love with the heroine because of her beauty, often at first sight—and physical appearance represents essential value. When Maria in *West Side Story* sings "I feel pretty," she isn't referring only to her appearance. Because she's in love with someone who loves her in return, she feels desirable and valuable.

I grew up hearing a family story that reflects this view of beauty. My father spoke often of his beloved grandmother, who helped raise him in Warsaw, Poland. After extolling her many wonderful qualities, he would add sadly that her husband never loved her. The one her husband had loved was her sister, his first wife, who died giving birth to their first child. It was his Orthodox Jewish tradition that required the widower to marry his deceased wife's sister. My father would conclude the story with this explanation: His grandfather had loved his first wife because she was beautiful, and he never loved her sister, his second wife and the mother of his next fifteen children, because she was not.

Appearance cuts so close to women's core sense of value that comparisons in this domain are especially pernicious. "You're almost as pretty as your sister," a grandmother blithely told a teenage granddaughter, thinking she was paying her a compliment. One woman recalls that her mother had her and her sister parade in front of the neighbors, inviting judgments of who was prettier. Although this impromptu beauty pageant is unusual, every day in the life of many sisters is a page from a fairy tale in which each asks, "Mirror mirror on the wall, who is fairest of them all—me or her?" Because comparison is so often assumed, a compliment to one sister can be heard as a slight to another. "Your sister is so pretty" may be taken to imply "and you're not."

"My mom will often tell me or my sister that we are beautiful," my student Genesee Herzberg wrote in an assignment, "often in front of each other, but never at the same time. When my mom compliments my sister, I immediately feel like I must look ugly." In Turkish, a language with many fixed expressions that are used in particular contexts, there is a prescribed expression to say when talking to one person and praising another who is not there: *sizden iyi olmasin.* It means, "may she (or he) not be better than you"—in other words, "I don't mean to imply that this compliment couldn't also be applied to you." This saying acknowledges and corrects for the universal tendency to feel slighted when hearing someone else praised. That's the emotion experienced by Genesee, who recalled, "I felt a pang of hurt every time my mom would compliment my sister." Sisters are in each other's presence so often, the chances are great that they'll overhear praise for the other and feel that pang of hurt.

Along with praise for appearance that implies one daughter is pretty and the other is not, sisters are attuned to praise that labels one, and not the other, as smart. Genesee experienced this too. She wrote: "When I would get my report card in high school, my parents would tell me how proud they were of me. Despite the fact that they would often say the same thing to my sister when she received her grades, she seemed to only notice what they said to me. Later she'd complain that I'm the smarter, better sister—and more loved." That is what all the comparisons come down to: Who is more deserving of the ultimate resource, parents' love?

Given the emphasis placed on appearance for women, it might seem that the sister who gets labeled the pretty one wins the contest. But in the game of life, the opposite may be true. A social worker envies her sister, who's a lawyer. "I wish to God I'd gone to law school," she commented ruefully. "It never occurred to me. It didn't occur to me I was smart enough." In her family, her sister was the smart one; she was the pretty one.

We're Close; We're Not; We're Different

"What are you writing now?" a woman asked me.

"A book about sisters," I said. "Do you have any?"

"Yes," she replied and added, "My sister and I have a fraught relationship. We were never close. We're very different."

I chuckled, then had to explain why. In this brief statement she had encapsulated what just about all the women I spoke to told me sooner or later—usually sooner: whether or not they and their sisters are close, and whether and how they are similar or, more often, different. Comments like, "People can't believe we're sisters because we're so different," reflected an assumption that sisters should be similar. But this is ironic, given how frequently women told me that they and their sisters are different.

When I was writing about mothers and daughters, I heard "We're the same" as often as "We're different." But when talking to sisters, while I also heard both, I heard "We're different" far more. I don't think this reflects how similar or different sisters are, compared to mothers and daughters, but rather how sisters tend to think of themselves. My student Hannah Yates commented that she enjoys seeing her mother get together with her three sisters, Hannah's aunts, because "I see my mom reflected in each of them and notice them in her." When Hannah showed her mother these comments, she responded, "What's most interesting to me about what you wrote, is that we each think we are so different from one another." She added, "As long as I can remember, I felt very different from the rest of my family. As a small child and into adulthood, I couldn't figure out how I was born into that family and often thought I would find my 'real' family. I thought of myself as this little spirit who was just anxious to have a body—hopping up and down just wanting to be born—and because of my impatience, I hopped into the wrong family!"

Many women will recognize this experience of feeling different, which in no way implies not feeling close. Women who told me they're close to their sisters said, "We're different," as often as those who said that they and their sisters are not close. Although a single example doesn't prove anything, I was intrigued when one of three brothers commented, "We're exactly the same." I never heard a woman say that of her sisters.

I was also intrigued by the ways a sister and brother who are the closest brother-sister pair I know described their relationship when I e-mailed to ask them about it. The sister wrote, "Although he and I are alike in many ways" (she named some), "we also appreciate the things that make us very different." She went on to discuss some of their differences and how they contribute to their mutual enjoyment and appreciation. The brother also enumerated many ways they enjoy and support each other, but he did not say anything about similarities or differences. For the sister, as for just about all the women I interviewed, telling me how they're alike and how they're different provided an organizing principle for her account.

For sisters, it seems, gauging closeness and assessing sameness or difference are ways not only to understand and explain their relationship but also to address the question that forms a canopy over all others: "Who am I?"

So Near and Yet So Far

In a sense, we ask of everyone we know or meet, "How close are you to me?" We array just about everything in the world along a continuum according to how close or distant it is from us. Linguist A. L. Becker calls this "the cline of person." He points out that we see the cline of person in grammar, beginning with the pronouns "I" and "you" and extending to linguistic pairs like "this" (close to us) and "that" (farther away); "here" (close to us) and "there" (farther away); "now" (close to us) and "then" (farther away). We also see it in other categories. For example, animals can be pets (close to us) or wild (farther away); people can be relatives (close to us) or strangers (farther away).

The categories close vs. distant are a "cline" because close and distant are not on/off characteristics but points on a continuum. People, things, and concepts are positioned somewhere along the continuum rather than firmly at one pole or the other. "Here" can refer to something you're holding or something in the room; "there" can be across the room or across the country. "Now" can mean this moment or the era we live in; "then" can be yesterday or the last century. The same goes for people. We don't have only two categories: family members and strangers. We have members of our "immediate" family or "extended" family and friends who are "like family." We also have friends, acquaintances, and "total" strangers. And some relatives are closer to us while others are farther away, either because of kinship (siblings are closer than cousins, first cousins closer than "distant" cousins) or affinity (a particular cousin may be closer than a particular sibling).

The cline of person—that is, how we array people and things as closer to or farther from us—is a fundamental way that we see order in the world and our place in it. That's why we're always asking the question, "Are we— and how are we—close or distant?"

Same or Different

At the same time that we're gauging closeness or distance, we are asking a related question, "Are you like or unlike me?" Women typically addressed these two questions together, saying they were close or not because of— or in spite of—being similar or different. The answers to these questions are continually shifting in response to changing situations. The question, "Are we—and how are we—the same or different?" has particular resonance for sisters because it sometimes seems as if they can hardly define themselves except in comparison with one another, as if sisters are mirrors in which they see themselves—or see what they might have been. One woman expressed this difference-in-sameness: "We're two peas from the same pod but we went through different digestive systems."

My sister Naomi was meeting me at the airport when I arrived for a visit. As I came through the doors to the waiting area, I quickly spotted her, and we hugged in greeting. Then we stepped back, looked each other up and down, and burst out laughing. We were dressed almost exactly alike, right down to our black high-top lace-up shoes. This sameness delighted us because it overrode many obvious differences: We don't see each other all that often, we live quite different lives, and there are eight years between us. We also look very different in many obvious ways. (My sister Mimi and I are closer in age and look so much alike that as children we were often mistaken for identical twins.) Naomi and I delighted in discovering we were dressed the same because we took it as evidence of the connection we treasure.

An eighty-year-old woman, Colleen Miller, told me about her beloved older sister Jeanne, who had passed away two years before. Although they had lived in different states for most of their adult lives, she and Jeanne were very close and very loving. Yet Colleen began by telling me about their differences, including life circumstances (Colleen married twice and had children; Jeanne never married and had none) and interests ("I'm a periodical reader; she's a book reader"). Nonetheless, Colleen said, "Deep down, we were very much alike." She stressed, for example, that they were both lifelong caretakers, "So I was emulating her I'm sure by always doing something for someone." She also described "habits" they shared: "You did your laundry on Monday and you did your ironing on Tuesday, and Thursday you cleaned the house. And we both had that habit."

Colleen related a phone conversation she had with her sister: Jeanne described a coat she had just bought, and Colleen exclaimed, "I have the very same coat! I just bought it over at so-and-so." Colleen told me, "We would do that. Yes, and we're a hundred miles apart. Not knowing. We would buy sweaters; they'd turn out to be the same sweater." To Colleen, having bought the same items showed that despite surface differences and living in distant cities, she and her sister were similar "deep down," and that similarity was evidence of their closeness.

Close: To Be or Not to Be

"Close" is the holy grail of sister relationships. I frequently heard "I wish we were closer" but never "I wish we weren't so close." Yet what exactly does it mean to be close? Here is an image of one kind of closeness.

Toward the end of Jeanne's life, Colleen convinced her to come and live with Colleen and her husband, George, so they could take care of her.

One of the images that sticks in my mind most poignantly from the many interviews I conducted is a scene Colleen described of herself and her sister during this time:

> George would get up and he's out getting breakfast or something and Jeannie would poke her head in the door and I'd say, "Come on in here."
>
> She'd say, "No, I'll just—"
>
> "Jeannie, come over here." Then I'd pull her down in the bed and she'd lie down beside me and I'd hold her hand. She had these tiny little hands, like a little bird, a bird hand. We'd lie there and we'd start to talk and we'd laugh; we did a lot of that growing up. We would lie down in the bed together and we'd just talk.

This scene has remained with me as a symbol of closeness: two elderly sisters lying in bed side by side, holding hands, laughing, and—the bedrock of women's relationships—talking.

Colleen and Jeanne's physical companionship is one of many forms that closeness can take. Another is "I'll be there for you when you need me." Some sisters feel close in that way even though there is no physical proximity and infrequent contact. On the other hand, there is the close of "I know who you're having lunch with today." That kind comes from the assumption that being close means caring about the smallest details of each other's lives. Sisters who share that type of closeness speak or e-mail daily. For many women, being close means, "We know each other's emotional temperature day by day." For them, telling each other about personal problems is a requirement of closeness. But Colleen and her sister Jeanne, so evidently and so movingly close, did not tell each other their personal problems. Colleen had been deeply unhappy with her first husband, but she didn't tell her sister about it until after he died. When Jeanne asked, "Why didn't you tell me?" Colleen replied, "Jeannie, you have your own life to live and I have mine, and I have to solve my own problems."

For Colleen, "you have your life and I have mine" did not lessen the closeness of her relationship with her sister. And the many ways they were different did not overshadow what she saw as their underlying sameness.

She's Me

Sally was on the phone with a prospective employer, trying to put her best foot forward in an interview for a job she very much wanted. It was one of those crucial conversations on which so much rides that you wish you had someone to help make your case, someone who can fill in when you draw a blank, bring up an important point that you forgot. And that's just what Sally had. Throughout the phone interview, her sister was on an extension speaking for Sally—speaking *as* Sally—whenever her help was needed. The two sisters could jointly hold one side of the conversation because their voices sound exactly alike; even their mother couldn't tell them apart on the phone. The joint effort worked. Sally got the job. It was a very real instance of what many women feel in a vague way: that the world sees you and your sister as one and the same person. And sometimes you see yourself that way too. Many sisters feel, at times, "She's me."

Two sisters, three and a half years apart, were telling me about their childhood. At one point, while recounting an event, one said, "Yeah, I was twelve." The other objected, "No! I was twelve!" The first replied, "You couldn't have been. You must have been eight." After trying in vain to place their ages, they gave up and went on to describe how they walked to school and walked home each day for lunch. Both of them. Sisters often ask, when recalling something from childhood, "Was that you or me?" The two are merged in memory, sometimes impossible to distinguish. A woman commented that it felt all wrong when her sister was in high school and she was still in middle school. She explained, "I wanted so bad to be in high school because I was older in my head." In her head she was the same age as her sister.

"In our early childhood we were almost like twins," said Alison, whose sister is slightly less than two years older. "We were dressed alike. I thought I was her. For many many years I kind of lived through her." When they were little, the sisters made up imaginary worlds they inhabited to-gether, as the Brontë sisters are known to have done. Also like the Bron-tës, they were each other's main company, perhaps more than most because their family moved often. When they were older, they shared written worlds. Both bookish, they went to the library together, returned with their books, then: "We'd be in our rooms after school, reading. She'd read through her stack and I'd read through mine and then we would swap." Again Alison added, "I felt for many years like she was me." This feeling was reinforced by another fact: "We were also almost always the only two black kids wherever we were." Alison said that when she realized boys had privileges denied to girls, "I was like, Oh, man, boys are so lucky. I wish my sister was a boy. I didn't wish *I* was a boy. I wished that *she* was a boy, so I could have that experience vicariously."

I Was Being a Grown-up

Alison also benefited, and not just vicariously, from her sister's efforts. For example, when their father didn't want his older daughter to wear high-heel shoes, Alison recalls, "That was a big big battle, but because she had the big battle, I got to wear heels." The same happened with wearing stockings: "Because she had the battle, then I could. So it was like what happened to her was happening to me." I heard many similar memories. For example, a girl had her ears pierced when she was fifteen, even though the family rule said she had to be sixteen. Her sister was over sixteen, and they went together. Having a sister who was old enough was the same as being old enough herself.

The privileges of an older sister may come to a younger one without much effort on her part, or they may come to her because she demands it, indulging the urge to be included, to be the same. A student in my class, Kathleen O'Hara, reported that she and her one-year-younger sister Laura are like equals, because Laura insisted on being equal when they were small. Kathleen explained in an e-mail:

> When I was 5, I got the training wheels off my bike, and she insisted on having them taken off of hers, too, so she rode a two-wheeler at 4, and I rode one at 5. When I got to stop riding in a car seat, she refused to sit in one anymore. She would climb out once the car started moving and my parents couldn't physically keep her in one, so they gave up, and she got to ride without a car seat a year younger than I did, too. She would never have tolerated going to bed earlier than I did, so we always had the same bedtime. The only thing I ever did earlier than she was going to school, and she

probably wouldn't have allowed that, either, if there had been anything she could have done about it. (And now she's considering graduating a year early!)

Kathleen went on to describe her sister as "the squeaky wheel who was always appeased." She later told Laura this theory, and Laura responded, "That's not being a squeaky wheel, that's being grown-up and assertive." This remark says a lot about how being and having a sister can affect your sense of yourself. When Laura said she was "being grown-up," she was referring to herself as a child of four. An older sister always seems grown-up in comparison, so being like her is tantamount to being grown-up too, even when she's only five.

Me and My Shadow

Alison, who said of her older sister, "I thought I was her," and described the many ways she benefited from their alliance, also noted a downside to their sameness: "I was the younger and the smaller. I always felt that I was the lesser of the two." She described how relatives contributed to this impression: They'd notice and greet her older sister first, saying, "'You're such a pretty girl, look how tall you're getting. Oh, look, such a beautiful smile; isn't she pretty?' And then they'd turn to me and go, 'Hi, Alison.' So I had this notion that I was invisible when I was with her." Alison felt, "I was always being compared to her and not measuring up."

Many of us, as children (and inside, as adults), have the feeling that somehow we don't measure up. The goal we can't reach may be amorphous, but if you have a sister, it can take her shape. How could a younger sister measure up? She is smaller (usually—though sometimes she's bigger, and that presents a different problem for the older one); there are facts she doesn't yet know, things she can't do, shelves she can't reach. We all come in frequent contact with people who are older and more capable, but only a sibling, especially one close in age and the same sex, is right there beside you all the time, a constant reminder of your shortcomings. (The same would be true of a brother, but a brother wouldn't be dressed the same and probably wouldn't be interested in playing the same games or reading the same books, so you're less likely to look at him and think, "He's me" or "I'm him—only less.")

There were many ways that women said they felt as Alison did: the lesser of the two. For example, Pat, whose sister seemed always to be embroiled in emotional crises, said, "I erased myself to make sure she was okay." And because her sister always had dramatic stories to tell about her life, Pat "kind of felt like my life paled in comparison." There is only so much conversational space at a table or in a family. If one sister talks a lot, another will talk less. We tend to attribute intentions to others and see ourselves as reacting, so it can be a surprise to learn of the intentions others attribute to us. An older sister, Janine, was shocked to learn, well into adulthood, that her younger sister had felt in her shadow and saw her as "dominating" and "monopolizing" dinner table conversation, of taking all the oxygen out of the room. Janine had been aware of no such intention. She was just being herself.

Sometimes a sister who tends to be the center of attention does know it—and may regret the effect this has on her sister. Candy was flamboyant; she had a gift for performance that came to her early. When she entered a room, all attention shifted to her and away from everyone else, including her older sister, Nadine. As a child she didn't think much about this, but when they grew older, she and Nadine talked about it. Candy liked being the center of attention, but she didn't like feeling she was hurting her sister, so when they were together she'd try to hold herself back, make herself smaller. But one day she thought, Hey, why do I have to do all the changing? If you feel small next to me, get bigger!

This makes sense. It's not Candy's fault that Nadine is shy. But it's not Nadine's fault either. Getting bigger is pretty much what comes naturally to Candy. But for someone who's shy and naturally quiet, being told to get bigger may be like being thrown into a pool when you can't swim.

Here's the view from Nadine. She said, "When I was a senior in high school, Candy was a freshman. I was shy and quiet, with a small circle of friends. Suddenly, people I never spoke to before would approach me and say, 'Oh, you're Candy's sister.' It was very weird. She was a cheerleader, she was popular, she had lots of boyfriends; she was even dating a boy my age. As soon as she walked into a room, I'd disappear." One of the benefits of growing up is that you can leave dynamics like these behind. But they can come hurtling back when you're with your family. That's what happens with Nadine. "I live in the Midwest now," she said, "and I feel like I'm pretty strong, effective, and confident. I've achieved a lot in my professional life. But when I get in front of my sister, every insecurity comes back. It's hard to feel the strength of my light in the glow of hers."

If a sister is there beside you as you're growing up, the way you feel beside her becomes part of your sense of yourself. It's the unavoidable result of juxtaposition. Objects can't help casting shadows, and lights can't all be the same wattage even if they want to.

Feeling Her Pain

Many women told me they felt as if they disappeared when their sisters walked into a room. And many felt that they merged with their sisters, so their sisters' moods became theirs. "There was a period in her life when she was unhappy," a woman said of her sister. "I felt so bad I could barely breathe. If she didn't have a good life I couldn't sleep, almost like I was experiencing it, or worse." If you and your sister are one, you feel her emotions. This deep connection can be deeply satisfying. But if she is hurting, then you hurt too. And it can be frightening to think that you *have* to be like your sister, especially if she is something you don't want to be.

The sense that your sister is you and you are your sister can be especially upsetting if your sister has physical, mental, or emotional difficulties. For Hallie, whose older sister had cognitive disabilities, the happiest moment of her life was when she was six and realized that she was *not* like her sister and the other children with even more severe handicaps at the school they both attended. It might seem surprising that Hallie was sent to the same school as her sister; Hallie explained that this was because the school was owned and run by a relative. Perhaps, in addition, their parents thought Hallie could look out for her sister, or both girls would be better off if they stayed together. Whatever the reason, being sent to the same school sent a metamessage: You and your sister are the same. No wonder Hallie was relieved to discover that they weren't.

Being the same is at one end of the cline of person continuum. It's an extreme form of the bond between sisters. The term "bond" is revealing, because it can be used in two different ways. There is the bond of "a close bond"—comforting connection. But there is also the bond of "bondage"—being tied up, lashed to a post or a person. A child whose sister has disabilities typically feels responsible for protecting her. Barbara Walters felt that way toward her older sister, Jackie, as she movingly describes in her memoir, *Audition*. Walters's life was limited by her sister's limitations: "I didn't join the Girl Scouts because Jackie couldn't join. I rarely had friends over to the house because they didn't know what to make of my sister." I heard similar accounts from women I spoke to. One told me, referring to a sister who is three years older, "The other kids would pick on her and she'd end up crying. I'd run in the house to get help." She added, "That was my job in life—to take care of my sister."

This woman, like Walters, had responsibility for protecting her sister even though she was younger. In many families, older or more able sisters protect younger or less able ones, because they were told to or because they took it upon themselves. But sometimes they resist that role. And sometimes one sister expects another to watch out for her, and is puzzled, hurt, or resentful when she won't. For example, a woman recalled that she was desperately lonely as a small child sent away to summer camp for the first time. Her older sister was at the same camp, and seemed to be thriving—and to want nothing to do with her. As adults, too, women sometimes expect sisters who seem to have it all together to bail them out, financially, emotionally, or in other ways. Yet those who appear invulnerable on the outside rarely feel that way inside.

In a family that experienced great turmoil because of a parent's suicide, the younger siblings believed that the oldest was untouched by the tragedy; it wasn't until they were all adults that they learned it had been as painful for her as it was for them. They hadn't known because she hadn't talked about it. What they saw as invulnerability was actually her effort to hold herself together. An older sister in another family helped me to see that if a child feels as if she's struggling to maintain her balance, having a sister hanging on makes her all the more likely to topple over. She said of her sister, who was a troubled child, "It was like we were in a boat and she was tipping it and I was afraid that I'd sink with her."

Feeling that you and your sister are bound together can also be comforting. Valerie recalls with delight this incident from her childhood: An older cousin asked her six-year-old sister if she would be a flower girl in her wedding, and her sister responded, "Yes, Val and I would love to be flower girls." The cousin didn't have the heart to tell her that a child of two and a half wasn't old enough, so both sisters were flower girls—the little one dragging a heavy flower basket behind her as she toddled down the aisle. Valerie summed up the story by saying, "My sister had just assumed that we came as a pair." And, as if reinforcing the continuity of this pattern, when I asked Valerie if I might include her name in the acknowledgments for this book, she suggested that I include her sister's name as well. (I did.)

Comforting closeness and perilous connection are two sides of the same coin. So are wanting to be the same as your sister or wanting to be different. In either case, you can't think of yourself without thinking of her.

Lost Sisters, Lost Selves

Losing a sister is another circumstance that shapes, and is shaped by, the depth of connection between sisters.

When Colleen Miller spoke of her sister Jeanne, who had passed away two years earlier, she frequently used the present tense, as in her comment, "I'm a periodical reader; she is a book reader." The present tense reflected Colleen's conviction that her sister's death did not end their relationship. "She's always with me," Colleen said. "She's in this room; she's here right now." I knew what she meant. Colleen described her so vividly, and the love she felt for her was so palpable, that Jeanne's presence was palpable too. Colleen added, "Do you know what I did within the last year? I called her phone number. I said to myself, Maybe I had a bad dream; maybe she'll answer. But she didn't answer."

When Jeanne died at eighty-six, Colleen had known her for seventy-eight years. No wonder her lost sister was still with her. Yet the same is true—maybe even more true, though in a different way—of women who had far fewer years with sisters who died young. In a "My Turn" column in *Newsweek,* Jessica Handler describes how poignantly she misses her two sisters, both of whom died of the same inherited blood disorder—one at twenty-seven, the other at eight. The pain of those losses is always close to the surface: "Little girls remind me of my sisters when they were very young. They stop my heart when they run across a playground or walk past me hand in hand. They turn back time in a way that nothing else can."

Eva Nagel, a psychotherapist, was thirteen when her three-and-a-half-year-old sister Laura died suddenly during the night. Eva went to bed one night, and her sister was fine; the next morning: "I woke up to a dead sister. And nothing, pretty much nothing, would ever be the same." Nagel explained:

> My childhood ended. I was different—all of life divided into before and after. She gave me an early wisdom and the seed of spirit that I may not have come to on my own. . . . Today, more than forty-five years later, Laura is still in my everyday conversations whether I am talking to a client about their recent loss or watching my exuberant granddaughter who attacks books with the same concentration I still remember in Laura. And yes, when you ask me if I have a sister, I will still, I will always, answer yes, definitely yes.

These sisters were snatched by death, but sisters can also be lost by choice—and the choice need only be made by one. A woman who severed all ties with her sister explained that she reached an age—she was in her thirties—when she asked herself, "How do I want to live my life? Where do I want my psychic energy to go?" She realized that the answer did not include her extremely difficult sister. This conviction crystallized when her son was born: She did not want her innocent child's life "sullied," as her own had been. She likened the ability to free herself from this debilitating relationship to other freedoms women gained in recent generations: to get divorced, to remain unmarried.

Though remaining unmarried affects only one person, getting divorced or cutting off a sister affects two. I was moved by this woman's account of making a tough decision that she felt was necessary to save herself and her family from a lifetime of pain. I was also moved by another woman's account of the pain she suffers daily because her sister cut her off. She described herself as "truly heartbroken," and I could sense this as we spoke. Following a visit to her parents' home, she said, "I saw the photos of my sister and me as little girls, as teenagers, and as young women, our heads affectionately pressed together, and I realized more than ever how much I miss her and long for that missing link." She doesn't understand her sister's decision and has done everything she can think of to convince her to change her mind. "I have apologized," she said. "I have professed love and regret." She added that the loss is compounded because her sister has children and she doesn't, so she lost not only her sister but also the cherished role of aunt. Finding herself not only without children but also without nieces or nephews deepens her sense of feeling "barren."

Both these accounts—of pain caused by being cut off by a sister and of pain that caused one sister to cut another off—are testament to the bond that being sisters entails.

"Get Your Barbies Out of My Side of the Room!"

Cutting off contact sets in relief the double meaning of "bond." If the connection weren't perilous, a sister wouldn't feel she has to sever it; if the tie weren't deeply comforting, a sister wouldn't find its loss so devastating. Losing a sister is a life-changing instance of the dynamic that is pervasive in sister relationships and pervades many mundane, daily encounters. A microcosm of this challenge—finding the right balance between the comfort of a close bond and the threat of bondage—is the common childhood circumstance of sharing a bedroom, as I did with my sister Mimi.

When we were small, Mimi made a proposal that sounded reasonable: She wouldn't go into my side of the room, and I wouldn't go into hers. I agreed. But there was a circumstance I hadn't factored in: The door was on her side of the room. I had just become Mimi's prisoner. I remember the incident because I felt tricked—and utterly trapped. The ties of sisterhood had me truly, though temporarily, bound.

Another woman who as a child shared a bedroom with her sister recalls, "We were always trying to figure out what we could put down the middle of it so we could each have a side. We never actually figured out how to do that." This struck me as a metaphor for the many ways sisters negotiate sameness and difference, closeness and distance: finding different areas of interest, living in different parts of the country—they all can be seen as trying to figure out how each can have a side.

Sharing a room presents opportunities for connection and conflict, just as there are two aspects of closeness and sameness—the connection that brings safety and the connection that threatens it. Beth and Amy had always shared a room, but Beth wanted her own. She lobbied so relentlessly that their parents eventually had a room built for her. Beth was thrilled. She moved all her belongings to the new room and settled in to spend the night. And that's what she spent in the new room: one night. She missed Amy and moved back the next day.

Another pair of sisters discovered the pleasure of sharing a room when a relative visited and one sister moved into the other's room so the visitor could sleep in hers. It was so much fun to be together, they made the move permanent. They continued to share one bedroom; the other was converted into a playroom. Years later, one sister decided she was old enough to have her own room, and claimed that long-empty second bedroom as her own. This time her homesteading lasted a year. After that, her clothes and belongings continued to occupy the second bedroom, but the sisters were back together, both sleeping in the first. They continue to share a bedroom when they're both home during breaks from—that's right—medical school.

There's a lot of appeal in sharing a room: someone to talk to after lights are out, and, when you're small, to protect you from ghosts and goblins that can sneak up on you if you're alone in the dark. Having a sister in the room can make you feel safe—and assure you that she's safe. A woman told me that when she was seven, her older sister moved into the bedroom next door. She was so scared that her sister would be kidnapped, she'd call through the wall, "Are you okay? Are you okay?" If you're used to having someone in the room with you, finding yourself alone can feel weird and wrong. Another woman told me that when she went off to college, one of the hardest things to adjust to was going to sleep in a room by herself; she kept looking for her sister in the next bed.

In addition to these and other comforts, there are also many challenges to sharing a room. For one thing, it gives the other easy access to things you value. She can borrow them, steal them, hide them, or break them. "Don't you *dare* touch my perfume," a teenager warned her younger sister, who, as soon as she was alone in the room, picked up the bottle of perfume—and dropped it. Sharing a room also provides opportunities to tease or torment. Jenny had rituals she had to observe before the lights went out. I say "had to" because that's the way rituals are; they must be carried out, and carried out just so, to work their calming magic. Jenny couldn't go to sleep until she heard the door click closed, saw the closet door shut tight, and got into a particular position that would take awhile to get just right. Knowing this, her sister would close the door without letting it click, leave the closet door ajar, and threaten to turn out the light prematurely because she was tired of standing with her hand on the switch.

These sisters are now in college, but they continue to share their old room when they visit home. The doors to the room and the closet have lost their magical power, but Jenny still needs to be in the right position before lights out. Now her sister patiently stands by the light switch and says, "Okay, get in your position!" and is happy to wait until her sister gives her the go-ahead to flip the switch. What used to be an annoyance is now a touching reminder of their shared childhood in their shared room, a reminder that they are a team—sisters. And the sister who broke the perfume bottle later gave her sister a new bottle of the same perfume—for her eightieth birthday.

Many sisters shared not only a room but a bed—and that closeness too can be revisited and reclaimed. When actor Ashley Judd broke her ankle, she stayed with her country-singer sister Wynonna while her ankle healed. She found healing, too, by sharing her sister's bed. "When we were growing up, we did the same," Ashley said in an interview. "We'd fall asleep holding onto each other's hair."

Sharing a bed or a room reflects the many ways that closeness and sameness can be too close for comfort or profoundly comforting.

Don't Tread on Me

One aspect of sameness can't be escaped: Siblings' ages progress in lockstep, so when one celebrates a birthday, the other is reminded of her own advancing age. A woman told me it was annoying that when she turned thirty, her sister didn't say, "Wow, you're thirty." Instead she said, "Wow, if you're thirty then I'm nearly forty. *Yikes!*" The thirty-year-old didn't like the feeling that her sister saw her first and foremost as a reflection of herself. But it's inescapable because their ages are forever linked.

"You should dye your hair," Holly urges Caroline. But Caroline likes her hair gray. Leaving it in its natural state is a point of pride, so she resents Holly's advice. Caroline thinks to herself, What I do with my hair is none of her business. But in a way, it is. If Caroline looks older, people will automatically see Holly as older too, especially when they're together. Unfair, yes, but unavoidable. (Though saying something about it isn't.) Any sign of connection that brings pleasure to one sister may bring discomfort to the other, or to the same sister in another context. Finding the right blend of sameness and difference, closeness and distance, is always a work in progress.

Rugged individualism is a distinctly American cultural value, tracing as far back as the American revolutionary war motto, DON'T TREAD ON ME. Most Americans take it for granted that each person, including each child in a family, should be seen as unique and standing alone. This conviction accounts for the standard practice of assigning twins to different classes at school. Only that way, the belief goes, can each develop the individuality required for adulthood. But other cultures make different assumptions. A woman raised in Greece noted that before she came to the United States, she had never heard the idea that parents have to nurture a child's individuality. And a woman raised in Cuba told me that her sister, who was a year older, was held back a year from starting school so the two of them could be in the same class. The adults who made that decision found it self-evident that both girls would be better off if each had the other for company and support in the strange new environment of school. American adults found a different conclusion self-evident: When they entered school in the United States, the sisters were summarily assigned to grades one year apart.

Individuals also find varying ways to reconcile the conflicting pulls to be like your sister and be your own person, to stick close to her or go your own way. A woman I talked to is lesbian and has a sister who is lesbian as well. I assumed that this similarity would be pleasing to her. She said it is, but there is also a part of her that would have liked to be the only one—the star in that role. Her response was a reminder that sameness and difference both have appeal. We don't seek one or the other, but the right balance of both.

Find Your Own Thing

In many American families there's an unspoken edict (or maybe a spoken one) that a sibling shouldn't horn in on another's domain. If your sister loves dancing, you should do something else. If your sister plays the guitar, you should play a different instrument. I've often wondered what would have happened if the Brontë sisters had made this assumption. Would we have been deprived of Emily Brontë's *Wuthering Heights* because her sister Charlotte had cornered the literary market with *Jane Eyre*?

Where do we get ideas about what is possible or appealing, except by watching the people closest to us? Seeing what your sister has is enough to make you want that very thing. No matter how much parents try to treat children equally, kids can spot differences and covet whatever the other has. "She got blue and I got pink," a woman recalls, "so I wanted blue." It had nothing to do with the inherent value of blue or pink; it was about green—in the sense that the grass is always greener in your neighbor's yard.

Though the one who got there first may feel encroached upon when a sister shows interest in territory to which she herself laid claim, the resulting competition is not always bad. A successful writer attributes her career to just this kind of competition. She encouraged her sister to develop her talent and take up writing, then realized that she had always wanted to write too. She'd been putting off taking the leap, but seeing her sister leading the life she herself wanted inspired her to take the leap as well. Sometimes competition and inspiration are one and the same.

Though some sisters are warned to avoid another's domain, others may feel they are pushed toward it. For every woman who felt stymied, discouraged from following her dream because her sister got there first, there is one who felt she had to do what her sister did even though it wasn't right for her. Paula told me that her younger sister Kristin went to the University of Wisconsin because that's where Paula had gone. A large university with lots going on was just right for Paula, but Kristin, who was less outgoing, felt lost there. Kristin would have been happier at a small college, but she never considered that option. She had assumed that the trail blazed by Paula was the one she was destined to follow. Kristin would have been better off had there been more of an injunction in her family to find her own thing.

Whose Clothes These Are I Think I Know

In photographs from our childhoods, Mimi and I are often dressed alike. Wearing the same clothes as my sister, who was two years older, seemed natural to me; I don't remember having strong feelings about it. But Mimi recalls how she felt about it: not good. When she saw that I had put on the same clothes that she was wearing, she'd change into something different. And if I changed my clothes to match hers, she'd head for the closet and change again. I can imagine why I'd want to dress like Mimi, who was older, faster, and more in control of the world. Maybe I thought I'd don some of her abilities and privileges with those clothes. But to Mimi, it must have felt like one more intrusion from this interloper who was always nipping at her heels—too much connection, not enough independence. If dressing like my older sister meant I got to climb up a rung on the ladder to stand beside her, to her it meant being pulled down a step to where her younger sister stood.

There's another reason Mimi might have been less than enthusiastic about our dressing alike: If I wanted to be like my older sister, she probably wanted to be like . . . herself—and to let others know who that self was. Choosing clothes is one of the most important ways women demonstrate their identities. To know what that identity is, you have to know how you're like and unlike your sister. Wearing clothes that are different or clothes that are the same—or are hers—can be part of that effort. When mothers (like Alison's and mine) dress sisters alike, "like twins," the sameness, I assume, is meant to reinforce closeness. And sometimes it works that way. The Olsen twins, Mary-Kate and Ashley, still wear each other's clothes; during one interview, Mary-Kate was wearing her sister's ring and shoes. But sisters who get angry when one wears the other's clothes may feel that it's too much closeness, blurring the line where one ends and the other begins.

Sharing, borrowing, and stealing a sister's clothes figured in so many of the stories I heard about sisters that at times I thought I could shape this entire book around that theme. My book about mothers and daughters is titled *You're Wearing THAT?* It occurred to me that this book might be titled *What You're Wearing Is MINE!* That's pretty much what a high school student said when she spied her sister wearing her cardigan at school one day. Then and there she made her sister take it off. A woman recalls that her older sister kept her clothes in much better condition than she herself kept her own, so she took advantage by helping herself to her sister's: "I didn't have to starch my blouses or collars (the kind you used to pin to your sweater) because she had already done it to hers," she said. Then she added, "My timing had to be good so I could take them when she wasn't there and suffer her wrath *after* I had worn them."

The comments of another woman articulated why one sister might object to another wearing her clothes. I asked the middle of three sisters very close in age whether she and her sisters ever took or fought over one another's possessions. Yes, she replied, especially clothes. "I probably was the most jealous of my clothes," she said. "I think I really was struggling how to be my own person." Her clothes were an expression of the person she was. If her sisters wore them, it was that much harder to distinguish herself from them and be her "own person."

A girl might want to wear her sister's clothes because she wants her body to be like her sister's, as did Eileen, who told me, "She was thin and I was chubby, and I would always try to fit into her clothes. If I could fit into something she wore, that was a sign that I had made it; I was doing okay." Her sister didn't see it that way. Eileen mimicked how her sister whined in protest, stretching out the word "clothes" as if to illustrate her accusation: "You're stretching out my clo-o-o-othes!" Eileen's sense of her own body—her conviction that she was "chubby"—was inseparable from her view of her sister's body, the yardstick by which she measured hers. Her sister's clothes were a stand-in for that comparison.

Another woman told me that sharing clothes with her older sister was so natural a part of her life growing up that it felt very strange to go off to college and have only her own clothes to choose from. "Hand-me-downs" are almost synonymous with the burden of being a younger sibling, but not everyone regards them that way. One woman told me she was thrilled when she inherited her older sister's clothes. And another said she loved it when her sister got something nice because she knew that eventually it would be hers.

If sharing—or swiping—clothes was common among sisters, it was by no means universal, and by no means the only way to express or achieve closeness. A woman who credited her mother with fostering lifelong devotion among her daughters told me that part of her mother's creed was *not* sharing clothes. In addition to telling all her children that they had to watch out for one another, their mother also warned, "Don't wear each other's clothes. Get your own clothes. That will create confusion." (The woman explained that to her mother, as to other African-Americans of her background, the word "confusion" meant serious conflict and turmoil.) The injunction not to share clothes springs from the same assumption: It blurs the borders between you.

Having a sister wear your clothes can feel like theft: She is stealing not just your sweater but your personality, encroaching on who you are. Wearing another's clothes is the closest you can come to being in her skin, because they actually were next to her skin. In clothes, closeness and sameness are rolled into one.

Where We Stand

I was talking to two of three sisters together. Here's a brief exchange that took place:

Nina: Yeah, all three of us really care about each other, but that
         doesn't mean we can't get into major disputes and that
         we're not quite different. I'd say our personalities are
Sylvia: Quite different.
Nina: *Quite* different.

The sisters' words sent the message We're different, but the way they said it sent a metamessage of connection: Sylvia and Nina jointly built a single sentence. When Nina repeated "*quite* different," she was accepting and ratifying the way Sylvia finished her sentence. The sisters were demonstrating in their conversation that they could speak as a team. By saying the same thing—that they are different—they were also demonstrating their closeness and shared conversational style.

We all seek to figure out for ourselves—and show the world—who we are. Having a sister adds an image that you see in addition to yours, when you look in the mirror. You can't help looking at that other image when you examine your own. A sister is you and not-you. Understanding who you are means figuring out who you are in relation to her. And to find your place in the world, you need to know how close to—or distant from—your sister you want to stand.

CHAPTER THREE

Looking Up and Talking Down
Competition and the Array of Age

.

Sister relationships change and evolve. As children you were best friends or fought or stayed out of each other's way. When one or both left home, you kept in touch or drifted apart. When one or both had children, the kids brought you closer or you lost touch because you were so busy. When your kids were grown, you talked more often or moved to another state and talked less. But there is one condition that never changes: the difference in your ages. Even twins are aware that one is older and one younger, if only by minutes.

The inevitable ranking by age is a family version of power dynamics that affect every relationship, every conversation. In addition to asking, "Are we the same or different? How close or distant do we want to be?" we also ask, "Who has more status and power?" This is where the competition among siblings comes in. If our wishes differ, whose desires win out? If we express different opinions, whose words count more? In conversations between employees and the bosses who can fire them, power trumps connection (though an employee may be more or less friendly with a boss). In conversations between best friends, connection trumps power (though one friend may accommodate more often than the other). Among sisters, growing up in the same family creates deep connection, while the immutable difference of relative age provides built-in hierarchy. Seeing how the dynamics of power and connection work together is crucial for understanding all relationships, but especially relationships among sisters.

Among my fondest memories from early childhood were times when my father put Mimi and me to bed. After tucking us in, he'd tell us stories he made up himself—stories in which we were the heroes who saved the day. We especially loved "stories with actions," when he moved around the room acting out the scenes and delighted us by rushing toward our laughing, upturned faces. Mimi is two years older than I, but we share this precious memory because when we were little, we went to bed at the same time. Alas, one day it dawned on Mimi that she should go to bed later because she was older. My parents couldn't argue the facts, so they agreed. I bitterly resented having to leave everyone awake and chatting, and go to bed by myself. Mimi didn't have to do anything to earn the right to stay up later. It was a privilege that came with her age—not her absolute age, but the difference between her age and mine. She wasn't concerned about what time she went to bed, so long as she stayed up later than I.

Connection in Status

My student Emily Sauerhoff devised a clever study to examine conversations between sisters. She and three of her friends, all nineteen-year-old college students, each called her younger sister (three were sixteen, one was twelve) and recorded the conversation. Emily gathered and transcribed the recordings. Looking over the transcripts, she noticed that in all four cases, the talk focused on the younger sisters' lives. One pair talked about the younger sister's trip to New York City, her report card, and the family cat. Another pair discussed the younger one's day at school, her friends, and her potential boyfriends. A third pair discussed the younger one's driving, basketball team, plans to visit Georgetown, and college applications. The last pair talked about the younger sister's school, friends, and weekend activities. In one case only, an older sister talked about herself, because her younger sister asked, "How's your life going?" and listened to the answer.

These conversations established the sisters' closeness and connection: They were keeping in touch while one was away at college and the other living at home; they talked about their personal lives; and they emphasized things they had in common, like the upcoming Thanksgiving break when they'd be together. But the conversations also expressed, reinforced, and created the status differences of their relative ages. All four focused on the younger sisters' experiences and included little or no discussion of the older sisters' lives. Revealing personal information is a sign of connection when it's mutual, but not when it's one-sided. Like a mini-interrogation, the one who reveals personal information becomes vulnerable while the one who only asks questions does not. In literal interrogations, suspects reveal information that may be used against them; questioners do not. Adults ask children questions to show interest and involve them in conversation; children typically answer but don't ask for information in return. "What did you do in school today?" is not usually followed by "We had a spelling bee. What did you do at the office?"

Emily noticed that when an older sister did say something about her own life, she quickly redirected the talk back to her younger sister. For example, one of the college students, Claire, said, "Guess what? I'm going to New York for a day during my study days." Then she added, "Do you have anything New Yorky that you really would like for Christmas?" Her younger sister, Hillary, asked a question that turned the talk to Claire: "Where are you going in New York?" Claire answered but then turned the focus back to Hillary: "We're just gonna go to Manhattan; y'know—see Rockefeller Center and the tree and all the storefront windows. I'll get you a designer purse." Claire stressed the gift she'd get for her sister just as parents might promise to bring their children gifts when they go on a trip.

The older sisters in these conversations also gave advice or offered insights based on their greater life experience, while their younger sisters didn't. Here too it's the one-way nature of the exchange that's key. Friends may give each other advice and comment on or interpret each other's experiences without compromising equality. But if only one gives advice and interprets the other's life, she comes across as more knowledgeable, experienced, and mature than the other—as an older sister usually is.

These phone conversations established connection between the sisters, but everything they said also reflected and reinforced the age hierarchy between them. They were talking like sisters, but one talked like an older sister and one like a younger. Status and connection were inextricably intertwined in their conversations.

Hierarchy Creates Closeness

Americans tend to assume that status differences create distance while equality creates close relationships. I myself saw it that way when I wrote *You Just Don't Understand.* I described the common conversation where a woman talks about a problem and is annoyed when the man she's talking to offers a solution. I commented that she's annoyed in part because offering solutions introduces a status imbalance. The person with problems is one-down, the person with solutions one-up, and that creates distance, whereas the woman's whole point in talking about problems is to reinforce closeness. It seemed self-evident to me that differences in status are distancing.

When I wrote that, I didn't realize I was expressing culture-bound assumptions. In many cultures, it is assumed that status differences don't disrupt connection but actually create and reinforce it. For example, in a study comparing American and Japanese college students in small-group discussions, linguist Suwako Watanabe concluded that the American students saw themselves as individuals engaged in a joint activity while the Japanese students saw themselves as members of a group united by hierarchy. When I read this, I was momentarily caught up short. United by hierarchy? Isn't hierarchy distancing? Yes, if you think of employers and their employees, but not if you think of families. Parent and child or grandparent and grandchild are very close and also very hierarchical. The hierarchy creates their closeness. The same goes for siblings.

Nearly all the American women I spoke to, as I noted in Chapter Two, focused their talk about sisters on whether they're the same or different, close or distant. In contrast, women I spoke to who had been raised in other cultures focused their comments on the respect and responsibilities that come with their relative ages. For example, a woman raised in Vietnam said that even though she's an adult with grown children of her own, her older sister visits and tells her what to do. She doesn't like it, but she can't talk back to an older sister, so she agrees pleasantly, then later ignores her sister's instructions. She didn't tell me that her culture forbids a younger sibling to talk disrespectfully to an older one; she took that proscription to be self-evident. Their relative ages shape the way she talks to her sister and the way her sister talks to her. The built-in hierarchy of age gives structure to their relationship and will continue to do so throughout their lives.

Sameness and closeness, on one hand, and the hierarchy of age, on the other, are two different types of glue that can hold families together. In one case you're close because or in spite of your differences and similarities; in the other you're connected by rights and responsibilities that come with your position in the ranking by age. If you're older you're responsible for younger siblings: to take care of, teach, and protect them (though you also may tease, exploit, or torment them). If you're younger, you look up to older siblings and, when you're small, do what they tell you (though you may also tease, harass, and pester them). These rights and responsibilities bind you together too.

A Filipino-American woman commented that, growing up as the oldest, she was expected to set a good example for her younger siblings. This injunction is based on the assumption that her younger siblings will emulate her; they'll want to be the same. Even if they determine to do the opposite, they are still operating on the axis of sameness and difference. The responsibility of older siblings to set a good example for younger ones demonstrates that the hierarchy dynamic grows out of and entails the sameness/difference dynamic.

Since Americans tend to focus on sameness and closeness when thinking and talking about family, they often assume that the hierarchy that comes with age will disappear with time. Those who grow up under the influence of cultures that tend to focus on the rights and responsibilities of relative age assume that the hierarchy defining their relationship will endure and ensure closeness.

Line Up by Age

A woman was telling me about her childhood in India and her sister. "I called her Didi," she said, "but Didi isn't her name. It means 'older sister.'" "Is there also a term for 'younger sister'?" I asked. Her answer was simple: "No." In India, as in China, Korea, Japan, and many other cultures, a younger sibling addresses an older one as "older sister" or "older brother," but the older addresses the younger by name. This continues throughout their lives—a daily reminder of their places in the lineup by age. In these cultures, the importance of siblings' relative ages is reinforced by the way people outside the family are addressed as well. In Korea, for example, women address friends who are older than they as *"enni,"* "older sister," and friends who are younger by their first name. And in India, Korea, and many other countries, any apparently older stranger is addressed respectfully as "older sister" or "older brother." The sibling relationship, in other words, is the paradigm for age relations by which a younger person shows respect to an older one.

Americans also show respect by addressing someone by title alone, while a person of lower rank is called by name. That's why parents call children by their names, but children call parents some form of Mom and Dad. And a police officer who stops you for a traffic violation may address you by the name on your driver's license but you will probably respond with "Officer" and certainly not with the officer's first name. But for Koreans and Indians, the words used to show respect remind everyone that the very notions of respect and responsibilities are based on siblings' ranking by age.

In Indian families, brothers' ranking by age extends to their wives, regardless of how old those spouses are. (Wives traditionally reside in their husbands' extended households.) The younger brother's wife has less status than the older brother's wife, even if she is older in years. These differences, too, are reflected in the Hindi terms by which relatives are addressed. Your father's sister is *bua,* his younger brother's wife is *chachi,* and his older brother's wife is *tayi.* Your mother's brother's wife is *mami,* and—my favorite—your mother's sister is *masi. Masi* comes from *ma jaisi,* meaning "like a mother," recognizing the special closeness of the sister relationship. But your mother's older and younger sisters are both *masi;* apparently their status is sufficiently determined by their husband's age-ranking in his family.

Each of these relationships reflects different combinations of status and connection; it's hard to know how to regard a relative unless you know their place in both. Shilpa Alimchandani, who was raised in the United States by parents born in India, learned terms for relatives in her parents' native Hindi. She finds the American terms for relatives hopelessly inadequate to convey relationships. In English, all these different relatives are lumped together as "aunts." In cultures that have reminders of status distinctions built into the language, relative age provides guidelines for families to function.

A couple born and raised in Korea treat their four American-born daughters according to their ranking by age. The mother calls each daughter on the phone weekly, oldest first, then down the line. As children, when the two middle daughters were given bikes, the older of the two got to choose the color she wanted first. And when the family moved to a house with four bedrooms, the two older girls were given their own rooms, and the two younger ones were assigned a room to share. This all makes perfect sense: The first daughter, eleven at the time, is eighteen months older than the next one down, and the youngest, at seven, is three years younger than the next one up. The two middle sisters are separated by . . . three minutes. Bridget and her sister Audrey are identical twins. Yet because of those three minutes, Audrey has always been given the privileges that come with being older.

The bedroom assignments were particularly interesting. Each room was decorated in accordance with the age-based assignments: the two girls given rooms to themselves chose the colors they wanted, and Bridget, the "younger" twin, chose the color for the room she was to share with the youngest. But when the time came to move in, the children sorted themselves differently. The twins moved in together, leaving the second single room to the youngest. The parents had done their duty by respecting the age-grading in assigning rooms. The children sorted themselves by connection.

Though a rigid system of hierarchy provides guidelines for sisterly behavior, it does not preclude rivalry, as Fern, the American daughter of Chinese parents, discovered when she visited cousins in China. The cousins, two sisters, had never left China and did not question the customs that gave priority to the oldest. But that did not mean the younger was ready to accept second-best; it just meant she had to be more creative in one-upping her sister. Fern wanted to buy gifts for her Chinese cousins, and she knew that the older sister's gift had to be more expensive, so Fern took her to a jewelry store first and invited her to choose a piece of jewelry. The value of this gift set the limit that the younger sister's gift could not exceed. When her turn came, the younger sister chose a pendant whose price was safely below the cost of her older sister's gift. Then she picked out an expensive chain to go with it. Though the combined value of the pendant and chain exceeded the cost of her sister's gift, she explained to Fern that this was not a problem. She would show her sister only the receipt for the pendant; her sister need never know about the chain.

The Expected Order

Though hierarchies that come with relative age are more obvious in traditional cultures like Korea and India, they are fundamental, if less apparent, in American families as well. Elise, for example, told me that she's the middle of three sisters. Her sister Linda is the oldest, and Sandra is the baby. Linda is four years older than Elise, and Sandra is younger than Elise by four minutes. Though Elise and Sandra are twins, there is no question in Elise's mind that Sandra is the baby sister. She got away with murder; their parents were easier on her; Sandra didn't get beaten the way Elise and Linda did. It's possible, of course, that Sandra was treated differently in part because of her temperament or other differences in how she behaved. Whatever the reason, the four-minute difference in their ages was enough for the twins to be distinguished as a middle and a youngest child.

Every twin I spoke to told me which twin is older, how their behavior reflects this ("I take care of her when she's sick," "I cook her dinner regularly"), and, often, how early the pattern emerged. A woman explained, for example, that she was like an older sister to her twin, even though their age difference was only eight minutes. She illustrated her point by saying that they have a photograph of her pushing her twin in a carriage when she was barely able to walk.

Part of the reason twins can't help thinking of themselves as older and younger is that they're constantly being asked. "It's the second question out of people's mouths," an identical twin said. "After 'Are you twins?' people always ask 'Who's older?' " Americans, too, can't think of sibling relationships without reference to the hierarchy of age. And the primacy of the older is reflected in the way the question is phrased: not "Who's younger?" but always "Who's older?" Children themselves are aware of and express this hierarchy, even when they're very small.

Three-year-old Tessa, prancing and strutting, announced, "I'm a princess." Her two-year-old sister Sarah mimicked her strutting and said,

"I'm a princess too." "No you're not!" Tessa corrected. After thinking for a moment she allowed, "You're a prince." Sarah wanted to be whatever her older sister was. But Tessa wanted to be a princess in order to be special, and she was not going to let her little sister horn in on her reign. If a princess was the best thing to be, she'd get that role, and Sarah could be something else. They both accepted and reinforced the metamessage of power that came with being older. Tessa got to be a princess and Sarah didn't. More important, Tessa got to decide what Sarah would be. Sarah didn't question this arrangement. She accepted the role of prince as well as her older sister's authority to assign it. This makes perfect sense to me. When I was little, my father overheard me asking Mimi, "Can I play in your backyard?"

When sisters grow up, the authority and deference that come with relative age may continue, morph, or even reverse. Reversals may come with added layers of discomfort, satisfaction, or combinations of both. According to biographer Sheila Weller, singer-songwriter Carly Simon felt guilty—in addition to feeling gleeful—when she achieved fame, because in her family her two older sisters had been considered the stars. For Carly to become the star "upturned the sisters' expected order of things."

Winner's Remorse

A few years ago, Mimi and I visited her best friend from grade school, Davina, now a grandmother and restaurant owner. Davina asked, with chagrin, if I bore a grudge because she and Mimi mistreated me when we were kids. In particular, she wanted to know if I'd forgiven them for making me eat cat food. I bore no grudge, and I didn't remember having eaten cat food until they reminded me of the game: They blindfolded me and gave me foods to taste; I had to guess what each was. When I recalled the game, I had a vague recollection of distaste associated with the fishy smell of canned cat food, but the emotion that came back most viscerally was gratitude that my older sister and her friend were including me in their game. In fact, all my strongest memories of Mimi and Davina's friendship are of times they let me play, helped me out, and saved my skin—like when we were all at summer camp, and Mimi and Davina snuck into my bunk during the night, took everyone's shoes, and piled them in one big heap with laces tied in mismatched pairs. I felt grateful and special because they had left my shoes undisturbed.

As adults, Mimi and Davina felt guilty that it had been so easy to push me around. (The cat food was only one example.) They suffered from winner's remorse. If you win a contest with strangers, you can feel unalloyed triumph. But if the contest is with a sister, it's not so simple because you're dealing not only with competition but also with connection. Mimi recalls that as a child she realized how much power she had over me. I always assumed she reveled in it. She tells me she did, but she also found it kind of scary. I'll bet that feeling is common among older sisters, and that it plays a role in winner's remorse

A set of twins both tried out for their high school basketball team. After tryouts, which their parents and older brother attended, the entire family was stunned; one sister made varsity and the other junior varsity. The family stood around the car, reluctant to drive home in the face of this unacceptable outcome. Then they came to a decision. The twin who made varsity returned to the gym and asked the coach if her sister could come to varsity practice with her. The coach agreed, and the second twin did so well that she ended up playing on the varsity team too. Neither twin fell behind, thanks to winner's remorse.

Younger sisters can experience winner's remorse too. When tennis champion Serena Williams beat her sister, Venus, in a quarterfinal match at the United States Open, she too experienced winner's remorse—and had to guard against its getting in the way of playing her best. She told an interviewer that when she plays against her sister, "I try not to look at her because I might start feeling bad. I want the best for her. I love her so much." Serena was clearly thrilled to win the match, yet she couldn't help but feel bad to see her sister lose. Serena is the younger Williams sister.

When adult sisters have children of their own, they have a whole new set of opportunities to compare: Which college are your kids attending? What profession have they chosen? Though some no doubt feel pleasure when reporting their children's successes to their sisters, they may also feel a twinge of winner's remorse. Carol was upset when her son dropped out of college, but when she told her sister the news, she felt almost relieved. Carol always seemed to have better luck than her sister, so in an odd sort of way she was glad of the chance to even the score by lowering hers.

Loser's Resentment

Rights that come automatically with age are institutional power—power conferred by social roles. But there is another kind of power, too: interactional power, created by an individual's actions. In a work setting, institutional power comes with a job description while interactional power is the influence that individuals create by their behavior. Someone whose opinion is respected may be listened to more often than someone in the same position whom coworkers regard as unreliable and flaky. A person who is quick to anger can also gain interactional power, because coworkers back off and back down to avoid an explosion. These patterns are also found in families. Being older confers institutional power in privileges and status; being younger confers institutional power to make demands. In either role, an individual can gain interactional power. Siblings can get their way because they're more outgoing or because they are favored or feared or more likely to throw a tantrum if they don't. A woman commented, for example, that her sister got a lot more attention than she did because "she did a better job of getting sick." Whatever the source of power, the sister who has it may not think about it all that much. But the one who doesn't may harbor resentment that leaks out in ways that take her sister by surprise.

A college student home for a visit was surprised when her younger sister opened the envelope containing her SAT scores and announced, "I did ten—no, twenty points better than you!" The older one had the luxury of forgetting that their parents often held up her achievements to motivate her sister. But the younger one was always aware of the burden of comparison, so her resentment was close to the surface, ready to pop out at unexpected times. Another older sister was similarly caught off guard. Pregnant with her first child, she told her sister the name she had chosen for the baby. Her sister burst out, "All my whole life you got everything I wanted first. I picked that name ten years ago."

If two people are walking single file, the one who is walking behind can always see that there's someone ahead of her. She has to adjust her speed with the other walker in mind, deciding how much space to leave between them, how far behind she's willing to fall, how quickly to walk if she wants to catch up. The one who's walking in front doesn't see the one behind her unless she makes a point of turning back. She can easily forget that the other is there. Just so, it's easier for an older sister to forget the competition so long as she's safely ahead, and to be surprised when her sister's awareness of it comes out in barbed remarks.

"My strong points are her struggle points," a woman said of her sister, "and vice versa." We all have strengths and weaknesses, things we're good at and things that don't come easily. But if you have a sister, you can't think of your strengths and weaknesses without thinking of hers. And that can explain not only the kind of thing a sister says but also the way she reacts to what others say. Karen told me, "I get really upset if someone corrects the way I say something or implies that I don't know something I should, like 'What, you don't know that?'" She traces this response to the way she compared herself to her sisters. She said, "I was the artistic, whimsical, athletic sister, who did well at school but wasn't brilliant." "Wasn't brilliant" implies that her two sisters—one older, one younger—were smarter than she. Karen sees that comparison as the source of her struggle point, what she calls her "Achilles' heel."

Pamela is successful by most any standards. She's got a PhD and a faculty position in clinical psychology. But that doesn't quite cut it in her own family, especially in the eyes of her older sister. For a time, her sister was a painter and made it clear she thought the lofty life of an artist superior to the mundane concerns of an academic. But her sister eventually gave up art and pursued a PhD in sociology. Then she let Pamela know that sociology, with its hard-nosed statistics, was superior to the wishy-washy field of clinical psychology. Pamela feels that comparison to her sister means she is a contestant in a lifelong contest in which she is bound to come in last.

I don't want to leave the impression that competition has only negative effects. Here's an example where an older sister was spurred to accomplish more by her younger sister's achievement. The older had always said she was satisfied with her position in middle management. But when her younger sister announced she was taking a new job with far more responsibility and remuneration, she changed her mind. Within a week, the older one had updated her résumé, put out the word that she was interested in moving up, and found a higher-level position within her company. Competition was inspiration. I suspect that the ladder of age was at work here.

Seeing a younger sister overtake you provides a jolt more powerful than the accustomed experience of the younger looking up and the older comfortably ensconced on a higher rung.

Size Places for Life

A number of women I talked to characterized themselves or their sisters as "a typical middle child—a peacemaker." Yet others saw themselves or their sisters as "a typical middle child" because she was rebellious, or neglected and therefore shy, or overlooked and therefore difficult. Women said "typical middle," "typical oldest," or "typical youngest" with very different ideas about what's typical. Sometimes "typical oldest" meant rebellious because she had to blaze the trail (like the older sister who skipped school, smoked, and dyed her hair orange), but sometimes it meant the oldest was a Goody Two-Shoes who always did what she was told. One woman said, "My sister is four years younger, and we were quite different as children. She was the outgoing one and I was the more withdrawn, typical older child." Though the specifics differed, what was constant was the assumption that a child's place in the array of siblings by age affects personality and that the effects last a lifetime.

A woman who is the youngest of four—seven, if you count her father's children from his first marriage—said that when she's with her friends or out in the world, she doesn't think of herself as shy and has no trouble standing up for herself. But come Christmastime, when her siblings all gather, she clams up. "I probably say three words the whole time," she explained. "I could not be in the room and it wouldn't matter." The feeling of being ignored is right there, ready to return when she's around her family. She believes this results from being the youngest.

In other families, older sisters feel ignored, as if they don't count. Marsha showed her older sister, Sheila, a physician's assistant, a worrisome condition on her hands: The skin around her fingernails was inflamed and cracking. "It must be a vitamin deficiency," Marsha said. "I'm going to see my doctor." Sheila looked at her fingers and said, "It looks like eczema. If you're worried, go to a dermatologist."

"I don't know," Marsha replied. "I think it could be systemic."

The next evening Marsha called her sister to give her the report. "You were right," she said. "My doctor sent me right over to the dermatologist, and he said it was winter eczema."

Instead of being pleased, Sheila was angry. "You never believe anything I say!" she blurted out. "You always have to hear it from someone else. My patients come to me with questions like that, and my own sister thinks I don't know anything! You never listened to me!"

Sheila's anger was less about this specific exchange than about the past, where she felt she wasn't listened to, even though—or maybe because—she was older. Whenever her sister visits, it's like their shared past is visited upon her.

You Totally Talked over Me!

Flare-ups over seemingly insignificant comments or actions can be a hall-mark of sisters' conversations. "Looking back, it was so stupid!" women often say when recounting an argument. The most trivial disagreements can provoke disproportionate responses because they reignite flames from long-smoldering embers.

Jennifer Kovach taped and analyzed a conversation she had with her boyfriend, Josh, and her year-younger sister, Lynds. The difference of a year in age would be immaterial between friends. But between sisters, the difference is vast. It gives the older obvious powers—and the younger less obvious powers—over the other.

Jen, Lynds, and Josh were talking about a topic that arises frequently among college students: how some roommates make messes they never clean up and, adding insult to injury, show no gratitude when another roommate does the cleaning for them. At one point in the conversation, Lynds emitted a loud sigh. Jen and Josh continued their animated talk, so Lynds made her complaint explicit: "Jen!" she barked. "You totally just talked over me like fifty times!"

Jen laughed, in keeping with the general goodwill of the conversation, but her remorse was genuine. "Sorry," she said.

Lynds, still annoyed, said, "Forget it!"

"Go ahead," Jen encouraged, but Lynds would not.

"No," she replied, "I don't want to anymore."

Jen didn't give up. "I didn't hear you," she said, and repeated, "Go ahead." At this point Josh became the bystander at a family feud and made a joke about watching the sisters fight. "Go ahead," Jen said for the third time, repeating her encouragement.

Lynds repeated her complaint: "I said, I was trying to say this, it's about the third time now."

Because this was a friendly good-natured conversation, and because Jennifer was taping it for a class (one she was taking with me), the three then indulged in a round of joking, playing on and playing up the absurdity that they all could see. After much shared laughter, during which Josh and Jen joked about the number of times Lynds had tried to say something, Lynds finally agreed to make her point: Messy roommates show little appreciation for roommates who clean because they don't care about the mess.

You may or may not feel that Jen did Lynds a disservice by talking over her attempts to make her point. Whether or not you think so probably depends on your own conversational style—or your own experiences with siblings. Jen and Josh continually talked over and interrupted each other, yet neither took offense; they were just talking. Some people feel that others should clear the field and give them a chance to talk. Some feel that talking at the same time makes for an enjoyable conversation. If you don't get heard the first time you try to say something, you just keep trying. (In one conversation I taped and analyzed I counted eight times that a speaker tried to make his point. On the eighth try he succeeded, and the conversation proceeded with no indication that he or anyone else saw anything amiss.) Apparently Jen and Josh were two of those, while Lynds had the other style. This could have happened between any two friends, and I'm sure it does. But because they were sisters, the interplay of their styles took on additional layers of meaning.

For one thing, Lynds blamed only Jen, even though Jen and Josh had both talked over her. Many of us feel it is our sister's job to watch out for us, and we blame her not only for what she herself does but also for what others do if she doesn't protect us. Jennifer also noticed that Lynds became the center of attention by refusing to talk. Had she made her point as soon as Jen apologized and gave her the floor, the conversation would not have centered, turn after turn, on Jen's trying to get Lynds to speak.

This fleeting exchange was not really a fight. It went by quickly amid much laughter and would have been soon forgotten had Jennifer not been recording the conversation for our class. But that is the beauty of recording and transcribing conversations: You get to see patterns that are always there but you otherwise wouldn't notice. I doubt it was by chance that Lynds's protest—and her feeling that she was being slighted, ignored, not listened to—occurred in conversation with her older sister. In her analysis, Jennifer noted that her sister's outburst was a kind of tantrum. By the same token, Lynds's refusal to talk reversed the built-in power dynamic, making her older sister "practically beg" her to say what was on her mind.

Money Is Love and Love, Money

Many arguments that unexpectedly erupt among sisters involve competition. The argument, if you can even call it that, between Jennifer and Lynds involved a competition for the floor. Often the competition is over possessions, at least on the message level. On the metamessage level, it is often about love—specifically, who got more of it from their parents. A conversation in Julia Glass's novel *I See You Everywhere* shows how this can play out in a mundane conversation.

Louisa, who lives in California, has just said that she misses the East. Her younger sister Clem responds, "So move back." Then Clem, as narrator, says, "Louisa gave me her iron-maiden look." Here's what Louisa says next and how the conversation proceeds:

> "*You* try to change coasts when you're always on the verge of broke."
> "I *am* always broke."
> "You're a student," she said. "That doesn't count. Dad bails you out."
> "So, he'd bail you out, too."
> "I wouldn't let him."

This brief exchange exposes some of the layers of paradoxical emotions and attitudes swirling around money. Louisa, who is self-supporting, resents their father giving money to her sister. The resentment leaks out when it's not really relevant, in one of those unexpected jabs with which family members can poke each other. In fact, it's two jabs, a double whammy. Jab one: Louisa reminds Clem that their father supports her. Jab two: With the phrase "bail you out," Louisa is ostensibly describing their father's action, but indirectly she's characterizing Clem as someone who gets into trouble—a metaphorical jailbird. Clem defends herself by exposing the baselessness of Louisa's resentment: their father would "bail out" Louisa too. Louisa's reply, "I wouldn't let him," illustrates why Clem sees her sister as an "iron maiden"—and why Clem elsewhere describes her as judgmental. Louisa implies that she's a better, stronger person for not taking money from their father. Moving to the metamessage level, Louisa's remarks become even more hurtful. When Clem said, "I *am* always broke," her metamessage was "I'm like you," a bid for connection. But everything Louisa says rejects the suggestion that Clem is like her, and therefore pushes her away. The depth of Louisa's resentment of Clem's taking more than her fair share of their father's money seems evidence that she sees her sister as taking more than her fair share of his love.

Even when parents are apparently treating their daughters equally, sisters can see unfairness. And unfairness is often there to see, because changing circumstances can make "the same" gifts very different.

In Greece, parents traditionally give each of their children a home—a house or apartment—if they can. It's common to build one apartment on top of another, adding a floor for each child as money becomes available. Let's say a couple have three daughters and give each an apartment when she marries. This is equal treatment. But the parents' changing circumstances, and the physical reality of construction, mean separate cannot be equal. The oldest sister will get the first apartment built, the one on the ground floor. As floors are added for the second and third sisters, each successive apartment will be newer and hence more modern, as well as higher up and therefore sunnier. The youngest sister will necessarily end up on top in more ways than one. And the contrast among the apartments will always be there for all to see, including the sisters themselves. Even if they don't live in these apartments but live elsewhere and rent them out, the differential treatment is tangible, because the higher, newer apartments fetch higher rent. The inferiority of an apartment can come to stand for all the ways one sister feels that another came out ahead. And this feeling may persist even though it's obvious that the inequity was unavoidable, an inevitable consequence of circumstance.

Knowing that their parents genuinely meant to be fair does not always change sisters' feelings. Intended or not, the results are there to compare. Any gift can be occasion for comparison. Patricia's parents gave her sister Regina an expensive cameo because Regina could not afford to buy one for herself. They gave no such gift to Patricia because she could. Patricia understood, but she still felt slighted. The meaning of money goes way beyond financial need. When it's flowing from parent to child, money represents love. And if the spigot flows more generously to one child than to another—even if the children are now adults—the comparisons can spark complex emotions. They may ask not only, Who got a better gift? but also, Whose children get more gifts or more approval or more attention? Whom does the parent visit more often or spend more time with? ("You watched my sister's kids for two weeks while they went on vacation. What about my kids? What about me?")

Last Chance for Love

The game of Who Got More? may not end when parents pass away. Losing parents is a painful experience; many sisters come together at this time, and after parents are gone, they can fill for each other some of the roles that parents filled before. Having siblings can make the loss more bearable. But sometimes, in the pain of loss, siblings vie for what is left. I was struck by how many of the accounts I heard about lingering resentments and even rifts among siblings resulted from disputes about inheritance. A friend who is a brother put it this way: "It's your last chance to grab the love for yourself." This is a context in which brothers and sisters, as far as I can tell, react pretty much the same.

In a column devoted to answering questions about ethics, *The New York Times Magazine* printed a letter that began, "My beloved sister . . . has long received financial help from our parents" and ended with the query, "May I ask them to make a reckoning of their aid to my sister, subtracting it from any bequest they eventually make her, so that overall, she and I receive equal amounts?" Randy Cohen, the ethicist, replied: "You may ask but they need not comply. This is their money, not funds they hold in trust for their heirs." Yet some heirs do feel that their parents' money or property is meant to be theirs and are concerned about getting their fair share of the inheritance, just as they were vigilant for signs that a sibling got more gifts, attention, or love when their parents were alive. And some who couldn't make their parents give over a fair share when they were alive can try to force them to do so after they're gone.

Claudia was grateful that her parents had helped her and her family buy a house. She knew that her sister Ida resented this, but she dismissed Ida's concerns, since Ida had a husband who earned well and didn't need their parents' help. So Claudia was caught off guard when their parents died, and Ida wanted Claudia to reduce her share of the inheritance by the amount she had received from their parents for the house. If the ethicist is right, then Ida was wrong. But the ethicist was talking about money—the message; Ida was reacting to the metamessage about love. In another family I heard a variation on this theme. A sister borrowed money from her parents and had not paid it back by the time they died. At that point she claimed that the money had not been a loan but a gift, so it should be ignored when she and her siblings divided the inheritance. These two scenarios highlight two different perspectives. In one case, parents gave a child a gift; after they're gone, another child wants to lay claim to it against the parents' wishes. In the other case, a child betrays the parents, and ultimately her siblings, by converting a loan to a gift after the parents can no longer speak for themselves. In both cases, the parents' money stands not only for money but also for their love.

There are innumerable ways that siblings might take more than their share—or believe that others took more than theirs—after parents pass away. One gets to the parents' home first and takes valuable furniture or jewelry before the others arrive, or begins taking things while the parents are still alive. Or everyone gets an equal share, but that seems unjust because one doesn't really need it. Even if there are no disputes about inheritance, arguments can break out because the pain of loss is great and a sister's gain makes the loss more poignant. I heard of passionate fights about possessions of little or no financial value—a needlepoint pillow, a cup. A rancorous dispute broke out in one family over a nightgown. That might seem absurd, but it's understandable, because a nightgown is about as close to a person's body, to her personhood, as a possession can be. And underneath, the conflict—like so many between siblings—was ultimately about who had rights to their mother's love.

I don't want to give the impression that all the stories I heard about parents' deaths involved conflict. Here's an example of how three sisters met the challenge of sharing a single item that had meaning for them all. After their mother passed away, the sisters divided her jewelry amicably. There was one bracelet, though, that they all wanted, so there was a chorus of overlapping protests: "You take it," "No, you take it." One sister proposed a way they could share it. Each would keep the bracelet for a year and then pass it on, in a continual cycle. The sisters agreed this was a fine solution, and one of them took possession of the bracelet for the first year.

Happy as this ending was, it wasn't the ending. When the sisters next gathered, the one who had gotten the bracelet first brought out three jewelry boxes. "I didn't feel comfortable having the bracelet while you two didn't," she said. "So I found the jeweler who made it for Mom and had him make two more." Each box contained an identical bracelet—and there was no way of knowing which was the original. Each sister took a box. Each inherited her mother's bracelet.

It's a Contest

The bracelet solution was a creative and unique way to solve the challenge of dividing an indivisible item. Inheritance is a particularly dramatic instance of the competition inherent in sibling relationships—a competition that can take many forms and be played out in innumerable ways.

"I spoke to Mom twice yesterday," a woman remarked. Her sister parried, "I spoke to her once, but we had a better conversation." They were joking—sort of. Sisters can compete not only about who gets more from their parents but also about who gives their parents more, who knows them better, who takes better care of them. In my own family, I'm not aware of feeling competitive with my sisters about who got more from our parents—either while they were alive or after they passed away—but I vividly recall feeling competitive with a sister about who knew our father better and who could take better care of him.

Naomi and I were both visiting our parents, and Naomi was preparing their breakfast. She placed eggs, toast, and a cup of coffee before my father. I knew he liked to have his coffee, together with something sweet, after he had finished his eggs. But I didn't say anything because it felt wrong for me to be telling my older sister what to do. I figured it was my father's place to tell her. This he did, when he finished his eggs and wanted a hot cup of coffee. At that point I couldn't resist saying, "I knew that. I thought of it when you gave him the coffee." Naomi was understandably annoyed by my remark and didn't hide her annoyance. This happened many years ago, but it stuck in my mind because I felt so many conflicting emotions. I felt awful that Naomi was mad at me, and I couldn't figure out if I'd been wrong not to say something in the first place. I knew I'd been wrong to open my mouth when I did. But overriding the whole interaction was a sense of satisfaction that I'd known my father's preferences better than she did.

I'm not proud to tell this story now. But it captures the way that Naomi and I sometimes banged into each other as we both hovered over our father. It was an odd combination of competition and connection. We were competing over who was more connected to him. At the same time, the competition itself was a kind of connection between my sister and me.

Taking the Show on the Road

Many grown sisters take vacations together, sometimes with spouses or children, sometimes without. It can be like old times, staying up late in your pj's, talking and laughing, being as silly as when you were kids. But vacations can also present opportunities to replay rivalries. If there are three sisters in a room with two beds, who has to sleep on the cot? When you make plans for the day, whose preference wins out? Then there's money; there's always money. One is more frugal so she wants to stay in more modest hotels, go to less costly restaurants, and leave smaller tips. And when it comes time to pay, what's a fair way to divide up expenses?

Following a family reunion, three sisters stayed on to spend several days together on their own. Now they were divvying up the hotel bill. Cindy, the youngest, was fuming. Esther, the oldest, felt Cindy should pay for the extra room because Cindy's two children did not want to share a room with her children. That would sound reasonable, except . . . well, there were several excepts. Cindy's children would have been happy to share a room with their cousins, but not a bed! And the only room with twin beds had been commandeered by the third sister, Betty, because she and her husband couldn't sleep in a double bed. So Cindy felt that it wasn't her children's needs that had required the extra room. Furthermore, she'd had the highest travel expenses, because she and her family had had to fly and rent a car, whereas her sisters had been able to drive. Then there was the matter of who could afford to pay more. Cindy's family had a higher income, true, while Esther's had low cash flow, but Esther lived on property that was worth a lot—far more than the value of Cindy's home.

The argument about the hotel bill was particularly tense because the sisters were already sore. So let's back up. Earlier in the day they'd gone separate ways. Betty was to pick Cindy up to go to lunch, but Cindy was late. And it turned out to be much harder for Betty to find a place to wait than Cindy had thought it would. Cindy felt she'd had a good reason for being late, which was out of her control. Because of her metabolism, when she gets really hungry she has to eat something. So she had to stop and get something to eat, and the service was slower than she could have predicted.

None of these extenuating circumstances changed the fact that her sisters, who were also getting hungry, were mad at her for being late. But she was mad at them too. She had needed to mail a package, and Betty, who does all the driving on the trips, had taken her to the nearest post office, but she had been tired and therefore unwilling to drive farther to find a UPS drop-off, which would have been cheaper. And that's not all. When the three of them travel without their spouses, they stay in a room all together, and Cindy is the one who usually ends up sleeping on the cot! She understands why—she's the youngest and has the strongest back—but still, it gives her the feeling that she's the odd one out. Which she always is and always has been, because she's more than six years younger than her next older sister, while they are only two years apart. They had each other for company growing up; then they both left home, and she found herself alone with parents who were older and grappling with depression as they aged.

If this account sounds convoluted, it's because family interactions often are. The current conflict is never the whole story. Every comment, every action, bears meanings from earlier ones—a lifetime of comments and actions. And everything has meaning not only on the message level but also on the metamessage level, where connection and power are negotiated.

Sharing Nutrients, Mingling Roots

There is a way of growing vegetables that's called "three sisters." It entails planting corn, beans, and squash together in a single mound, so the special attributes of each make them all grow better. One gardening Web site assigns birth order roles to the crops: "Corn is the oldest sister [who] stands tall in the center. Squash is the next sister [who] grows over the mound, protecting her sisters from weeds, and shades the soil from the sun with her leaves." (Elsewhere I read that "the spiny squash plants also help discourage predators.") "Beans are the third sister [who] climbs through squash and then up corn to bind all together as she reaches for the sun." The beans also add nitrogen to the soil.

The sisters metaphor explains how planting corn, beans, and squash together improves the chances for all to thrive. If three crops are rooted in a single patch of earth, it would seem obvious that one or more will suffer as they compete for nutrients. Instead, each plant contributes to the others' growth. Sisters too can thrive in the context of apparent competition. Though they are rooted in the same patch of earth—parents and other adults in their lives—the love each gets needn't mean less for the others. Crops don't only take from the earth; they also give to it. So too do sisters enrich the soil in which the others grow. And just as planting the crops together strengthens them all, the built-in hierarchy of relative age strengthens the connection among sisters.

CHAPTER FOUR

Whose Side Are You On?
Understanding Alignment

Luci Baines Johnson and Lynda Johnson Robb were teenagers when their father, Lyndon Johnson, was president. Many years later, Lynda Robb described how she and her sister navigated the White House to protect each other. "Luci and I were of the age to be entertaining dates, and, of course, you didn't particularly care to be discovered by your father. When one of us saw him, we would try to message ahead that he was coming your way. We would go up the back staircase, figuring we might be able to get there quicker than Daddy could on the elevator." By working together to keep their father from intruding on their dates, the Johnson sisters formed an alignment that connected them to each other in opposition to him.

Every family is a network of constantly shifting alignments, as if each member were a dot in a children's drawing book. The dots can be connected with solid dark lines or thin faint ones, with dotted lines or crooked ones, as individuals become closer or more distant, more connected or independent, and assume varying stances toward one another from moment to moment. Two parents may align with each other, creating a bulwark that the children cannot penetrate or bring down. Children may align with one or more siblings in their joint stance toward a parent, or with one parent in a stance taken toward the other parent. For example, a woman told me, "My sister got spanked more. If my mom spanked me or yelled at me, I would call my dad. And he'd play the part of my ally versus my mom instead of playing my mom's ally." A common alignment is the one between

Luci and Lynda Johnson, an alliance of sisters in their dealings with one or both parents. And a common way of creating and reinforcing that alignment is talk.

"When my mother's been visiting, the minute she leaves, I'll call my sister," Joan commented. "I'll say, 'Can you believe what Mom did?' or 'You won't believe what Mom said.' Sometimes I won't even wait till she leaves. The minute she goes out for a walk, I'll run to the phone and call. My sister is the one person who knows what it's like and why it drives me up the wall." Anytime two people talk about a third person, they are creating an alignment that links them to each other and excludes the one they are talking about. Joan and her sister create an alignment simply by talking about their mother. Even more, they align with each other by taking the same stance toward her, agreeing on how they react to what she says or does. Knowing that her sister understands—and shares—her reaction reassures Joan that her view of their mother is accurate, her response to her mother reasonable. That reassuring alignment is one of the most precious gifts of having a sister.

But there can also be a special disappointment, a unique feeling of abandonment or even betrayal, when sisters take different stances toward their parents. If Joan's sister had responded, "It doesn't bother me when Mom says things like that; I know she doesn't mean anything by it," Joan would have felt frustrated rather than reassured. And if Joan's sister thinks Joan is way too critical of their mother or not appreciative enough, she will be aggravated by Joan's complaint. The concept of alignment helps explain a source of frustration with a sister, when you seek or expect a connection based on a shared stance but don't find it. When you do find it, alignment helps explain the special comfort of being sisters.

Sisters Talking

In her story "White Horse," Margaret Atwood portrays the way sisters can demonstrate their alignment and create a shared universe through talk. Lizzie, who makes her home in the city, is visiting her sister Nell on the farm where Nell lives with a longtime partner who has not gotten around to divorcing his wife. Reading a section of dialogue between the sisters, I found myself increasingly confused; then I realized that Atwood had accurately represented the way sisters talking together create a shared world that no one else can enter. In the following scene, Atwood recreates for readers the experience of overhearing a conversation between sisters.

> "This air's so great," said Lizzie, breathing in. "You should stay here forever. You shouldn't even bother going in to the city. When are you going to get rid of that rusty old machinery?"
>
> "It's lawn sculpture. That would suit *them*," said Nell. "They'd never have to see me again."
>
> "They'll get over it," said Lizzie. "Anyway they live in the Middle Ages. Is it a harrow?"
>
> "They might like Gladys [the horse]," said Nell hopefully.
>
> "Gladys is beside the point," said Lizzie.
>
> Nell thought about that. "Not to herself," she said. "I think it's actually a disker. The other one's a drag harrow."
>
> "They wouldn't like Howl [the dog]," said Lizzie. "He's too craven for them. What you need is a rusty old car."
>
> "We've got one, we're driving it," said Nell. "He's mentally deficient. I can see their point though. Everything's different now. They aren't used to it."
>
> "That's their problem," said Lizzie, who despite her fragility could be tough when it came to other people, and especially other people who were doing wounding things to Nell.

The first time I read this passage I was befuddled. The words "drag harrow" and "disker" were unfamiliar, but I could figure out from the context that these are terms for farm machinery. But who were "they" and "them"? I turned back and reread the preceding pages to see if I had missed a reference to characters the sisters might be referring to, but I found none. The Middle Ages? Everything's different now? What on earth were the sisters talking about?

I read on. Atwood presently explains:

> When Lizzie and Nell spoke together, they often left out the middle terms of thought sequences because they knew the other one

would fill them in. *Them* meant their parents, in whose books—outdated, prudish books, according to Lizzie—only cheap, trashy women did things like living with married men.

With this insight, I reread the passage. It was like watching a blurry picture come into focus. In addition to understanding that "they" and "them" referred to Lizzie and Nell's parents, I also understood that Atwood was showing how the sisters reflected and created an alignment between them through talk. By using pronouns without ever mentioning the nouns they refer to, the sisters demonstrated and reinforced the bond of a shared background. Their parents didn't need to be introduced into the conversation because they were always there, like hovering ghosts that only the sisters could see.

Also always hovering is the knowledge that their parents disapprove of Nell's living with a man who's married to someone else. That's why when Lizzie said that Nell should never leave her country home, Nell thought immediately that this would mean not seeing her parents: both sisters knew that their parents would not visit her there. When Lizzie said, "Anyway they live in the Middle Ages," she aligned herself with Nell, dismissing their parents' disapproval by exaggerating how outdated it was. And when Nell said, "Everything's different now," she built on her sister's comment to say she understood why it was hard for their parents to accept her doing something that was unthinkable in their time.

This conversation illustrates the sisters' alignment in another way too: They jumped back and forth between two topics—parents and farm machinery—without signaling the switch. When Nell said, "It's lawn sculpture. That would suit *them*," it's not the lawn sculpture that would suit their parents but Nell's never going to the city. When Lizzie responded, "Anyway, they live in the Middle Ages. Is it a harrow?" she went from the parents back to the farm machinery. A reader can follow the conversation, separating topic threads as you would untangle a knot, because Atwood has so accurately depicted the way many sisters talk—and why a woman commented that when she's hanging around with sisters she always ends up feeling left out: Their conversation contains opaque references, unstated assumptions, and conversational habits gleaned as members of the same family.

Shared Memory, Shared Conversation

Whenever I interviewed two or three sisters together, I had a chance to observe shared conversational styles and references like those portrayed in Atwood's story. When sisters told me about events and people from the past, they often repeated and expanded each other's words as if they were jointly building a sculpture, shaping it together. I'll give examples from three sets of sisters of different ages and backgrounds.

Frances, Millie, and Wendy, seventy-six, seventy-four, and sixty-seven years old respectively, were telling me about growing up in a small town in Indiana. As they recalled an incident involving their mother, they built on one another's words so their joint dialogue had the rhythm of poetry. The main speakers were the two older sisters.

> Millie: Remember the dog?
> Frances: You got her a dog!
> Millie: It was the ugliest thing you could ever see!

Millie then recalled that she and Frances had bought the dog as a birthday present for their mother. She concluded her account by returning to the theme of the dog's appearance, and Wendy echoed Millie's words in agreement:

> Millie: And then of course, this is the ugliest dog!
>
>   . . .
>
> Wendy: It is *ugly*!

Millie and Frances, two years apart, had bought the dog together. When Millie asked, "Remember the dog?" Frances could have said, "Yes." Instead she replied, "You got her a dog!" In this way, she didn't only tell her sister (and me) that she remembered; she also joined her sister's universe of words by repeating the phrasing and rhythm of her question. At seven years younger, Wendy wouldn't have been with them, but she joined the conversation as a chorus member by picking up the theme of the dog's appearance: "It is ugly!" It would seem odd for Wendy to use the present tense when referring to a dog who lived decades before, except that she was echoing the phrasing her sister had just used.

Later, all three sisters recalled that their father successfully invested some of the family's money in the stock market and significantly increased its value. Their mother disapproved of such risky behavior because the money he had invested before the Depression had all been lost in the crash. Her disapproval applied as well to the man who sold her husband stocks. Frances told a story, and her sisters took part by chiming in, showing that they shared the memory and the knowledge of their mother's attitude, but also their conversational style. Wendy supplied the stockbroker's name, and Millie supplied the motivation for their mother's antipathy.

> Frances: So they were living out in the country and this broker came from Louisville about every other week.
> Wendy: Mr. Rivers!
> Frances: And Mother was—as if he was into drink or something, that's how Mother felt about Mr. Rivers. "Oh, there's that old Rivers again. I don't like him around here!" you know.
> Millie: She knew!

Though Frances told the story, Wendy and Millie made it their story too by adding information ("Mr. Rivers!") and corroboration ("She knew!"). Their interjections cheered Frances on in her account. On the message level, the sisters communicated information about their childhoods; on the metamessage level, telling it together conveyed their sisterly alignment.

Let's move down a generation, across the country, and over to a different cultural background: two African-American sisters in their fifties who grew up and still live in the Washington, D.C., area. These sisters, Michele and Gae, also spoke as if they were jointly holding one side of the conversation while I held the other on my own. For example, when they told me they had bought a condo in Florida together, their two comments would make just as much sense had they been said by one speaker:

> Michele: We have a relative down there.
> Gae: My mother's cousin.

Each picked up the other's words to continue her thought:

> Michele: She looked at the same complex. So she looked at it and
>   a friend of hers was there.
> Gae: Yeah, Wilma.
> Michele: Wilma, and they decided. . . .

And here again (the third person driving to Florida with them is a niece):

> Gae: We drove
> Michele: We drove down, yeah, the three of us.
> Gae: We drove down a couple weeks ahead of them.

The sense that the sisters were together holding one side of the conversation persisted even when they were telling me about a disagreement that
arose as they furnished their jointly owned condo.

> Gae: The only thing that we were really disagreeing about
>   was the fan, remember?
> Michele: Oh, yeah yeah! Because I wanted it in the middle
> Gae: And I was like *"No! No!"*

These are just a few examples of the impression I got throughout this
conversation—both at the time it took place and later, reading the
transcript—that Gae and Michele were not only telling me about their
lives as sisters but also demonstrating their sisterness. On the message
level they told me they had participated in the same past experiences; on
the metamessage level, the way they talked about those experiences ex-
hibited—and created—an alignment between them.

Finally, let's move down another generation to a third and last example
of sisters co-speaking. Chika and Amara, both in their twenties, were
telling me about their international background. Their father, from Nigeria, and their mother, from Grenada, had met as college students in Min-
nesota, where Amara was born. The family then moved briefly to Nigeria,
where Chika was born, before they returned with their mother to live in

the United States. The sisters often spoke as one, finishing each other's sentences.

> Chika: So then they had me over there, and then she came back here, and we were raised
> Amara: We were raised here in Washington, D.C., but we lived in Grenada for about two and a half years.

Amara picked up Chika's words, "we were raised," repeated them, and completed the sentence with no hitch in timing and no interruption, just the two of them together holding one side of the conversation.

Chika then took the floor again, acknowledging that her older sister remembered more of their time in Grenada, but she added her own perspective—and her sister repeated her words, just as a chorus in a Greek drama repeats characters' words to reinforce them:

> Chika: Yeah, she has a better recollection at that point than I do. But I remember a lot.
> Amara: She remembers a lot.

Here's another example of one sister completing the other's sentence seamlessly, the two of them speaking with one voice:

> Amara: One thing about me is that if you ask me to do something for you, I'll do it, but I'm still going to
> Chika: Put up a fight.
> Amara: Yeah (*laughs*).

You don't have to be sisters to co-converse like this. Any family members can do it, and so can friends. Whenever two or more people agree on when it's appropriate to chime in, they can pick up each other's words and rhythms to have the pleasurable experience of talking in unison, like dancing together. But when two people speaking as one are sisters, the conversation yields a special pleasure. The connection created by shared conversational style reinforces on the metamessage level the connection of shared memories expressed on the message level at the same time. What they're saying and how they're saying it combine to create a solid line of alignment between them.

And Mother Makes Three

The sisterly alignment created by Nell and Lizzie in Margaret Atwood's story consisted in part of a shared stance toward their parents. Most parents are gratified when their daughters are close, but they may also feel a twinge of discomfort if that closeness is based partly on an alignment that leaves them out or even establishes a critical stance toward them. Had Lizzie and Nell's parents been eavesdropping on their conversation, they would not have been pleased by the way their daughters were talking about them. Perhaps it is to guard against this uncomfortable possibility that some parents treat their children in ways that disrupt or prevent their mutual alignment.

One mother never allowed her two small daughters to play together out of her sight. Her motivation may have been to make sure they were safe or did not engage in activities of which she disapproved. But it also may have been to forestall their forming an alliance that excluded her. Whatever her motive, if the sisters couldn't talk to each other out of their mother's earshot they couldn't form such an alignment. And these sisters never did.

Writer Joyce Maynard recounts and explores her relationship with her older sister, Rona, in a personal essay that appeared in *More* magazine. (A parallel essay written by Rona appeared alongside it.) Joyce and Rona love each other deeply but have also caused each other pain. Joyce writes, "So often, the story of my sister and me has been one of signals missed, of feelings registered but never expressed." As an example, she recalls and regrets that she did not attend her sister's wedding. Rona had decided to marry on short notice, and Joyce had "begged" her parents to let her go with them to the wedding. Their mother insisted it was more important that Joyce not miss any of her college classes. Looking back, Joyce realizes that her sister knew nothing of this conversation: "Rona knew only that her sole sibling didn't show up." Joyce's desire to go had not been expressed to her sister, because each sister had an alignment only with her mother, not her sister (and their mother apparently chose not to tell Rona that Joyce had begged to attend). Hurt and distancing between the sisters resulted not only from Joyce's absence at Rona's wedding but from the absence of a direct alignment between them. Had such an alignment existed, Joyce would have talked to Rona directly, whether or not she took their mother's advice about staying away.

Maynard also mentions another example of "signals missed" and "feelings never expressed." Joyce dropped out of Yale at eighteen to live with the writer J. D. Salinger. She learned years later that Rona had worried that Joyce would suffer terribly when the relationship ended, as it did—and as she did—in less than a year. Rona expressed her concern, but not to Joyce. She expressed it in letters to their mother. In both examples, Joyce and Rona were the principals, but the alignments created were with their mother. Their mother was like the hub of a wheel with separate spokes running back and forth to each daughter but no way for the spokes to intersect.

These examples show how conversations—who spoke to whom—can reflect, reinforce, or disrupt alignments and, consequently, relationships. At the same time, they provide an inspiring example of how alignments can be formed and relationships restored, as the Maynard sisters demonstrate in their piercingly honest, deeply moving matching essays.

Negotiating Alignments

Alignments are negotiated in conversation moment by moment, forming, shifting, and re-forming. You can see how it happens in a conversation between two sisters that was taped and transcribed by Courtney Ivins for a paper she wrote for my class. The sisters, Jessica and Becky, are college students. They also have a third sister, Katie. At eighteen, Becky is a younger sister to twenty-year-old Jessica and an older sister to fourteen-year-old Katie. Jessica and Becky both live at the colleges they attend, but Jessica's college is close to the family's home, while Becky's is farther away. At one point in the conversation, the sisters were talking about how the youngest was faring as the only child still living at home. Jessica said, "She called me a couple weeks ago and she was like, 'You have to get me out of here. Mom and Dad are ganging up on me.' So she came to visit." What followed captures Becky's coexisting but potentially conflicting alignments as younger sister to Jessica and older sister to Katie:

Becky: I can't do that.
Jessica: Yes, she can come visit you.
Becky: I can't come visit you whenever I want.
Jessica: I know iss sad.

The confusion over what "that" refers to reflects Becky's conflicting alignments as the middle sister. Jessica assumed that when Becky said, "I can't do that," she was aligning herself with Jessica as older sisters to Katie. So Jessica assured her that she too could invite Katie to visit. But that wasn't what Becky had in mind when she said, "I can't do that." She was aligning herself with Katie as younger sisters who want their older sister's company. When Jessica realized this, she reassured Becky again, but in a different way. She quickly realigned with Becky by saying that she also regrets that they can't visit: "I know iss sad." She then suggested that they could "Skype it up": talk to and see each other using computer technology.

The spelling "iss" in "I know iss sad" is not a typo. It represents a special language that Jessica and Becky sometimes use when they talk to each other; they call it "sisterspeak." Using that private language in itself was a way to repair, on two levels, the separation introduced into the conversation. One level was the reminder of the sisters' physical separation: They attend different colleges. By using their shared language to say she too is sad that Becky can't visit her, Jessica offers a salve to Becky's sadness. But their shared language also reinvokes the alignment between them that Jessica temporarily forgot when she misinterpreted Becky's remark as reflecting her alignment with their younger sister rather than with Jessica.

Later in the conversation, we again see an alignment fractured and then restored. Becky tried to align with Jessica by criticizing Katie for not keeping the bathroom she uses neat and clean. Rather than accepting this alignment by joining in the critical stance toward Katie, Jessica defended Katie's right to keep the bathroom any way she wants since she's the only one using it. Watch how Jessica aligned with the absent Katie:

Becky: She's so the bathroom mess-maker! She would always deny it but she absolutely is. Go up to the bathroom and it's so gross.

Jessica: It's fi— I didn't even notice.

Becky: And my bathroom stuff is so neat.

Jessica: I didn't even notice it.

Becky: It's so gross!

Jessica: (*in low silly voice*) I didn't even notice it.

Presently Jessica told Becky that if the bathroom bothers her, she should clean it herself. Becky finally succeeded in getting an "eww" out of Jessica by telling her that Katie leaves toothpaste sticking to the sides of the sink. With this, Jessica and Becky were again aligned as older sisters sharing a critical stance toward the youngest. The concept of alignment provides a way to talk about—and see—the subtle shifts in connection and competition that the sisters negotiated in their conversation.

Sister by Your Side

In the eyes of the world, and of their own families, sisters are often seen as a unit. It's common to hear sisters referred to collectively by their shared last name, as in the book title *The Beecher Sisters*. Within the family, sisters are often referred to simply as "the girls." In the eternal struggle between connection and independence, being thus merged can be comforting—or discomfiting.

The comfort can come from having someone by your side so you're not alone, someone who understands your life and how your family history led you to it. This is especially evident in dramatic circumstances. Gisela was a Jewish child living in Berlin in 1939 when her family was desperately awaiting visas so they could leave Germany and join relatives in the United States. At thirteen Gisela was lucky to be included in a Kindertransport: Jewish children who were taken out of Nazi-controlled Europe to spend the war years in England. Her parents and older sister eventually managed to leave Germany for the United States in 1941, but Gisela was not able to join them until after the war ended, in 1946. By then, she was a young woman of twenty who had made a life for herself in Yorkshire. It was with reluctance that she left that life and the English family she had come to love. Her mother, thrilled to be reunited with her younger daughter, could not understand why Gisela had wanted to remain in England or why, when she arrived in the United States, she wanted to go back to Yorkshire. Gisela's salvation was that her sister understood how she felt. Ironically, her sister's understanding of Gisela's ties to her foster mother and her English home made it possible for her to break those ties and remain in the United States with the family she had been separated from for seven years.

But sister ties can also cause discomfort. Bobbi and Rose were home-schooled until Bobbi was nine and Rose seven. Suddenly attending a large school peopled by a horde of strangers was a challenge to both girls, but it was harder for Rose because she was not only younger but also shy and fearful—so fearful she couldn't find her voice to speak. If Rose had something to say, she whispered it to Bobbi, who would say it for her. And when, for the first few days at the new school, she cried inconsolably, the thoughtful school administrators placed a chair next to Bobbi's and allowed little Rose to sit beside her in Bobbi's classroom. When I think of this scene from Rose's point of view, I am touched by her trust in Bobbi to speak for her and the comfort she found simply by being in her sister's presence. But when I think of it from Bobbi's perspective, the picture shifts. Imagine a nine-year-old, herself overwhelmed by the challenge of a strange new world, being responsible for a seven-year-old—and trying to establish her place in a class full of peers with a weeping little sister stuck to her side. The alignment between them was comforting to Rose but discomfiting to Bobbi.

It is in the nature of alignments that connecting any two or more people can leave others out. An image from a wedding I attended has remained fixed in my mind. All the wedding guests were delighted and impressed when the groom and his two sisters took the microphone from the professional musicians and sang in three-part harmony. But the two women singing with him weren't the groom's only sisters. He had a third sister; she was seated among the guests, looking utterly dejected. I don't know why she didn't join in the singing, but it was a dramatic example of how an alignment among some siblings can exclude others.

Sister on Someone Else's Side

Sisters can align with one another, or they can align separately with one or both parents. And a sister's alignment with parents rather than with another sister can cause disappointment, hurt, and distance. I winced on reading an account of how a twelve-year-old joined her parents in belittling her seven-year-old sister for the offense of . . . playing with dolls.

Anthropologists Charles Darrah, James Freeman, and J. A. English-Lueck followed a number of American families closely, observing them as they went about their daily lives. In their book *Busier Than Ever,* they show that each family is a unique world in which parents imbue their children with their worldview and values. To show how families' use of and attitudes toward objects play a role in this process, the authors introduce a seven-year-old girl, Hettie, who loved to "play Barbies" with her friends. Hettie used a computer to design clothes for her dolls. Playing with dolls and designing clothes for them is such a common activity for girls her age, it probably wouldn't be remarked on in most families. A girl might even be praised for her computer skills and doll-fashion designs. Hettie's parents indulged her fondness for Barbies, but they also "gently rebuked" her for it, making clear their disapproval of the stereotyped gender roles the dolls represent. The authors note that Hettie's twelve-year-old sister Sonya "took on the attitudes and demeanor of her parents. She scornfully dismissed Hettie's Barbie art as 'not very creative.'" Sonya could have aligned with her little sister without rejecting their parents' values, perhaps by saying something like, "Lots of girls her age play Barbies. She'll grow out of it." Instead, Sonya aligned with their parents, reinforcing Hettie's isolation within the family.

At any age, an older sister's alignment with parents rather than with a younger sister can cause disappointment, hurt, and distance. When Emma decided to move in with her boyfriend, she knew her parents would disapprove, and she braced herself for their reaction. But she was not prepared for the letter she received from her sister. Madeleine, three and a half years older, warned Emma that this move would be a disastrous mistake. She cautioned that it is crucial for a woman to remain a virgin until her wedding day; that's what she herself had done and that's why her marriage was happy. Emma's boyfriend (who later became her husband) was incensed; he felt Madeleine was interfering in something that was not her business. Emma agreed, but she also felt betrayed. By writing that letter, her sister aligned with their parents rather than with her. Emma received a letter from her parents too, but when she told me this story decades later, she didn't even remember what her parents' letter had said. It was the letter from her sister that stuck in her mind—and her craw—because it violated the sisterly alignment she had expected.

A sister need not agree with a parent to be seen as violating an expected sisterly alignment. Just arguing their case can come across that way. Two sisters got caught up in a tangle like this when one of them, Patty, recently divorced, decided to buy a rather expensive two-family house. Though the price was significantly more than she had planned to spend, the income from the rental unit would help cover the mortgage payments. She was stunned and angry when her father argued adamantly against her decision. As a single woman, he said, she had no business becoming a landlord. Dealing with renters was a bigger headache than she realized; if an unsavory character moved in, she and her children would be vulnerable, and what if the unit sat empty for a period of time? She might find herself unable to meet the mortgage payments and lose everything. He had promised to help her make a down payment on a small single-family home, but he said he couldn't in good conscience contribute if Patty went ahead with this reckless move. Patty was so angry she stopped talking to her father—and to her mother, who she believed could have talked sense into him if she'd wanted to.

Patty's mother, in turn, was stunned. She knew her daughter needed her more than ever at this time, and being shunned by Patty meant being cut off from her beloved grandchildren as well. She asked Patty's older sister Diane to intervene. "She'll listen to you," their mother said. "Make her understand that I had nothing to do with this. Why punish me?" Younger sisters do often listen to older ones. But in this case, it didn't work. Though Diane thought she was simply representing their mother's point of view, Patty saw her as aligning with their mother—and by implication with their father—when she had expected her sister to take her side. Instead of relenting and talking to their mother, she stopped talking to her sister too.

Whose Side Are You On?

A family consists of so many overlapping and sometimes conflicting alignments that it can feel like a giant spiderweb: necessary for the spider to
snare nourishment but also sticky and, if you don't negotiate carefully, potentially entangling as you ask, of yourself and others, Whose perspective
are you taking? Whose side are you on?

Cynthia and her boyfriend were moving to California, where they
knew only one person: Stan, her sister Tracy's former husband. Cynthia
asked Tracy if it would be all right for her to contact Stan. Tracy said it
was, and she meant it. Her divorce from Stan had been amicable; they
were on good terms. But when Cynthia and her boyfriend not only contacted but actually stayed with Stan, Tracy (in Cynthia's words) freaked
out. From Tracy's point of view—a view she didn't have until the scene
materialized before her eyes—her sister's alignment with her former husband, when her own alignment with him was severed, felt like a betrayal.
Cynthia had been thinking of her own alignment with Stan: They'd always
liked each other; he'd been a family member for many years. But this
alignment conflicted with her alignment with her sister.

Judy was also caught in conflicting alignments. Her daughter had
given birth to her first child. With her husband in the army and a baby who
wouldn't stop crying, she was overwhelmed and exhausted; she wanted
her mother to come and help. Judy wanted to, but she was helping her
own two sisters clear out the accumulated possessions that remained in
their mother's home after their mother had passed away. Judy had a responsibility to do her share of the work at their parents' home, and she
wanted to share in the excavation of memories they were uncovering with
their parents' possessions. It was a once-in-a-lifetime activity, and it
couldn't be put off. But her daughter called daily, begging her to come. In
the end, the heartstrings of Judy's alignment with her daughter could bear
no more pulling, and she left her sisters to help her daughter. But she always felt she'd let her sisters down. There was simply no way to honor
both alignments; she had to choose one.

What seems like an alignment between two sisters may actually involve
three people. There may be a shadow figure tangling up the lines: a sister's

spouse. Alexandra and Lenore together inherited their parents' home when their parents died. They had the house appraised, and Lenore's husband, a professional landscaper, observed that the front and back yards looked unkempt. He offered to replace the dying azaleas, trim the old rosebushes, and generally spruce up the grounds, which their mother had left untended in the last years of her life. The real estate agent agreed that this would raise the value of the house, so Alexandra gratefully accepted her brother-in-law's offer. But when she went to see the house several weeks later, she was horrified to discover that the beautiful old rosebushes had been decimated, the azaleas and every other flowering plant had been taken out, and the entire yard had been torn up—but nothing new had been planted. It looked worse than unkempt; it looked like a construction site. Her brother-in-law had decided that the grounds needed completely new landscaping and had begun the work, but after ripping things out, he stopped, because he got a large commission. Working on his wife's parents' house was no longer his priority. As a result, the house was sold for far less than it had been worth before. Alexandra's position was clear: She was furious at her sister. But Lenore was torn between alignments to her husband and her sister. Though she too lost money because of her husband's work on the house, she ultimately came down on his side.

Alexandra and Lenore argued vehemently. "Why did you let him tear it apart if he wasn't going to finish the job?" Alexandra demanded.

Lenore defended her husband: "He had every intention of finishing it. He didn't know he was going to get that big contract. There are more important things in our lives than that house!"

As they argued, both sisters dragged the past into the present conversation—or, rather, they verbalized the past that is always present in families.

"It's not an isolated incident," Alexandra accused. "You both start things and leave them undone. That's your business, but this time it's my business too."

Lenore shot back: "Why are you making such a big deal about it? It's not like you need the money. You have way more money than we do." Then Lenore said something that could only be said by siblings—and that siblings can say at any time: "You always got more than I did. You were the favorite!"

The favorite—that perennial threat and frequent demon of sibling relationships—is the jewel in the crown of family alignments.

Playing Favorites

A woman who was one of five siblings, three sisters and two brothers, told me that her mother referred to her as her "A-Number-One Child," leaving little question that she was the favorite. Another woman said that her father favored her by buying gifts for her and only her when he traveled, and when he was home he invited her and only her to accompany him in activities he enjoyed. These examples of "playing favorites" are obvious. Few examples I encountered were this apparent, and few parents claim to have favorites among their children. Many go to great lengths to treat all their children equally. In some cases this works perfectly: several women told me that they and all their siblings each felt like the favorite. But the majority of those I spoke to readily told me which of their siblings was favored by which parent, though they didn't always agree on who it was.

"My sisters think I was our mother's favorite," a woman said. "I didn't see it because she beat me." How could a child be the favorite of a parent who beats her? The answer may lie in the concept of alignment. Whether the line running from one to the other is made of approval or disapproval, of expressions of love or antagonism, the alignment is created by the focus of attention on that child and the intensity of the feelings between them. Another woman told me that her father often says, "No one can make me as angry as you." Though this comment may seem extremely negative, she added, "Even in his anger I feel special." (Between sisters, too, fighting can reflect or create alignments. A woman who is the eldest of six commented, "I have more fun with the sister I fight with.")

A child whom parents fight *about* rather than *with* can also seem like the favorite. Gail recalls hearing her sister shout at their father, "You only have one child in your mind—Gail!" But Gail herself thought her parents hated her. Gail and her sister were both responding to the same dynamic. Gail had been a troubled child, unable to sleep, chronically unhappy and hyperactive. Gail believed her parents hated her because she could hear them arguing loudly in their bedroom about how to deal with her. Her sister knew only that most of her parents' attention was focused on Gail. The concept of alignment helps explain how Gail could think she was hated while her sister saw her as the favorite: A parent can "play favorites" not only by showering approval or gifts on one child more than another but also by devoting more time and attention, regardless of the form that attention takes.

Rosalyn's parents did everything possible to avoid playing favorites, and this too resulted in her feeling slighted. One year Rosalyn asked her mother to prepare a special treat for her birthday: the honey cake that Rosalyn had always loved. Her mother said she couldn't. If she made a honey cake for Rosalyn, she'd have to make cakes for Rosalyn's two sisters, and she didn't have time to make three cakes. In the end, her mother did give Rosalyn a honey cake on her birthday—a really small one, because she split the batter for one cake into three parts, to treat her daughters equally. Rosalyn felt she'd been shortchanged. It was, after all, her birthday; couldn't she be singled out on one day of the year? A parent's admirable efforts not to play favorites can itself mean that no child gets the whole cake of parental love.

Divorce: The Great Shake-up

Divorce can shift family alignments like a great shake of a kaleidoscope. And like the unpredictable rearrangement of a kaleidoscope's colored pieces, there are many different ways that divorce can leave family members re-sorted and realigned.

A woman, the youngest of four, was eleven when her parents divorced. She said of herself and her siblings, "We were sort of each other's comforting." In fact, she remarked, "My primary family in my life has been my siblings." Divorce strengthened the alignments of mutual support among them. But divorce can also fundamentally change alignments. Taylor was twelve when her parents divorced. She recalls, "At that moment I grew up. I filled in the gaps." The gaps she filled in were the needs of her ten-year-old sister, Joanne. As a result of their parents' divorce, Taylor's alignment with Joanne changed from sisterly to motherly. She saw herself and her mother aligned as two adults responsible for a child, her sister.

The realignments following divorce are even more complex if there is a new stepparent, especially if the stepparent's relationship with the parent preceded (and therefore, in appearance or reality, precipitated) the breakup. And the realignments can affect siblings differently, depending on their ages and temperaments and how they were aligned before. Evelyn was closer to her father than her sister was. When he left the family to live with and then marry another woman, her sister would have nothing to do with him or his new wife. But Evelyn did not break with him, and for this her sister could not forgive her. She had kept her alignment to him rather than shift to an alignment with her sister that cut him out.

Having had a special relationship with a father who leaves the family does not always lead a daughter to be more forgiving of him. It could have the opposite effect. In another family, one of two sisters had been favored by a father who abandoned his wife for a much younger woman. In that case, it was the previously favored daughter who was so angry that she cut off contact with him. The other sister kept in touch—and enjoyed the chance to be the focus of her father's attention, a position that hadn't been open to her when her sister had filled it.

For a daughter who had found it hard to penetrate the alignment between her mother and her sister, the appearance of a stepmother can be an opportunity to step into the role of Mom's favored daughter. Before their parents' divorce, Roberta and her sister, Carolyn, both knew that Roberta got better treatment from their mother. Enter their father's second wife, whom he married immediately after leaving their mother. Roberta felt honor-bound to be cool to the intruder out of loyalty to her mother. But Carolyn, who'd previously felt slighted by her mother, felt no such obligation. She formed an alignment with her stepmother that excluded Roberta. Since their father had realigned with his new wife, Roberta was now excluded twice over. Leaving aside her rejection of her stepmother, which was her choice, she also lost her alignment with her father and her sister.

In another family, too, divorce created a major realignment involving two sisters, though the specifics differed. The younger sister, Iris, got along better with their father than her sister, Lauren, did. So when their father left the family and set up housekeeping with another woman, the impact on Iris was more severe. She was the one who had basked in the glow of affection her father had lavished on her, all the more because he was not lavishing any on his wife. But now his new girlfriend was the focus of his affection, so for Iris, a spigot of love was suddenly turned off. Lauren took a position she thought of as above the fray: "This is the new order, you might as well accept it." But this stance wasn't really neutral. Because she was accepting his new situation, Lauren aligned with their father and broke her alignment with Iris. Later, Lauren came to agree with her sister that their father was behaving badly. Only then did she realign with her sister, replacing the connection to their father that Iris had lost when their parents divorced.

Choosing Up Sides

In all these examples, divorce required sisters to choose sides. Not all divorces have this effect; many are negotiated with a minimum of contention between the parents. And a family needn't go through a divorce for this to happen. Children can find themselves choosing sides, or being assigned sides, when both parents are at home.

The younger two of four sisters, in separate interviews, helped me understand their family by describing the seating arrangement at the dinner table in their childhood home. Their mother and father sat at opposite ends of the table; the two older girls sat to the father's right and left while the two younger ones sat to the right and left of the mother. This wouldn't be unusual, except for the conversations: There were two separate ones. At his end of the table, their father spoke to the two older daughters about politics, current events, and other intellectual topics. The two younger daughters talked only to their mother. The seating arrangement, and parallel conversations, established lines of alignment that split the family into two discrete teams.

Though these mutually exclusive alignments were unusually stark, the sense that children are aligned with one parent or the other was not unusual among the women I interviewed. In another family, Chris described herself and her two sisters almost like captains choosing players for volleyball teams. She sorted the sisters in relation to their parents based on personality, appearance, and interests. "I could handle our father better," Chris said. "I could tell when he was going to get angry and mollify him." She and her sister Ruth were further aligned with their father's side of the family by appearance: They resembled him and his relatives, while their sister Ellie looked more like their mother. (I have often thought that this common impulse to seek out alignments by physical resemblances must be challenging for children who were adopted.) Finally, Chris described alignments by interests: Ellie and their mother were word people who loved reading, while Chris and Ruth liked working with their hands: fixing or building things, painting, sewing, or knitting.

It was almost universal among the women I interviewed to describe themselves and their sisters by alignment with parents. "She got our father's sense of humor" or "our mother's temper" were common ways of saying that a sister was funny or volatile. And the way families assign interests and characteristics to align children with one parent or the other sometimes seemed imposed as much as discerned. In one family, for example, a sister was aligned with her mother, a talented seamstress, because she, too, made clothes—and because she married a man in the clothing business. Focusing on the nature of her husband's business (clothing) rather than the nature of his profession (business) reflected and reinforced the sense that this sister was aligned with her mother.

By separating siblings into teams aligned with one parent or another, we seek parallels—similarities and differences—to make sense of our families. It's one more way we look to siblings as we try to see ourselves.

Trickle-Down Alignments

I heard a mother say to her daughter, "You and I are the same. Your sister's different. You and I have the same body type. We have to watch our weight." The alignments created by and reflected in this brief exchange are not simple. Sorting family members by physical characteristics is rarely neutral. Aspects of appearance almost always imply value judgments. When the characteristic that aligns a child with a parent is one that the parent—or the child—dislikes in herself, the alignment can feel like a put-down, whether it's intended that way or not. In this case, the daughter responded, "You like my sister's looks—she's so pretty and thin—and you're repulsed by me." The daughter believed that her mother's distaste for her own body type was trickling down to her.

A woman's alignment with her sister can also trickle down to her own children, especially daughters. If you see in your daughter traits you liked in your sister, the similarity is a positive thing. "Somehow I had my sister's child," a woman told me. She admired her sister's industriousness and intelligence and was glad to see these traits in her daughter. She perceived a shadow alignment between her daughter and her sister, so the positive feelings she had about her sister were transferred to her daughter as well.

Sometimes, however, the marks left by a sister relationship can be more like a burn than a balm. It's usually comforting to hear from a friend, "I know just how you feel; I had the same experience." But sometimes that reassurance is not reassuring. Kayla recalls that she came home from high school one day and told her mother that her teacher had said, "Well, you won't be going to the college your sister Vivian went to." Her mother responded, "I know how you feel. I had a sister who was smarter than me too." Kayla's mother had always felt intimidated by her own older sister, Kayla's aunt, and Kayla believed that she took the same stance toward Vivian. Her mother's alignment with her own older sister had trickled down to her daughters.

Eleanor harbored a similar though smaller-scale grievance resulting from her mother's alignment with her own sister, Eleanor's aunt. When Eleanor was growing up, her mother worked in a dress factory. She sometimes brought dresses home for her daughter and her niece, her younger sister's daughter. And she always gave her niece first choice. As if that wasn't bad enough, one time when Eleanor's mother displayed two dresses she had brought, her niece said she wanted them both—and Eleanor's mother let her have them. From one point of view—and this was Eleanor's—her mother was favoring her cousin over her. But I suspect that in her mother's mind, it had nothing to do with the girls and everything to do with their mothers. Eleanor's mother had always taken care of her younger sister; taking care of her sister's daughter was an extension of that, so giving her niece first choice or even both dresses was simply extending to her sister's daughter the same self-sacrificing care she had always shown her sister.

I better understood this view when I spoke to another woman who explained a similar impulse, which she and her sister refer to as "lamb chops." If there's only one lamb chop left and both their children want it, she explained, they face a choice: "Whose kid is going to get it?" This woman adored her sister, so her choice was obvious: "Of course I'd give it to hers." She said this in the context of telling me how much she loves her sister, not how much she slights her children. Lamb chops, like the gift of dresses, illustrate how alignments can trickle down to the next generation.

I heard a particularly dramatic account of a mother's alignment with her sister being passed down to her daughters from a psychotherapist, Judith Kellner. Judith's mother was born in Hungary. When the Germans invaded her town during World War II, she was eleven and had been left alone with her eighteen-year-old sister. Their father had died, their mother was in Budapest, their brother had vanished, and their home became the Germans' headquarters. The older sister managed their survival by successfully hiding their Jewish identity. She also protected her sister by making her look even younger than she was: She insisted the girl bind her breasts to conceal them, keep her hair in pigtails, and carry a doll with her at all times. Judith grew up hearing her mother speak of her older sister, not with gratitude for having protected her but with resentment for being "controlling" and having treated her unfairly. Judith thus imbibed a deep sense that she had to make up for her aunt's mistreatment of her mother by being a better substitute-mother to her own sister, who was nine years younger than Judith. And her mother's childhood alignment trickled—or cascaded—down to her daughters in another way too: She re-created it by giving her older daughter responsibility for her younger one, thereby ensuring that the younger daughter would re-create it in turn by resenting Judith.

Let Me In, Let Me Out

The alignment I heard about more often than any other was the one between a mother and her oldest daughter—as described to me by younger ones. Many younger daughters told me that their mother and older sister formed a unit they could not penetrate. It could take many forms. Sometimes they shared interests; sometimes the mother had higher expectations of the oldest and paid more attention to how she did in school; sometimes she respected her opinions and engaged her in conversation; sometimes she worried more about her. Understandably, many younger sisters were hurt by this. But attention can become scrutiny, and many second sisters said they felt liberated by this exclusion: Their mothers were so busy focusing on their sisters that they themselves had more freedom to go their own ways.

While the younger daughter may see only the alignment that links her mother and older sister, the older sister may see another that excludes her. More than one alignment can coexist; since sisters are peering from different perspectives, they may see different ones. It's hard to conceive of a tighter alignment between a mother and her oldest daughter than the one between country singers Naomi and Wynonna Judd. For years they traveled as a duo, harmonizing, performing, winning awards. Yet Wynonna sees a different alignment. Speaking of her younger sister, she said, "Ashley is the part of my mom that [my mom] likes best. She's intellectual, organized, such a hostess." The world saw an alignment of action between mother and oldest daughter traveling and singing together. Wynonna saw an alignment of affinity: her mother seeing in her younger daughter aspects of herself. And the sisters will always have an alignment of shared history and memory, because they spent their childhoods together moving constantly with their mother from place to place.

Alignments are key to understanding what goes on between sisters when they are growing up, and alignments help explain how patterns evolve or endure when sisters are grown.

CHAPTER FIVE

"I'll Be the Princess, You Be the Frog"
Younger Sister: The View from the Frog

I was working with Naomi and Mimi, my two older sisters, in Naomi's kitchen. We were preparing lunch for our extended family, gathered at her home in the Adirondack Mountains. Mimi was cutting cabbage for coleslaw, Naomi was molding chopped meat into hamburgers, and I was the eager assistant, repeatedly asking if I could help and doing whatever task I was assigned. Mimi's husband, Bruce, came in and stood opposite her.

"I'm going to take a walk," Bruce said. "Would you like to come?"

Without stopping what she was doing, Mimi asked, "Where are you going to walk?"

"Well, if you come," he replied, "I'll walk to the pond up the road. If I go by myself I'll hike into the hills."

"I need to cut this cabbage," Mimi said. She continued to cut and Bruce continued to stand across the table from her, looking expectant.

I was watching this scene with my usual interest in human behavior. I noticed that Bruce wasn't leaving because he really wanted his wife's company. I could see that Mimi wanted to join him but didn't feel she could abandon her task. Then suddenly I realized I didn't have to be a passive observer. "Why don't you take a walk with Bruce," I said, "and I'll cut the cabbage."

Mimi dropped that knife almost before my sentence was finished, and she and Bruce were out the door a second later. I was ashamed that I hadn't thought of that obvious solution earlier. Why did I delay even a moment, watching as if I had no power to act? And why did Mimi assume it was her job, and hers alone, to cut the cabbage? Why didn't it occur to her that I could do it just as well? The answer to these questions is the ecology of the family, and the array of siblings by age. Mimi is older; she's competent; it's second nature to her that if a job needs to be done she should do it. I tend to feel incompetent around my two older sisters (and, by extension, in anyone's kitchen other than my own). I wait to be assigned tasks not because I'm reluctant to pitch in, but because I don't want to do something the person in charge doesn't want done or do something the wrong way: choose the wrong knife or bowl, cut the slices too thick or too thin.

As I took over cutting the cabbage, I heard in my mind the voices of older sisters who complained that their younger sisters don't do their share of work but just sit there and expect to be waited on. Like a medical student who thinks she has every disease she learns about, I saw myself in nearly all the bad-sister stories I heard. Now I thought that I, too, must seem lazy or self-indulgent. I reassured myself that I never sit around doing nothing; I always ask if there is anything I can do and do whatever is suggested. And I always voluntarily wash dishes, a job I know I can do without worrying that I might do it wrong (though I always ask which sponge or cloth my host prefers I use). Still, I wondered how often the women seen as lazy by their older sisters were sitting by passively not because they felt entitled to be waited on but because they felt incompetent or didn't want to intrude on their sisters' turf, like stepping over the line into her side of the bedroom they shared as kids.

The ending of this story was happy for everyone. Mimi and Bruce got to take their walk, and—absurd as this may sound—I loved cutting the cabbage. It was such a simple, mindless, no-big-deal task, I doubt that performing it gave Mimi any particular pleasure. But taking it over made me feel buoyant and happy. That was partly because I was glad I'd been able to help my sister and her husband do what they wanted. But it was also because doing that simple task made me feel competent. For once I wasn't just setting the table, fetching a bowl, or performing some other ancillary task I'd been assigned after meekly asking, "Is there anything I can do?" I'd seen a need and stepped in.

The Ecology of Family

When I took over cutting the cabbage, I was exhilarated because I had changed the way I usually interact with my sisters. I'd tried out for—and got—a new role in the family play. Often, though, when adult sisters get together, they take their usual role or find that a play they thought was different is really just another version of the same play they've been in their whole lives.

Here's another encounter that illustrates the enduring nature of family ecology. It too took place in a kitchen, a frequent site of sister conversations because it's the symbolic center of a home—and a room where women often gather. This experience was described by psychologist and writer Rona Maynard in an essay about her relationship with her younger sister, writer Joyce Maynard. (I quoted Joyce's essay in Chapter Four.)

Rona agonized about Joyce's impending visit. Joyce had an event to attend in the city where Rona lives, and she wanted to stay at her sister's house. Rona was reluctant because Joyce's previous visit had left her feeling invaded and overwhelmed. The intrusion was encapsulated by the way Joyce had taken over Rona's kitchen: "with the phone under her chin, a pastry blender in her hand, flour everywhere and the stereo at full volume." Rona faced a dilemma. She knew that Joyce would be terribly hurt if Rona told her she couldn't stay. "I couldn't bear to hurt my sister—or to lose myself placating her," Rona wrote in her essay. She hit upon a solution: Joyce could stay in Rona's home, but Rona would not. She and her husband would stay at a nearby hotel.

This solution seemed perfect to Rona but not to Joyce. Joyce, the younger sister, had always longed to be accepted by Rona and had always (as Joyce wrote in her accompanying essay) felt rejected by her. That same dynamic was being played out again. Vacating her own home so Joyce could stay in it was an admirable (one might say heroic) effort not to disappoint her sister. But it is also a perfect example of re-creating rejection in apparent welcome. Joyce wanted to stay with her sister, not just in her sister's house. By moving out, Rona turned down the most important element of Joyce's request—her desire for closeness—and Joyce ended up feeling rejected again. That's family ecology. Even when you're trying to change the dynamics, you can end up replicating them.

Who'll Make the Pie?

A scene in Patricia O'Brien's historical novel *Harriet and Isabella* dramatizes how a youngest sister can repeat and reinforce her place in the family, even as she's trying to change it. And each sister's behavior—exactly
the behavior that frustrates the other—is in part a reaction to that other's
behavior, in a mutually aggravating spiral.

O'Brien's novel is about Harriet Beecher Stowe, author of *Uncle Tom's
Cabin,* and her sister Isabella Beecher Hooker, the youngest of ten
Beecher siblings who was active in the suffragist movement. In this scene,
seven Beecher siblings have gathered at Harriet's home to confer about a
looming family crisis. Isabella goes for a walk, comes upon a blackberry
patch, and decides to gather the ripe, luscious berries. She hadn't planned
to pick berries, so she has no bucket with her and collects the berries in
her apron. Then she has an inspiration: She'll make a pie! Pleased with
this plan, Isabella eagerly anticipates how surprised and impressed her
two older sisters will be, since they see her as domestically challenged.

When she returns to the house, Isabella is greeted by an impatiently
waiting Harriet, who informs her that all the siblings are seated in the
salon for a family meeting. They've been waiting for Isabella to return so
the meeting could begin. Isabella rushes into the parlor to join the meeting, forgetting the berries in her apron until Catharine, the oldest sister,
exclaims, "Bella, what in heaven's name is in your apron? I believe it is
leaking on Harriet's carpet!"

"Blackberries," Isabella explains. "I'm going to make a pie for dinner."

Catharine dismisses Isabella's plan: "When did you last make a pie,
dear?" She then tells Isabella to get baking soda and a cloth to clean the
carpet, and adds, "I'll make the pie."

Isabella's response? She stands up, walks through the house to the
back door, opens the door, and dumps the berries into the dirt.

When Isabella decided to make a pie she was hoping to change the
ecology of her family. She would show her older sisters that she was not
the incompetent, impetuous baby sister they believed her to be. But
everything she did reinforced the impression that she was. First she kept
everyone waiting. When she finally appeared, she thoughtlessly brought
an apron filled with blackberries into Harriet's parlor and allowed them to

drip on the carpet. Then she threw the perfectly good berries into the dirt. As Harriet told her, "When you do something like that, you only make the others question your judgment more."

In the scene O'Brien depicts, Isabella was indeed impetuous and incompetent. But every move that gave this impression was a reaction to a move made by an older sister. Isabella threw out the berries because Catharine had announced she would preempt her pie-making. Isabella forgot the berries in her apron because Harriet greeted her at the door with such impatience and urgency. And why did Isabella disappear in the first place? This, too, was a reaction to an older sister's provocation. She went out for an unplanned walk to escape Catharine's harping disapproval of her suffragist activities.

But each step of the way, Harriet and Catharine were reacting to Isabella's behavior too. Harriet greeted Isabella impatiently and rushed her into the parlor because Isabella had disappeared without telling anyone where she was going. And Catharine spoke scornfully to Isabella, issuing peremptory orders, because Isabella brought dripping berries into the parlor and was oblivious when they leaked onto the carpet. It made sense for Catharine to doubt that Isabella could make a pie, not only because she knew that Isabella had little or no pie-making experience but also because Isabella had just demonstrated that she didn't know how to handle berries properly.

Each sister accurately saw her own behavior as provoked by another's, but none saw that the other's offending behavior was provoked by her own.

Every family has its own ecology, each member reacting to—and provoking reactions in—the others. But the specific pattern of mutual aggravation that O'Brien describes in this scene is common (though by no means universal) to older sister/younger sister dynamics. The oldest, Catharine, is critical of her younger sister and assumes it's her job to complete whatever tasks need to be done, including, or maybe especially, those begun by her younger sister. The youngest, Isabella, is impulsive and seemingly incompetent. (Joyce Maynard, too, was considered, in her own words, "the flighty, impulsive sister.") I recognized this pattern in many of the accounts I heard from women I spoke to—and in my own experience. I was never considered flighty or impulsive (I checked with my sisters), but I saw myself in the youngest sister who was incensed that her older sisters didn't think she could make a pie.

I'm Not Helpless, You Know

When my sister Naomi was twenty-five, she planned to take a five-week trip to Europe. Our parents didn't want her to go alone. Mimi, nineteen at the time, was engaged to be married, so it was decided that I would accompany Naomi, though I was only seventeen. I anticipated this trip with great excitement. I worked evenings and Saturdays at Macy's so I could contribute to the cost. Naomi and I had never experienced conflict. I admired and adored her. The prospect of spending time with her was as enticing as the prospect of seeing Europe.

We did have many wonderful experiences together on the trip, but there were also times when I was angry at her—at times very angry. One reason was my feeling that Naomi acted as if I was incompetent—or simply not there. Whenever there was something to be done—a request to be made, a transaction to be conducted—Naomi did it, leaving me to bring up the rear like the caboose on a train. Naomi had studied French in high school, so she had good reason to take the lead when we were in France. She also knew some Yiddish, because our Yiddish-speaking grandmother had lived with us until she died, when Naomi was fifteen but I was only seven. So it also made sense for Naomi to do the talking in German-speaking Switzerland. Nonetheless I felt that Naomi was depriving me of the fun of being in a foreign country—talking to local people—and acting like I didn't exist.

There was one language, though, that I spoke and Naomi didn't: Spanish. I'd studied it in junior high and high school and could speak it pretty well—far better, in fact, than Naomi could speak either Yiddish or French. So I decided we should add Spain to our itinerary. It wouldn't cost any more since we had Eurail passes that allowed us to take trains anywhere in Europe. But it did mean a very long train ride, so at first Naomi reasonably resisted the change of plans. She eventually agreed, and we headed for Barcelona. Over the many hours that the train made its way from Italy through France to Spain, my excitement mounted as I anticipated being in a country where I'd be the one who knew the language. Finally, our train arrived and we stepped onto the platform. Naomi headed for a station employee and asked for directions—in French.

If anger describes how I felt about my older sister doing all the talking before, I'd have to find a new word to capture what I felt then: fury maybe, maybe rage. I'd resented her taking charge when she could speak the language and I couldn't. But here she was trying to talk to someone in a language he didn't understand, while right beside her was someone who spoke his language—me. I plotted revenge. A few days later we met a group of young Spanish men. I was chatting away with one of them in Spanish when Naomi asked me to help her out by translating something her new friend was trying to say. I refused. I remember thinking, You thought my Spanish was useless at the station, you can't suddenly decide it's useful now. Go ahead, make yourself understood in French!

Writing this, I cringe to think of how spiteful I was. It's obvious to me now that when Naomi used her French to ask directions in Spain she wasn't trying to dismiss me and my language skills. I doubt she was thinking of me at all. She was just doing what she had always done, what she'd always been expected to do as an oldest sister: She saw a need and tried to fulfill it any way she could. (Furthermore, though I thought I was an adult at seventeen, she no doubt saw me as the teenager I was, a kid she was responsible for.) And I didn't need to respond by silently seething and seeking revenge. I could have stepped forward and said, "Hey, Nae, gimme a break! I can speak Spanish, remember?" That option didn't occur to me at the time. That's the strange nature of family ecology. You think you're reacting to the behavior of others in the only way possible. You don't see that you could react differently, causing others to react to you in a different way too. All I could see at the time was that my older sister was acting as if I wasn't there.

Hello! I'm Here Too

Returning from the trip, Naomi and I landed at Kennedy Airport (then called Idlewild). At that time, the customs area was open to view. Anyone who came to meet passengers arriving on an overseas flight could watch from a balcony as arriving travelers went through customs. When we got into the customs area, we saw our parents up there, waving to us. I later heard my father telling someone that we had sailed through customs, the agent never asking us to open our luggage because Naomi had flirted with him. I was incensed. I had chatted with the customs agent too. My father was talking as if I hadn't been there at all. This scene too is illuminated by hindsight. I can see now that my father would not want to think of his seventeen-year-old daughter as flirting. But at the time it was just one more example, among many I had accumulated, of my father seeing only my oldest sister, as if I wasn't there.

When my parents were in their eighties they moved to Florida. Closing up the home they had lived in for many years, they unearthed photographs, documents, and memories that had long been filed away. One item they unearthed was an old photo album with thick black pages containing pictures affixed by little corner tabs. Each page had four baby pictures, and under each one was a little poem, handwritten in tiny print that I recognized as my father's. The baby in the pictures was Naomi; my father had written the poems for her. When I saw the album, I felt slighted. My father had written no poems to accompany baby pictures of me. In fact, there were very few baby pictures of me, period. When I went through the drawer of old photos, all the pictures I found were of Naomi: Naomi as an infant, Naomi as a little girl sitting on a pony, Naomi dressed in a nurse's costume. On and on.

When I looked at these pictures I felt as if I had been intentionally left out. But that made no sense. There was no me to be left out because I hadn't been born yet. But it still felt that way. And when I wrote above that "my father" had written the poems, that too was inaccurate. Naomi's father had written them; he wasn't "my" father at the time because I didn't exist. When I chose the pronoun "my" I wasn't reflecting reality but revealing the way I felt about it.

Some years ago I wrote a play based on my family that focused on my father. In preparation, I asked my sisters what they remembered about Daddy from their childhoods. Naomi described one touching scene after another. One time she hurt her knee and Daddy scooped her up, carried her inside, and carefully bandaged her knee. He taught her to fold a sheet of paper in half when she had to make a decision, and write the pros on one side and the cons on the other. He would toss ideas back and forth with her the way other fathers play ball with their kids, having debates in order to teach her how to argue and think logically. Hearing Naomi's tales, I marveled—and envied—that my father had so much time to spend with her. My memories of him are overwhelmingly of missing him because he wasn't home. When Naomi was a child, he worked normal hours so he was home evenings and weekends. When Mimi and I were children, his work kept him away most evenings and many weekends. (Here I'm reminded of an advantage I had: When I wrote "Mimi and I," it was comforting to recall that Mimi was beside me, keeping me company and sharing my fate.)

I also asked my father if he remembered what my sisters and I were like as children. Of course, he said, and proceeded to tell me specific incidents—all involving his first child. He recalled, for example, when Naomi had chicken pox. He said, "The doctor warned us, if you scratch you're left with scars. So you mustn't scratch. And she was suffering. She said, 'Itch me, Mommy. Itch me.' And we said, 'No, you mustn't scratch.' She was such a good girl, she didn't scratch. Now they have cream; I put on cortisone, and it stops the itch. It's amazing. Every time I have an itch and I put on cortisone and it stops the itch, I think of Naomi. If we had a little cortisone, it would have solved it." I asked about when Mimi and I had chicken pox. We must have itched too! He had no memory of when Mimi and I had chicken pox.

I knew that the photo album, the poems, the time Naomi spent with Daddy when she was a child were the result of changing circumstances. Though we were born into the same family, it was not the same family when each of us was born. But changing circumstances aren't the whole story. There is no escaping the primacy of the first child. For every experience you've had, there's a special resonance to the first time you had it. In her novel, Patricia O'Brien quotes Harriet Beecher Stowe: "The first child is pure poetry. The rest are prose." Many children who are not firstborn sense this. Some spend the rest of their lives trying to achieve poetry. (Sometimes they succeed so spectacularly that their firstborn sisters spend the rest of their lives wondering how they got reduced to prose.)

Anthropologist Roy Grinker writes about his own two children in his book *Unstrange Minds*. After their first child, Isabel, was born, Grinker remarks, he, his wife, and Isabel were "three, a unity so perfect that it blinds you." When their second daughter was born, Grinker observes, she was "an outsider in the way that all second, third, and fourth children are outsiders." If you've ever been close to (or been) a woman or a couple expecting a first child, you know the excitement (as well as the trepidation). How can later children ever hold the same place in their parents' imagination? Even grandparents often gravitate to the oldest. One grandmother admitted, "She's the most interesting to talk to, we've known her the longest, and she was the first, so we have a special feeling about her." This is the reality that later-born children sense.

Easy for You

I've been talking about ways that younger sisters face greater challenges than sisters born first. But the reverse can also be true. Changing circumstances can make life easier for later-born children. The family's finances may improve, so younger children grow up in better houses with more amenities. The parents may be more relaxed and more lax about enforcing rules. They (and the older children) may dote on the cute little newcomer. The narrator of Tillie Olsen's short story "I Stand Here Ironing," looking back on how she raised her children, regrets that her firstborn child, Emily, got short shrift, while Emily's younger sister Susan had an easier time—and was herself a factor in making Emily's life harder. The mother recalls how her own difficult circumstances redounded on Emily's childhood:

> She was a child seldom smiled at. Her father left me before she was a year old. I had to work her first six years when there was work, or I sent her home and to his relatives. There were years she had care she hated. . . . She was a child of anxious, not proud, love. We were poor and could not afford for her the soil of easy growth. I was a young mother, I was a distracted mother. There were the other children pushing up, demanding.

There was also another circumstance that provoked a "corroding resentment" in Emily. Whether it was the result of their different upbringings or genetic chance, "Her younger sister seemed all that she was not." Some of Susan's offenses were in her actions. She was "not able to resist

Emily's precious things, losing or sometimes clumsily breaking them." Susan also had advantages that resulted from her personality: "Susan telling jokes and riddles to company for applause while Emily sat silent (to say to me later: that was *my* riddle, Mother, I told it to Susan)." Some of Susan's advantages were accidents of birth: Emily was "dark and thin and foreign-looking in a world where the prestige went to blondeness and curly hair and dimples, she was slow where glibness was prized." Susan was "golden- and curly-haired and chubby, quick and articulate and as-sured, everything in appearance and manner Emily was not."

Differences in appearance and personality can distinguish sisters in any constellation. But the sisters in this story had drastically different child-hoods largely because their mother's circumstances were drastically differ-ent when each was born. Emily's mother became an impoverished single parent—and a psychologically anguished one—when Emily was a year old. Susan's mother was happily remarried and financially secure. Emily and Susan were born into different families, because the family's circum-stances had changed—and the changes favored the younger child. Emily might have understood what a woman said to me about her relationship with her older sister: "I've been a little ingrown toenail to her all her life."

In Olsen's story, family circumstances changed for the better when younger children came along. It is certainly possible, and common, for change to go the other way: the family's means and emotional well-being could decline rather than improve. There is, however, one circumstance that disproportionately affects younger sisters in families that have only daughters.

The Girl Who Should Have Been a Boy

My father loved to tell this story about the day I was born. He was waiting expectantly in the hospital (at that time fathers were not permitted in the labor or delivery room). The doctor appeared with a glum face. He began, "I'm sorry, Mr. Tannen." Here my father would pause, so his listeners could experience the fears that ran through his mind when he heard that opening. Then he'd resume, "I'm sorry, Mr. Tannen. It's another girl." At this my father would laugh and continue: "I said, 'But that's what I wanted! I like the other two so much, I wanted another one.' But he didn't believe me. He kept on apologizing, as if it was his fault that the baby was a girl.'"

The doctor who delivered me was not alone in assuming that the birth of a third girl must be a disappointment, especially to a father. When I tell people I'm the youngest of three sisters, they frequently ask whether my parents had me in hopes I'd be a boy. If I tell them this story as evidence that it wasn't so, some suggest that my father only said that to make me feel better by masking his true desires. That's how certain they are that all fathers want a son. There's good reason for this assumption. Many women told me that the third, fourth, and fifth sisters in their families were conceived in hopes of having a boy. One woman said of her parents, "They kept trying until they got a son." Her parents succeeded on the fourth try. But if they were winners with the fourth child, the third daughter was a loser. The woman explained that when her brother was born, "All the attention got focused on him," and the third girl "just kind of got lost. We sisters weren't paying attention to her, and I don't think my mother was paying much attention to her." Sadly, there can be losers without winners. I heard of cases in which the boy never came, and the parents, or the fathers, showed little regard for the later-born girls who came instead.

In many cases, a last-born sister, or another sister, was treated as a boy. I heard of three such cases one after the other at a gathering of six women. At the start of the discussion I asked each woman to introduce herself by saying her name then listing her siblings and where she fit in the constellation. One woman began, "I have three sisters and no brothers. I'm the second of the four girls. And my father always desperately wanted a boy." She went on to explain that when the fourth sister was born he gave up, "so he basically turned to me to be his boy." She was given a boy's nickname, her engineer father taught her to use a slide rule, and she caddied for him on the golf course.

On hearing this, another woman said, "I have two sisters. I'm the youngest. And my parents, like yours, wanted very badly for the third child to be a son. When my mother was pregnant they used to refer to me in Yiddish as *der yingl*, the boy, and of course I turned out to be me but again my father kind of treated me as a boy. I was always the one whom he shared business experience with, and he taught me how to take care of finances." Yet another woman at the gathering, the second of two sisters, picked up on the theme: "My father was looking for a boy also," she said, "and took me fishing with him because I was the only one around so I was sort of a substitute boy."

These women were in their seventies, eighties, and nineties. At first I thought their ages might explain why their fathers so badly wanted boys. Surely things have changed. But I heard similar tales from women of all ages. For example, a woman in her forties who is one of four sisters—and an identical twin—also commented that her father often said outright that she was his son. When she and her twin sister were given stuffed animals, her sister got a fluffy French poodle and she got a Saint Bernard. And more was expected of her. The decision to label her the boy reflects assumptions about gender. Her father said she was the son because she had a stronger personality and was more stubborn. It began when she was born weighing a bit more than her twin sister. But she had mentioned that she was born second. Wouldn't the one born first be seen as more aggressive? The word in her family was that she pushed her sister out.

Many daughters are glad to have been treated like sons. A woman who is the oldest of three sisters recalls, "Every time my mother was pregnant, my father would make planes. He gave us cars and guns. We had a gas station instead of a doll house. When we finally got dolls, we didn't know what to do with them." She said this without regret; she is very successful in her career and attributes her success in part to the pressure she experienced "because my father didn't have the boy."

I don't know whether being treated as a boy is more a good or a bad thing. It probably can be either or both at once. Certainly it's preferable to being mistreated or ignored, as were many later- or last-born girls in families where a boy was wanted. That makes sense in a way, but in another way it doesn't. Every sister was born female rather than male. But the onus often falls on the girl born last. The middle sister of three told me that they all always knew that their father had wanted a son, but "the boy issue" hit the youngest sister hardest.

Surprise, Surprise!

There's another way that I know I don't owe my birth to my parents' desire to have a son. Having heard so many people make this assumption, I decided when I was in my twenties to find out once and for all. I began a conversation with my parents: "If I ask you a question, will you promise to tell me the truth?" My father's response was swift. "I won't," he said, "but your mother will." In this he was truthful: My mother always said exactly what she thought, whereas he—sometimes for better, sometimes for worse—always took into account the effect his words might have on his listeners.

Thus encouraged, I went on: "When I was born, was there some part of you, any at all, that hoped I'd be a boy?"

Now it was my mother whose reply was swift. She said, "I didn't want another child at all. It didn't cross my mind to think whether it would be a boy or a girl."

Writing this now—a story I've told many times—makes me chuckle aloud because it reminds me of qualities I treasured in my parents: my father's wry humor, my mother's ruthless honesty. Some of the stories from my childhood that I've written in this book are painful to recall, but this one isn't. The knowledge that my father wanted another child but my mother didn't no longer hurts, though at one time it did. This conversation was not the first I'd heard of that circumstance of my birth. I'd known it as long as I could remember; my parents spoke of it openly. Some people are surprised, even shocked, to hear that. "How come your parents told you?" they'll ask in disbelief. But talking to women for this book, I discovered that my family's openness was not unique. Many women told me that they or their siblings had been unplanned or even unwanted. One woman said, "I was not supposed to happen. My parents needed another kid like a hole in the head. The story goes that there was a hole in the diaphragm."

Surely knowing your birth was not planned could be hurtful. It might seem wise to keep such knowledge from the children implicated. Ironically, however, the knowledge may be more hurtful if it's hidden or referred to in whispers. Anything kept secret comes with the metamessage, "This is so terrible it must not be spoken aloud." In contrast, anything openly talked about comes with the metamessage, "This is a normal part of life." I was struck not only by how often I was told that a later-born child was unplanned, but also by the vast range of ways in which this information was framed, and the equally vast range of attitudes and assumptions associated with it.

A woman told me that her younger sister doesn't know it, but the pregnancy that led to her sister's birth had been accidental whereas her own had been planned. Their mother had confessed this to her and her alone; of course her sister was never to know. On one level, keeping a daughter from knowing that her birth was unplanned is a way to protect her and prevent her feeling hurt. But by telling the secret to the other daughter, the mother reinforced the alignment with her. As a result the younger daughter was excluded twice over: first by being unplanned, and again by being kept in the dark. In fact, she's excluded thrice over, because her sister's knowing while she herself doesn't know ups the ante of exclusion. For her part, the older sister was not glad to have been told. Once she knew that her mother regarded this information as secret, she always wondered whether she herself had been unplanned, unwanted, or both.

Another woman who told me that her birth had been unplanned and unwanted did so in the context of explaining why her mother had treated her badly and made no secret of preferring the woman's older sister. I had been about to write, in the previous sentence, "she had been unplanned and unwanted." But that would not have been accurate. "She" refers to a person, an adult who was once a child. It was her birth that was unplanned, an abstract idea of a baby that was unwanted, not the actual baby she turned out to be or the actual adult she became. In this case, though, the woman felt that her mother's negative attitude toward her birth extended from the idea of another baby to the actual baby born and the child that baby became—her. Though by no means universal, that was not unique either.

I heard another account of a family in which the last child suffered grievously from having been unplanned, because it was during the Depression and her birth made tough times tougher. The oldest of three sisters was telling me that her youngest sister was hard to deal with. She traced this sister's difficulties to the circumstances of her birth:

When my mother realized she was pregnant, she was frantic. Times were terrible, there was no work for my father, and she tried every home remedy to abort the fetus, but to no avail. When the baby was born, she was little and cried and nursed constantly. I think my mother was harassed and it was a sad time. She was definitely not wanted and as the years progressed, she felt it.

The fact that this youngest sister had been unwanted trailed her for the rest of her life, because her birth coincided with disastrous economic circumstances.

The baleful tone of this tale, like the assumption of secrecy, wasn't the only spirit in which I was told of a baby being unplanned. This circumstance too could be out in the open and spoken of with humor. It was with a laugh that one woman said, "I was a surprise! My mother always said that." Good humor also characterized a similar remark made in a group discussion. The speaker was the woman who told me that her parents kept trying until they got a boy. Here's the comment I quoted before, with its conclusion: "They kept trying until they got a son, and then I was the accident after the son." At this the women who were gathered around the table all laughed. She repeated, "I was just a mistake. After four kids there's no way you're like 'Woo! Let's have another child!' There's no way." But later in the conversation she added, "Even though I was an accident, I never felt like I was a leftover. I felt like a youngest child and got the benefit of being youngest." In this family, the youngest sister's birth having been accidental was not a secret.

The same circumstance can be handled very differently in different families, each assuming that there is no other way. I was struck by the lighthearted tone in which this woman announced, "I was just a mistake," because it reminded me of another woman's remark about her sister: "Imagine going through life knowing you're a mistake!" She was assuming that this knowledge could only be painful. For the woman in that group, clearly it was not. Nor was it for the youngest sister in another family, as I got to see firsthand.

I was talking to five siblings, three sisters and two brothers, all at once. I began by trying to get a sense of where each was in the lineup by age. When I got to the youngest, a sister, she placed herself: "Yeah, and then there's me. I'm four years later." Before she had quite finished her sentence a brother finished it for her: "A mistake!" Amid general laughter, a sister concurred: "She was a mistake!" and added, "She had to sleep in the closet!" The youngest sister didn't dispute this, but explained: "We had a nice big walk-in closet—really—and that was my room. And I loved it." I can't know for sure that the laughter and teasing weren't covering up hurt, but it felt to me that the mirth was genuine. The ease with which this family talked openly about it sent a metamessage that being unplanned was not a stigma for the youngest sister. I later checked this impression with her, and she replied:

> You got it right. I absolutely have no problem with that. As a matter of fact my mother is always saying that she was glad she didn't stop at four, even if it was a mistake. I recently wrote down what she said on the phone when we were saying goodbye. She was particularly happy and thankful for all my husband and I had done for her the day before at her house—lots of yard work, etc. She said, "I'm glad something didn't work and I got you." The "something" was the diaphragm.

A child in any sibling position might be unplanned or unwanted. A national survey found that, in the United States in 2001, half of all pregnancies were unintended. But the likelihood increases—in reality or expectation—with the last child born. It's one more assumption that comes with the territory of being the youngest.

You Be the Mop

When they were small, Tina and her sister, Georgette, who was four years older, played a game they called Mop. Georgette grabbed Tina by the feet and dragged her around the house, her long blond hair spreading out like a mop. They also played a game inspired by a Nancy Drew mystery in which Georgette was a Scottish noblewoman named Lady Douglas, and Tina was her housekeeper, Morag. Tina as Morag would do anything Georgette as Lady Douglas told her to do, even something that Tina as Tina had just refused to do. Doing it as Morag was part of a game, and Tina loved to play games with her older sister. It was fun being Morag, just as it was fun being dragged around the house by her feet like a mop. And it must have been fun for the ten-year-old whose twelve-year-old sister found a way to get her to make lunch: The older one would suggest they play waitress, and the younger one would get out a notepad, take her order, then make sandwiches and serve them.

Colleen Miller recalls that when her older sister, Jeanne, and Jeanne's friends put on plays, she'd take whatever part no one else wanted, "an animal or something." She didn't mind; she was just happy to be included. Another youngest, Andrea, told me that her older sister organized plays and cast herself as the princess. Andrea got to be the witch, the dwarf, the prince, or the frog. An older sister might claim the role of princess even if she wasn't putting on a play. A Ukrainian woman, Nadia, recalls that her sister, Sofia, over eight years younger, always wanted to be with her, even if it meant just sitting in the corner listening when Nadia was with her friends. So sometimes Nadia proposed they play "princess," meaning Nadia was the princess and Sofia was her servant who did whatever she was told. One thing Nadia often told her servant to do was give her money. Though servants don't typically have more money than their masters, Sofia hoarded money and Nadia was a spendthrift, so when Nadia ran out she'd get more by asking her little sister.

Another woman who saved money as a child, Lori, told me that her older sister used her as a bank, but her sister didn't withdraw money from the bank—she robbed it. Her sister took Lori's money without asking.

Children can be creative in taunting younger sisters. For example, Lauren Treadaway recalls that her little sister particularly loved a beanbag animal she'd named Howie: "I would take Howie, climb up on her bed, put him on top of the fan, and then go, 'Hey, Kate, watch!' and turn on the fan, and Howie would go *fwoom, woo, woo, poom!* Like into the corner of her room." Though Kate would get angry and cry, the beanbag animal wasn't damaged. It always survived—to be used the same way on another occasion.

Not all possessions targeted by older sisters are as resilient as Howie. Jesse's favorite thing to do was stay in her room and play with her paper dolls. She'd make clothes for them, arrange and rearrange them, make up stories about them, and move them around as she told the stories out loud. One day Jesse came home and saw something odd. Her older sister was standing over the barrel in which the family burned trash, but it wasn't a trash-burning day. So Jesse walked over and peered into the barrel to see what had been burned. What she saw were the charred remains of her paper dolls. "They were messy," her sister explained. "And I didn't want to listen to your stupid stories anymore." Jesse was in her forties when she recalled this incident from her childhood. After telling it, she said, "I love my sister. I'm proud of her. But there's part of me that still . . . *paper dolls!*" As she said this, Jesse's body language and tone of voice conveyed how she felt when she discovered what her older sister had done to her treasured paper dolls—and how remnants of that feeling could still be found in the barrel of their adult relationship.

The Little Bully

It isn't always the older sister who pushes the younger one around. A younger sister can be a bully too, especially if she's bigger, bolder, or has a more aggressive temperament. The little sister who insists on playing horsey gets to sit atop her older sister and clobber her! And many younger sisters have an advantage that their older sisters vividly and bitterly recall: Their mothers always saw the younger as the victim and automatically chastised the older in any dispute. Knowing this, younger sisters can blame almost anything on older ones. A very young child looked up from the changing table to her mother, who was fastening her clean diaper. Indicating the diaper she had dirtied, the child accused her older sister: "Maddy did it!"

In a conversation recorded by my student Kathleen Hewett, a college student named Meredith recalled the injustice of always getting blamed. She said of her younger sister, "She'd run up and bite me, and then when I'd start to chase her she'd run into Mom's room. And I was like 'Mom, she just bit me!'" Adding insult to this literal injury, Mom never believed her— or didn't care. Being bigger and stronger, Meredith always got the blame. But smaller, weaker children can inflict considerable damage. Tatiana, a six-year-old Russian girl, was trying to be playful with her two-year-old sister who was sitting in her high chair. "Boo, boo," Tatiana cooed, putting her face close to her baby sister's. At just that moment, the baby managed to get her hands around a vase on a nearby surface and slammed it into Tatiana's face. The blood that gushed from Tatiana's forehead was eloquent testament to the power a younger sibling can have over an older one.

Gwen and her family went to live in Nigeria when she was fifteen and her sister, Anita, was eleven. Anita was just entering her mischievous tomboy stage, while Gwen was beginning to feel and act like a grown-up girl: She polished her nails, wore frilly clothes that she kept nice and clean, and always washed her face with sweet-smelling soap. One day, Anita went with a friend to watch a goat being ceremonially slaughtered in a neighbor's yard. Gwen decided to forgo that sight and stayed home. When Anita returned, she found Gwen quietly reading in her room and merrily tossed the goat's eyeball into her lap. As an adult recalling this experience, Gwen summed up her response: "I thought they were going to have to institutionalize me."

Throwing a goat's eyeball into her sister's lap was a particularly creative way to do what nearly all younger sisters do occasionally or often: try to distract an older sister who's reading, doing homework, or otherwise engaged in an activity that leaves her younger sister out. Nadia recalls that if she was doing homework, she had merely to leave the room for a few minutes to discover on her return that Sofia had raced into the room and scribbled on every page of her notebook. Another woman told me she'd sneak up behind her studious older sister and throw a blanket over her head. And three different women told me they used to hide behind the couch when their older sisters entertained dates, then choose the most impressive time to jump out and make their presence known.

These are only a few of the many examples I heard of younger sisters harassing older ones. I also heard tales of younger sisters getting older ones into trouble by tattling or making false accusations. And it was often with true bitterness that older sisters told me of younger ones who had only to shriek and adults within earshot would rush to their rescue, comforting the guilty and chastising the innocent older sisters.

Don't Blame Me

Considering these many ways younger sisters make mischief, perhaps it is not surprising that while adults tend to blame the oldest, older sisters tend to blame the youngest. We can see evidence of a younger sister's umbrage at being falsely accused in a conversation that took place among three sisters in 1952. How on earth can we listen in on a conversation that took place so long ago? The sisters, who had lived together their entire lives, were tape-recorded by a nephew when he was seventeen and they were seventy-eight, sixty-three, and sixty-one. Half a century later, the nephew still had the tape and gave it to his cousin Catherine Davies, who, lucky for us, is a linguist at the University of Alabama who studies conversation. Davies picked out for analysis a story that the sisters told about an incident that had occurred during a visit to the 1933 World's Fair. In the following excerpt, the youngest sister is talking, and it's clear that for her the main point of the story is that she was accused of a crime she didn't commit.

In 1933 a nephew named Daniel was driving the sisters and a friend of theirs from their home in Pennsylvania to the World's Fair in Chicago. The middle sister sat in the rumble seat, a seat that opened out from the back of the car, exposing the passenger to the elements. At one point it started to rain, so the sister in the rumble seat got wet, and the hat she was wearing was ruined. She wasn't worried, though, because she had brought an extra hat—or so she thought. It turned out that the box containing her spare hat, as well as other clothes, had been left behind. On discovering this, she blamed her younger sister, Bessie, for failing to bring that box, when in fact the nephew Daniel had decided to leave it behind because he couldn't fit it in the car.

When Bessie retold the story two decades later, she focused on—and repeated—the injustice of her sister blaming her:

> . . . and she blamed *me* for it, and I had nothing to do with it. It was Daniel doing it . . . and he took it, it wasn't me, and I heard her say, "That was our Bessie, that was our Bessie done that." He took it . . . glory be and I hadn't anything to *do* with the thing. . . . It was *him* carrying them. I had nothing to *do* with it. I didn't even *know* until we were about starting.

A few turns later Bessie repeats, "She went and blamed me. I had nothing to do with it. Nothing whatsoever to do with it." The transcript describes her as "sounding agitated."

There were other adventures that resulted from the sisters missing clothes they had packed, but for Bessie, those many years later, what was most memorable—and what still smarted—was her older sister unfairly blaming her. That feeling of powerlessness and of lingering resentment is common among younger sisters.

Where's the Middle?

When I planned this book, I assumed that the chapter on older sisters would come before the chapter on younger ones. But while writing this chapter, I suddenly thought, Why? Why does the oldest have to come first? I decided to put this chapter first, more or less the way I reversed the expected order when I chose the subtitle *Women and Men in Conversation* for my book *You Just Don't Understand*. My seditious reversal did little to change expectations of the "natural" order; I often see the subtitle written "Men and Women in Conversation." I've even heard people read it aloud that way while holding up the book. So I have no illusions that placing this chapter on younger sisters first will change anything either. First sisters come first by definition, and by definition the youngest comes last. But putting this chapter first gave me a little blip of satisfaction, like getting to sit in the front seat of a car where the oldest usually sits.

Before I turn to older sisters, shouldn't the next chapter be about middles? But there are so many different middles! My grandmother was the third of sixteen. Was her family composed of one oldest, one youngest, and fourteen middles? That doesn't feel right. Second oldest is surely different from second youngest. There are innumerable combinations and constellations of positions in between. Even the terms "oldest" and "youngest" are inadequate. Many factors influence what it's like to be in these positions, such as how many other siblings there are and how many years separate them. Here's an example that helped me to think about sisters who are neither oldest nor youngest.

I was attending a luncheon hosted by a women's organization. When I mentioned to my neighbor that I was writing about sisters, she pointed out three sisters who were all in the room. Two were seated at one table, a third at another. She walked me over to the sister sitting separately, Lilia, and introduced us. Lilia told me that she's the second of four. She explained that she's close to her two younger sisters, who were seated across the room, but she doesn't talk much to the oldest, because with that sister, "it's her way or no way." The younger two are in touch with her, she said, because they are happy to listen to her; they look for her approval. Later, as I typed up my notes from this conversation, I realized that the way the three sisters had seated themselves at the luncheon reflected what Lilia had described. The younger two were a pair, while she stood apart, differing in how she responds to the oldest. And in wondering why Lilia is made uncomfortable by the oldest sister's authority while the two others are not, I realized that with four years between herself and the oldest, and two younger sisters below her, Lilia is an older sister herself.

I began this chapter with an incident where my two sisters and I were preparing lunch. Though we are three, the scene I described was not really of a youngest, a middle, and an oldest. I was the youngest, yes. That explains, at least in part, why I was taking the role of helper while Mimi and Naomi were both taking charge. That's right; they were both taking the role of older sister. Naomi is six years older than Mimi, who is two years older than I. With six years between her and Naomi, Mimi is an older sister in relation to me. But she is also a younger sister to Naomi.

Those who aren't the oldest or youngest aren't something else entirely. They are older to some and younger to others. Every "middle" is a unique combination of those two roles. With that understanding, I'll turn now from younger to older sisters.

CHAPTER SIX

Gateway to the World
Older Sister: The View from the Gate

I was standing on the platform in a train station when a family of four arrived and took a place close to the tracks. Along with the parents were two little girls. One seemed to be about three, the other about five. The five-year-old glanced at the abyss where the train tracks ran, then looked at the three-year-old, who was trotting about, oblivious of her surroundings. She drew her little sister to her, wrapping her arms around her from behind in an affectionate hug—a hug that she did not release until the train arrived and they boarded it. The older sister had done just what a parent might do: She used the guise of affection to keep her younger sister safe. At five (she might well have been younger), this little girl would herself have been the child to be protected had she not had a sister who was even littler. Because she did, she was the protector.

Ten-year-old Kira was cutting a hard-boiled egg for her four-year-old sister, Sophie. Carefully wielding a knife, she first cut the egg in half, then laid the two halves facedown and cut each dome into quarters. She then asked for Crazy Salt to put on Sophie's egg. Later, as I chatted with her mother, Kira brought in a list of items for Sophie's upcoming birthday party. Each item was numbered: Play-Doh, dance, piñata. Her parents told me that Kira is like her father, logical and methodical. She is also like her father, I thought, in taking care of her little sister.

Of the many circumstances that shape children and influence the adults they become, among the most powerful is their place in the array of siblings by age. Youngest; oldest; middle of three; somewhere among four, six, or ten—each position affects the lives of those who fill it. But the position of oldest sister stands apart. Early in the process of writing this book, I kept a list of examples and notes that were relevant to each topic I planned to cover. The longest list was the one titled OLDEST SISTER; it ran to seventeen single-spaced pages. (By contrast, the list titled YOUNGEST SISTER was three pages long.) The oldest-sister position comes with the most extreme privileges, expectations, liabilities—and perhaps the greatest injustice. In exchange for fulfilling expectations placed upon them, oldest sisters are often admired and adored but also sometimes exploited and resented. A word I heard applied repeatedly to oldest sisters was "bossy." This word (used far more often for women than men) encapsulates a punish-the-victim aspect of being the oldest. "Bossy" is someone who tells others what to do. Telling younger siblings what to do is typically expected of oldest sisters from the time the younger ones come along.

The Ant and the Grasshopper

In his memoir *Dreams from My Father,* Barack Obama describes the day he became a member of the United States Senate. After the official swearing-in, he writes:

> In the Old Senate Chamber, I joined my wife, Michelle, and our two daughters for a reenactment of the ceremony and picture-taking with Vice President Cheney (true to form, then six-year-old Malia demurely shook the vice president's hand, while then three-year-old Sasha decided instead to slap palms with the man before twirling around to wave to the cameras).

The Obama girls behaved in ways that reflected their relative (not their absolute) ages. Malia, at six, behaved just as the adults in the receiving line did. Sasha, at three, did her own playful thing, then basked in the limelight. The way their father described them emphasizes the contrast: the older sister "demure," the younger one not just turning to the cameras but "twirling."

Reading this, I thought of a woman, the eldest of six, who said, "I was accused of being old in spirit," and added, "Sometimes I felt envious of my sisters' and brothers' lightheartedness." I thought, too, of another who described her younger sister as a "blithe spirit." It's not that all older sisters are demure and well-behaved, like Malia. Many were described to me as rebellious, flouting rules while bushwhacking a path, like the one who became a black-clad goth with spiked hair and piercings. But even if they were more alternative than traditional, older sisters were never described as "lighthearted," "blithe spirit," or anything like it. Referring to generations of women in her family, one woman put it this way: The older sisters were antlike, hardworking and responsible; the younger ones were like grasshoppers. Whether their temperaments were cause or effect, most of the oldest sisters I talked to or heard about were expected to take, or chose to take, a parental stance toward their younger siblings.

Oldest brothers also sometimes care for younger siblings, especially if there is no sister near him in age. But among the women I spoke to, if the oldest was a brother and the next a sister, it was typical for her, and her alone, to be given caretaking responsibilities. In one family it was explicit: When they were children, the oldest of four, a boy, and the next in line, a girl, decided that she was better suited to being the oldest, so she would take that role. They thought of this in terms of their personalities, not their genders, but similar switches occurred—without the children discussing it—in other families I encountered.

Though we wouldn't want to draw direct parallels, it's intriguing when primate behavior echoes our own. The greater inclination of sisters to be caretakers of younger siblings has been observed in nonhuman primates. According to primatologists James Higley and Stephen Suomi, female primates often hold their younger siblings, while males never do. Suomi also observed that females spend a lot of time grooming younger siblings, whereas males spend time playing with them. And as the age gap increases, the more motherlike older sisters become: The greater the age difference, the more likely older sisters are to groom younger siblings. (In contrast, as the age difference increases, older brothers lose interest in their younger siblings; they become less likely to play with them.) It's important to remember that these patterns indicate tendencies, not absolute differences. And the same goes for humans. I spoke to older and oldest sisters who told me they never took care of their younger siblings. The majority, however, did, to a lesser or greater extent depending on their parents' expectations, the family's needs, and their own proclivities.

Mini-Mom

If you've seen photographs of children in traditional societies, you've probably seen many in which a child who looks no more than six holds a baby on her hip. Though this image is surprising to many Americans, older sisters are often put in the position of taking care of younger ones here too. One woman in her thirties is still called Bama by her family because as a child she was like a baby mama to her little sister. I especially like this nickname because it captures how the parental older sister is often little more than a baby herself. Older sisters as mini-moms are looked up to and depended on by younger siblings, but sometimes they are also resented because, as many a younger sibling protests, "You're not my mother!" Maybe not, but older sisters have an awful lot in common with mothers, including in many cases how they talk to their younger sisters.

For a class she was taking at the University of Mary Washington, Gwynne Mapes recorded, transcribed, and analyzed a conversation she had while playing cards with two sisters, Kaylie and Melissa. Gwynne observed that nine-year-old Kaylie spoke to seven-year-old Melissa just as a mother might. At one point, little Melissa tried to improve her chances to win the game by grabbing Gwynne's cards and looking at them. Kaylie gasped, "Lissa!" showing disapproval in her accusatory tone but tempering it with affection and indulgence by using her sister's pet name.

Gwynne, with her college-student authority, cautioned, "No no no no, Lissa. You can't do that."

Kaylie echoed Gwynne's words: "No, here, you can't do that," then went on to teach her younger sister a lesson: "That's called cheating."

Melissa, objecting to the rules that Kaylie was trying to enforce, yelled, *"Play it my way!"*

Kaylie responded with patience: "Lissa." Gwynne Mapes described her tone as "gentle and understanding" and noted that Kaylie assumed a stance of "instruction and slight condescension"—in other words, a motherlike stance—toward her sister, who was only two years younger.

Reading this transcript, I had to go back and remind myself that Kaylie was only nine. The way she spoke to her sister kept giving me the impression that she was older than that.

A woman recalls that from the time she was twelve she was encouraged to take a motherlike stance toward her younger sister. For example, when their mother went out, she'd put the older sister in charge of the younger by saying, "Protect her, watch out for her, but don't let her know, and don't tick her off." These instructions epitomize the challenge many older sisters confront. How do you watch out for someone without letting her know that you're doing it? How do you avoid ticking her off, if you're exercising motherlike authority but are actually a sister? The one aspect of this role that many older sisters do manage well, often by their own choice, is the injunction, "Protect her."

My Sister, My Protector

The woman I was talking to stood up, stretched both arms out at her sides, and straightened her torso. She was dramatizing for me the way her older sister had always protected her, making a bulwark of her body and symbolically placing herself between her sister and any potential threat. Older sisters sometimes fight physically to protect younger ones, other times fight verbally, and sometimes just speak up to take their side when parents disapprove.

Few situations could be as frightening as the one faced by Vanessa when she was sixteen and living with her family in Knoxville, Tennessee, during the racially tense 1960s. Vanessa and her family, who are African-American, lived on a heavily trafficked corner with a large yard behind their house that was on higher ground. One day Vanessa saw a group of hostile-looking white men approaching their house, accompanied by a policeman. Their mother wasn't home, so Vanessa, the oldest sibling, greeted them at the door. The men were angry because someone had thrown a rock at their car, and they surmised it had come from the yard behind this house. Vanessa assured them that no one in her household had done any such thing, but they insisted, became angry, and called Vanessa a racial epithet. She met their anger with anger. Here she was, a sixteen-year-old girl, taking on a phalanx of menacing white men. Recalling the incident, she told me, "I'm talking as if I'm six feet tall," even though she was quaking inside. In the end, the accusers left. Vanessa had successfully defended her siblings. (Decades later she learned that the rock had indeed been thrown from their yard, by a group of boys together with her quiet little sister.)

Here's another example of a child leaping—literally—to the aid of a younger sister. Edie, the oldest of three, was in the kitchen of their childhood home when she saw through the window that the paper boy was taunting her sister Wanda, who is four years younger. While Wanda sat passively on their stoop, the boy was perched on his bicycle, shooting peas at her through a straw. "It made me so mad," Edie recalls, "I flew out the front door, over the hedges, and grabbed the straw out of his hand, knocked him off his bicycle, and started smacking him hard." But in addition to being mother-bear protective, Edie was older-sister judgmental. "I don't know who I was more mad at," she said, "him for doing it or Wanda for not standing up for herself."

The protector/caretaker role can start almost as soon as a new baby is born. One of Leona's earliest and most cherished memories is being in her crib with the chicken pox when her sister Kay climbed into her crib to comfort her. Kay wasn't the oldest, but she was the next up in age from Leona. In some ways she was the best situated to take the role of comforter, because she was small enough to climb into her baby sister's crib. And she didn't have to worry that she'd catch the chicken pox, because she already had it.

This real-life memory is similar to a fictional scene in Julia Alvarez's novel set in the Dominican Republic, *In the Time of the Butterflies*. Throughout the novel, Patria protects and helps her four younger sisters. And Alvarez shows how early it can start. She has Patria recall a tale she's heard their mother tell: At two Patria shared a crib with her one-year-old sister, Dede. Patria recounts, "One morning, she found me changing Dede's wet diaper, but what was funny was that I hadn't wanted to disturb Mama for a clean one, so I had taken off mine to put on my baby sister." The scene is touching as well as funny because a child so small was performing a motherly task, changing the baby's diaper, but also because, like a mother, she was putting the baby's welfare ahead of her own.

Take Her, She's Yours

On an Internet site devoted to sisters, a woman posted this comment describing how she feels about her older sister: "When she gets home I'm like an excited puppy to his/her owner. I really am it's kinda funny. I get all happy and I would probably definitely wag my tail if I had one ha ha." How flattering to have someone love you so much that she's like a puppy wagging her tail when you walk into a room. But puppies can also be pests, always underfoot. The same could be said about the metaphor of planting vegetables the three sisters way, where corn is described as the oldest sister and beans the youngest. In the words of one Web site: "Corn provides a natural pole for beans to climb." Natural, yes. But surely there are times when the cornstalk isn't in the mood to have beans climbing all over her. The resentment is likely to be aggravated if you're forced to put up with it, as many sisters are when their parents cajole, "Take your sister with you," or even, as one woman told me her mother admonished, "You take her or you don't go." "I'd take her," the woman confessed, "but I'd try to leave her places." (She added, "But she learned to keep going quick.")

Some older sisters choose to take care of younger ones in a motherly way; some have motherness thrust upon them. "Even though we weren't that far apart in years, I felt like a mother to my two sisters," said Rochelle. "I felt like I was assigned the role though I didn't choose it, so I wasn't thrilled about it. I felt like it was a role that I had without any of the perks." Because her mother worked the night shift, Rochelle's duties were legion: "bathing them, putting them to bed, making sure they got their homework done, making sure they got fed." There were perks that went to the eldest, but that wasn't Rochelle; it was her older brother. He wasn't expected to take care of the younger ones, but he still got first-child privileges, like being the first to get a bike. Even worse, if there was a sacrifice to be made, Rochelle was expected to make it. One year there were not enough Christmas presents to go around, so her father told Rochelle to give hers to her sister.

More than one woman told me, ruefully, "My mother gave her to me," explaining how she was assigned responsibility for a younger sister. Yet other older sisters told me that their motherlike activities were their own choice. Marianne, for example, thought her little sister was her personal possession. Marianne loved to dress her up the way other girls dressed their dolls. And, better than playing with dolls, she could put makeup on her. The line between choosing and being assigned the caretaking role is not always clear.

When Mimi and I were kids we fought, as children close in age often do. I remember how Naomi, six years older than Mimi and eight years older than I, turned a fight into a game. She had Mimi and me pretend to be boxers in a ring, sent us each to a corner, then rang a bell to signal the time for us to come out fighting. Mimi won by holding me down for the requisite count—with one foot on my upper arm. It didn't take much: I couldn't get up off the floor because I was laughing so hard.

Naomi often took care of Mimi and me, not only organizing and overseeing games but also taking over housekeeping and cooking when our mother was away. That's why she sometimes refers to herself as a parentified child—indeed, a QPC: a Quintessential Parentified Child! But until recently, I didn't ask whether she took that role voluntarily. She tells me now that sometimes she did. And she doesn't recall resenting it, because she got a lot of praise for being mature, responsible, indispensable. But she also had little choice. Our mother, emotionally fragile and easily overwhelmed, often shifted responsibility for her two younger children to her oldest one. "I can't handle them," Naomi recalls her saying. "You take them." As Naomi's creativity in turning our fight into a game shows, she handled us extraordinarily well.

Charlotte is the oldest of five. She too was assigned the role of substitute mom for a mother who was often not up to the task. If their father was out of town and their mother feeling down, as she often did, Charlotte would put her youngest sister in the stroller and lead the entire flock of kids to the local diner for dinner. In many ways she was a better mom than Mom was. When her little sister Tammy was eight, she and her friends were throwing water balloons; one landed in an open convertible. The driver stopped his car and got out to yell at the miscreants. Tammy took off for home, and the driver took off after her. As she neared home, she prayed, "Dear God, don't let Mom or Dad be home. Let it be Charlotte. She'll make it okay." Charlotte, at the time, was all of twelve.

My Sister, My Judge

Serving dinner to her children and grandchildren along with two of her siblings, a woman placed a carton of milk on the table. "Don't tell Adrienne," she said, drawing laughter from the group, many of whom had been reprimanded by her oldest sister for failing to observe proper etiquette. I lost count of how many women told me that their oldest sisters are judgmental, or how many oldest sisters told me that they are seen that way. "My sister thinks I'm judgmental," one commented, "but I'm just giving advice." Giving advice and pointing out ways to improve are part of caretaking; being judgmental is the flip side of that coin, a potential side effect of being protective. "Judgmental" can mean seeing accurately how the people you love could improve their lives and themselves and caring enough to tell them.

Julia Glass's autobiographical novel *I See You Everywhere* is told in the alternating voices of two sisters. Here's the voice of the younger, Clem: "Louisa's worst side is the one I call the Judge. À la Salem witchcraft trials. There's this look she gets on her face that tells the world and everyone in it how completely unworthy it and they are to contain or witness her presence." Clem then recounts an occasion when Louisa was arriving by plane and Clem drove to meet her. "When I pulled up at the airport, that's the look she was wearing, firm as a church hat, beaming her world-weary scorn clear across the state of Vermont." Clem adds, "I was late, okay, which didn't help." There you have it: the younger sister's exaggerated view of her older sister's tendency to be judgmental, but an admission that her sister had reason to disapprove; Clem was late picking her up.

Remember Wanda, the little girl whose sister Edie ran out and stopped the paper boy from shooting peas at her? I know this story because Wanda, the middle of three sisters, e-mailed me about their relationship and had her two sisters do the same. She followed up her original e-mail with a second one, saying, "I neglected to share my maiden name with you, and my older sister scolded me for it." She used the word "scolded" tongue in cheek, drawing on the stereotype of older sisters "scolding" younger ones much as mothers scold children. It made me smile; Wanda, when she wrote this, was sixty-two. But Edie was still four years older. As for identifying them, Edie had taken no chances; she'd told me her sisters' married names.

Faye was sending a funny attachment to everyone in her e-mail address book. But before pressing SEND she deleted her older sister Norma's name from the list. She'd had a flash that if she left Norma on the list, she'd have to make sure there weren't any typos in her message. Her friends would ignore them, but Norma would point them out. And if Norma had trouble opening the attachment, she was sure to question Faye about how she'd sent it, assuming Faye must have done something wrong. It could just be that Norma is a picky and critical sort of person. But that wouldn't quite tell the story. Pointing out typos and teaching how to send attachments can be helpful, and helping a younger sister is exactly what an older one is expected to do. That's the bind older sisters often find themselves in: Any offer of help implies criticism, and the metamessage of criticism is the one Faye hears loud and clear.

Another woman, Krista, one of four sisters, has a similar reaction to her oldest sister, Lois. Krista adores Lois and is deeply grateful to her for innumerable ways Lois has guided and helped her since she was small. Nonetheless, Krista doesn't invite Lois to visit as often as she invites her other sisters, because she has to prepare for Lois's visits by spending days cleaning. And she knows she won't get compliments for the results. Instead, she'll hear about how she could have done better. Her house is never tidy enough; her clothes are never quite right; the pictures on her wall aren't straight or would look better somewhere else. Whatever Krista does, Lois thinks there's a better way to do it. On the first morning of one visit, Krista asked Lois how she'd slept and Lois said fine but added that Krista should try adding fabric softener when she washes her sheets. Lois admired Krista's garden but suggested she plant hosta, which grows well in the shade. Krista doesn't doubt that Lois's advice might be helpful, but that's only the message level. Lois's advice conveys an unpleasant metamessage: that Krista isn't as knowledgeable or competent as her oldest sister.

There's an irony in both these examples. From the perspective of the older sisters, the unjust reward for the extra effort of caring is being left out. In the first case, Norma was left out of her sister's group e-mail—an omission she wouldn't know of and might not mind if she did. But Krista's sister is sometimes left out in a more significant way: receiving fewer invitations to visit. The ability to leave someone out is a kind of power. Ironically, the cause of Lois's being left out traces back to her own power as an older sister.

The Power of the Elder

Many of the complaints I heard from older and younger sisters reminded me of patterns I'd observed between mothers and grown daughters respectively. One such pattern is the complaint of younger sisters that their older sisters are critical. For example, a woman complained that her older sister continually critiques her weight with remarks like "Those pants are too tight." Another said of her older sister, "I could put a stopwatch on. In ten seconds she would say something nasty—usually about my hair: 'It's ugly, why do you wear it like that?'" These could have been examples in my book *You're Wearing THAT?: Understanding Mothers and Daughters in Conversation.* And the older sisters' parallel complaints reminded me of what I'd heard from mothers: "Why is she so sensitive?" The reason many daughters are sensitive to their mothers' suggestions and comments is that their mothers' opinion carries so much weight. A mother's words have far more power than she may realize, because her daughter wants her approval so much.

The same dynamic can occur between sisters, with the older one in the mother position—regardless of whether she wants that position or even knows she has it. One who didn't remarked to me, "I've finally figured out that my sisters all seem to be seeking my approval, I guess because I'm the oldest. It's a role I really don't want and that I feel has been foisted on me by an accident of birth, sort of like sibling noblesse oblige." And, as with mothers and grown daughters, each tends to overestimate the other's power and underestimate her own.

Oldest sisters are often unaware of how much influence their words can have. One of Vanessa's younger sisters commented that a nephew broke their family tradition by buying a toy gun for his son. "What do you mean, family tradition?" Vanessa asked. She was surprised when her sister explained, "You always taught us not to play with guns, so we never did."

Though she knew she'd often cautioned her younger siblings against playing with guns, Vanessa had no idea how seriously they'd taken her words, let alone that her injunction had become a family tradition.

If an older sister's offhand remarks are taken to heart when the sisters are grown, imagine their power when the sisters are kids. An older sister might toss off a remark with little thought and be astonished to learn years later that her younger sister remembers it, perhaps even made a life decision based on it. If an older sister teases, her taunts can stay with a younger one for life. The temptation to tease a credulous younger sibling is sometimes irresistible. If she's a little chubby, you call her fat. If she wears glasses, you call her Four-Eyes. No matter what she's like, you tell her she's dumb. How is the older, just a child herself, to understand the lasting effect that her words can have? A woman still feels slightly embarrassed when she runs because her sister made fun of her, telling her she waddled like a duck. "Whenever she tells me something it sticks with me," the woman said. "I believe it until she tells me otherwise." When you're both adults, there may seem little logic to this imbalance of power, but it makes perfect sense if you think back to childhood, when even a small difference in age gave one sister enormous power over the other.

She Can Do It!

There was a belief in one family that Martha, the oldest, could do anything. When all the siblings were converging on their parents' home because of a family emergency, Martha's plane was making a stop in Chicago, where Lily was going to change planes and join her. Lily's plane was late, and Lily was sure she'd miss the connection. But when she rushed to the gate, she found the plane still there and the doors not yet closed; Martha had managed to convince the pilot to hold up the plane for her sister.

Being given adultlike responsibilities at a young age can engender confidence that stands an oldest sister in good stead for the rest of her life. But it also brings a sense of obligation and a host of expectations. Grace didn't think twice when, after college, her year-younger sister asked her to take a test for her, a typing test required by the company where her sister was applying for a job. "No problem," Grace replied. She took the test with all the confidence of one who always does what's needed when it's needed. Both sisters were caught by surprise when Grace flunked. Later they laughed about it, realizing that Grace didn't type any better than her sister did. If anything, she was worse. Though few people would think of asking their sisters to take tests for them, many younger sisters automatically assume that their older sisters can do everything better than they—and the older ones do too.

I had a cousin, Erica, two years younger than I, who had never been told that she was adopted. A talkative aunt had revealed this secret to me when I was a child, and my parents had warned me, along with my sisters, never to tell Erica. I was over thirty when Erica approached me at a wedding, talked about facts in her life that just didn't add up, and ended by asking, "So what I want to know is, am I adopted?" I didn't say yes. Without planning or thinking, I said, "Ask Naomi. She would have been old enough to know what was happening when you were born." I was sure my oldest sister, who could handle anything, would know the right way to tell Erica. I was surprised to learn later that Erica did ask Naomi, and Naomi responded, "Ask my mother." That evening our mother called Erica—after first clearing it with her brother, Erica's father—and told her all she knew about her adoption.

Perhaps that was the best possible outcome, as our mother really did know more about the circumstances and could give Erica more information. But I have always felt that I let Erica down by passing her off to my sister. I believe that Erica asked me because we were closest in age and had spent the most time together growing up. It must have been hard for her to get up the courage to ask. I should have repaid her trust by answering truthfully. It makes me feel a little better to know that Naomi passed on the responsibility to our mother. I relate this experience in part because in it the younger sister/older sister dynamic replicates the relation of a daughter and mother. I turned to Naomi; Naomi turned to her mother. But I relate it for another reason, too. If I wasn't going to answer Erica's question myself, it would have made sense for me to suggest she ask my mother. But I didn't. The person who came to mind—the person I thought could handle anything—was my oldest sister.

Keep It Up

Surely there is a reward for being the one who always comes through. Well, yes. One reward is that you're expected to continue coming through without fail. Leanne always helped her younger sisters when they needed it. If they had a medical problem, she found the best doctor and got them an appointment. If they needed financial help, she wrote a check. So when a sister's teenage son got into trouble, everyone expected Leanne to drop everything and go fix it. Leanne couldn't; her company was facing a crisis that absolutely required her presence. But her sisters knew only that she was supposed to solve their problems, and they were angry that she didn't. To Leanne it felt terribly unfair: Rather than getting thanks for all the times she came through, she got grief the one time she couldn't.

Another oldest sister, Amanda, had a similar experience. She was incredulous to learn that one of her younger brothers bore a grudge because she hadn't organized a family dinner on the Friday night preceding his wedding. When Amanda protested that he'd never asked her to, he explained that she always organized family gatherings at holidays, so she should have come through for his wedding, too. Amanda said she would have been happy to arrange a gathering had she been asked, but how could he blame her for not doing something she didn't even know he wanted?

The difference in perspectives between Amanda and her brother comes down, I think, to different definitions of the wedding occasion—and expectations placed on an oldest sister. In his mind, I suspect, this was a family occasion, like holidays, when Amanda always took charge without anyone telling her to. In her mind, a wedding was a different sort of occasion; taking an organizing role would have been presumptuous. (I encountered an example where an oldest sister was resented for trying to do that.) Yet this brother's expectation wasn't entirely without logic. It is often assumed that the bride's family is responsible for the wedding, while the groom's family hosts a dinner the night before. Whether or not he thought this explicitly, it seems that her brother expected Amanda to take the role their mother might have been expected to take, more or less the way I assumed that my oldest sister should tell our cousin about her adoption rather than my mother.

Though Amanda had willingly taken responsibility for corralling the family at holidays, she thought that expecting her to plan her brother's wedding without being asked was over the top. Many of the oldest sisters I spoke to told me of times that their younger siblings' expectations outpaced their ability or willingness to serve.

To Help or Not to Help

Another way that older sisters sometimes chafe at expectations placed on them sheds light on how the hierarchy of age interacts with dynamics of connection. Women often talk about problems as a way of connecting, yet younger sisters often ask older ones for advice and help. So a sister accustomed to solving problems and giving advice may be uncomfortable when expected to just listen. Angela doesn't mind that her younger sister Linnie often calls to discuss concerns about her job: the difficult boss, the lack of responsibility commensurate with her skill, the knowledge that she is underpaid. But when Angela suggests solutions, Linnie has a reason to reject every one. Talk back to the boss? Too risky. Go over his head? Unthinkable. Ask for a raise? The company is in dire financial straits, so it won't happen. Quit? She might not find another job. Look for another job before quitting? The community is so small that her boss would surely learn of her inquiries. No solution is possible? Then accept it and stop whining! But there's no way Angela could get away with saying that. Linnie would protest, "You're my sister; you're supposed to listen and care." Angela does care, but as an older sister she never felt she had the luxury of just listening; she was always expected to do something when Linnie needed help.

If two sisters live in the same city while their parents or other relatives live in another, the out-of-towners can only stay with one sister when they visit. The sister not chosen may feel slighted, while the sister chosen may be more aware of the extra work that comes her way. Camille and Zoe are in that position. When relatives visit, they always stay with Camille, so she gets the job of host, which includes preparing and serving meals. Perhaps relatives choose to stay with Camille because she's older or because she's more organized and predictable (which might not be unrelated to her being the oldest). In any case, she gets the extra work of hosting and cooking for visiting relatives.

One year Zoe offered to help by providing a meal for the relatives staying at Camille's house. Zoe would prepare the wonderful Greek spanakopita she had recently learned to cook. Camille accepted her offer with relief. She was grateful that there'd be one less thing for her to worry about. On the appointed evening, Zoe arrived a comfortable hour before dinnertime. But she had with her not spanakopita but grocery bags containing the ingredients to make it. She washed the spinach, chopped the onions, opened packages of phyllo dough, and spread everything out on Camille's kitchen counter. Then she opened all the cupboards searching for a pot that was right for cooking the spinach and a pan to spread the layers in. She found what she needed but in the process removed all the neatly stacked and sorted pots and pans and returned the ones she didn't need to cabinets willy-nilly in a jumble. She did the same with the spice rack and the drawers containing cooking utensils. The spanakopita was indeed wonderful, but dinner was served at nine o'clock. Camille didn't doubt Zoe's sincerity in wanting to help, but she made a vow that the best way Zoe could help in the future would be to continue letting her older sister do all the work.

What's most unfair about all these scenarios is that the oldest sisters themselves aren't getting the kind of support and help that they're so used to giving.

Sister Knows Best

In the paper she wrote for her class at the University of Mary Washington, Gwynne Mapes also analyzed e-mail exchanges between adult sisters, Rosalie and Rachel, who were fifty and forty-five years old respectively. At one point in a longer e-mail, Rosalie invited Rachel's children to accompany her and her own children to a basketball game. She wrote, "I would love to go to the Pulley game on 2/22," and offered to "take any of your clan that could go." In a reply, Rachel turned down the invitation: "We aren't able to go to the Pulley game since it's a school night." Reading this exchange, I assumed the topic ended there. I was surprised to read Rosalie's response: "Are you sure you wouldn't consider letting the kids miss school on Friday to go to the game Thurs night? We could meet you at Pulley Friday if so and then I could drive part way. Just something to think about. . . . I'll try to buy the tickets soon."

When I saw that Rosalie pressed her proposal after Rachel had rejected it I was reminded of a comment made by a woman who is one of three sisters. Trying to decide on the best way to celebrate their parents' twenty-fifth anniversary, the sisters were exchanging e-mails cc'd to all. The youngest received an e-mail that did not have a cc. It was from the middle sister and read: "Look, we'll all say what we want to do, and then we'll do what Mary wants"—Mary being the oldest. Mary had many ways of getting to do what she wanted. One was just what Rosalie had done: suggest ways to get around any objections her sisters raised. Another was a tendency to forget that a plan she favored had been rejected and keep proposing it again.

Another younger sister told me that her older sister has to get her way "not only in action" but also "you have to see her perspective on things. You have to agree that she's right about how things are." She went on, "If you say, 'Okay let's agree to disagree,' it's like 'No, but but you have to see . . . '" One thing that's easy to see is how annoying this trait might be. But it's also easy to see that knowing more and being right can be habit-forming for an older sister, who really did know more and really was more likely to be right for all those years when they were growing up. Perhaps, too, she is continuing to exercise responsibility for ensuring peace and harmony in the family.

A Living Bridge

When Yvonne was in high school, her parents were embroiled in a divorce, so they weren't available to help her navigate the path to college. Filling out forms and filing applications, visiting campuses—she had to figure it all out for herself. So when her younger sister, Dale, got to that point, Yvonne showed her the way. She is happy that she was able to help Dale, but she also feels a twinge of resentment because Dale had it so much easier than she did. It would have been awfully nice had *she* had an older sister to provide guidance, to be a bridge to the potentially overwhelming outside world.

I feel very fortunate to have attended Hunter College High School, an academically demanding school run by Hunter College in New York City.

I passed a test to be admitted, but where did I get the idea to take the test? Not from my parents, who came to the United States as children and had to leave high school before graduation to help support their families. (My father eventually became a lawyer, but that's another story.) It was my sister Naomi, studying for her master's degree at Hunter College, who knew about Hunter High and suggested I take the test. This was just one of a myriad ways that Naomi was a bridge to the American world that my parents couldn't be and provided me with opportunities they couldn't provide.

When parents are immigrants, the oldest child born or raised in the United States is likely to be a bridge not only between younger children and the world outside but also between the parents and their new world. Grace, born in the Philippines, was a year old when her parents emigrated to California and took up farming. Her parents never learned to speak English well. They continued to speak their Philippine language at home when Grace was small. As later children were born, the family gradually began speaking English at home, so the three younger siblings never became fluent in the Philippine language, as Grace was. This is just one of many ways that Grace, as the oldest, was like a bridge between her parents and her siblings, as well as between her parents and the outside world.

Grace had responsibilities to take care of the younger children but also to record the farm's income and expenditures. Beginning when she was in third grade, she learned how much things cost, how much the day laborers were paid, and how to write everything down in a systematic way. By fifth grade, she was doing it on her own. One day, when she was eleven, Grace got off the school bus to find her father waiting for her. They entered the house together, and he introduced her to a man who was sitting in the office, then left the room. The man was an auditor from the IRS. Her father had told him that his daughter kept the books and would show them and answer his questions when she returned. Grace laughed when she told me this, recalling the surprise on the IRS agent's face when the daughter he'd been waiting to confer with turned out to be a child of eleven. But it seemed quite natural to Grace. She was accustomed to serving as mediator between her parents and the world that to them was unfamiliar territory but to her was a native land. Having read these two paragraphs, you will understand why Grace and her sister took it for granted that if a typing test had to be taken, Grace should take it.

Mediator Between Generations

Though immigrant families make particular demands on oldest siblings, any older child can be a bridge between parents and a younger sibling or between parents and the changing world. The pattern can emerge in just about any family and in the most mundane conversations.

In connection with a seminar she took with me, Leslie Cochrane recorded a conversation in which a couple and their daughter, Quinn, were talking about Quinn's younger sister, Justine, who was a freshman in college. The father was recounting, with approval as well as surprise, that Justine had called to ask how to prepare chicken. But then he mentioned something he did not approve of. He said, "And then it became apparent that she was texting while she was talking." Quick to defend her sister, Quinn said, "Oh, yeah, you know Justine can do that." She added, "And I remember in college I used to talk on the phone and instant-message on my computer at the same time." By saying, in effect, I did the same thing, Quinn implied that her father should not judge her sister harshly; Justine was just doing what all college students do. (He responded sarcastically, "That's really nice.")

On one level, this is a typical example of an older sister defending a younger one, trying to make herself into a verbal bulwark between her sister and her parents. On another level, although this was not an immigrant family, the older daughter was functioning as a bridge between her parents and the world outside that was more familiar to her than to them. Communication technologies like texting are new to their parents' generation but second nature to Quinn and Justine. You might say that they have native-language proficiency in text messaging, and Quinn was acting as an interpreter between her parents and her younger sister.

Here's another example recorded and transcribed by a student in my class, Elizabeth Sutcliffe. In this conversation, Elizabeth and her friend Eliza, a fellow college student, together take the side of Eliza's high-school-student sister Susannah in relation to her and Eliza's father. Susannah has just shown a project she's been working on to her mother, her sister, and Elizabeth, a visitor in their home. All three warmly praise her work. She then goes to show her project to her father in another part of the house. Soon she is heard stomping up the stairs and slamming the door to her room. Her father joins the others in the kitchen and explains that Susannah got angry because he pointed out mistakes: "She misused 'its,' and wrote 'water' twice." Both Eliza and Elizabeth defend Susannah, each in her own way:

Eliza: That's what daughters are for, Dad.
Elizabeth: It's late. I always make mistakes when it's late.
Father: Yeah, well.
Elizabeth: She's tired. It's late.
Eliza: That's her job to get mad at you.
Father: Yeah, okay.
Elizabeth: It's late. I can't think straight when it's late.

In analyzing this example, Elizabeth pointed out that Eliza mediated between her father and her younger sister by defending her sister without criticizing her father: He was doing his job as father by correcting her, and she was doing her job as daughter by getting angry when he did. That's just the way the world is. Elizabeth was a fellow mediator, but she took a different tack. Much like Quinn in the previous example, she took the stance, "I do the same thing." Elizabeth stressed—and repeated three times—that she too makes mistakes when it's late in the day. Note that Elizabeth, who is not a member of this family, addresses only the daughter's mistakes, not the father's role as critic. Nonetheless, together Eliza and Elizabeth took the role of older sister as mediator between the father and the younger sister, Susannah.

Both Sides Now

Abby was a sophomore in college when her sister Stephanie was a high school senior, but she heard about the uproar when she talked to her parents and sister on the phone. Stephanie wanted to go to Cancún with her friends during spring break, but her parents were against it. They thought she was too young, and they worried about the risks of drinking and sex. Stephanie swore up and down that her companions would be girls only, and they wouldn't drink. Finally, a compromise was reached: Stephanie could go, but her mother would go too, and Abby, whose college spring break coincided, would meet them there. Abby and their mother would stay in a different hotel, so they wouldn't intrude, but they'd be near enough to keep an eye on things.

When Abby arrived, she went first to the hotel where Stephanie and her friends were staying, thinking she'd say hello to her sister before joining her mother at the other hotel. Because they had the same last name, the desk clerk gave Abby a key to Stephanie's room. She didn't find her sister in it, but she did find a couple of surprises. The bathtub was filled with bottles of liquor, and an adjoining room was filled with boys' clothes. That evening, when Abby and her mother sat down to dinner, her mother put Abby on the spot: "I want you to tell me the truth. What did you see in that room?" Abby couldn't lie. And her mother couldn't contain her anger. She resolved to punish Stephanie by forbidding her to attend her senior prom. Abby convinced her mother that the senior prom was too important an event in her sister's life to deprive her of, and her mother settled on a different punishment.

Whose side was Abby on? She had taken both her mother's and her sister's sides, mediating between them. She took the perspective of a parent when catching Stephanie with liquor and boys, and she aligned with their mother by revealing her discovery. But she took her sister's perspective in arguing the importance of a senior prom and aligned with her in convincing their mother to find a less severe punishment.

Vicky is an American whose parents were born in Greece. She is the only one of three siblings who no longer lives in Boston, where their parents still live too. In some families moving to a distant city is taken for granted, but in Vicky's family it's a source of distress for everyone. Her parents continually remind her that they want her to come home, and though she protests their pressure and maintains her right to stay where she is, she feels guilty for having abandoned the family. Her older sister Penny defends Vicky's decision to their mother. "You need to let her do what she wants for her own life," Penny says. "And don't forget, you left your family to come to the United States." But when Penny talks to her sister, she herself lets fall little digs about Vicky having abandoned the family. Penny is smack in the middle, defending Vicky to their parents but taking the same stance as their parents when she talks to her younger sister.

Parents' Ambassador

There needn't be a conflict for an older sister to represent parents' perspectives to a younger sister, as well as the reverse, as if she is an ambassador or special envoy from one's world to the other's. Teresa, a graduate student in the United States, informed her family in Mexico that she had fallen in love with an American and planned to marry him. Concerned that her daughter might be making a mistake, her mother sent Teresa's older sister Carmen to check things out and return with a report. Carmen did this, but the report she submitted was prepared in conference with Teresa. Together they agreed on which aspects of Teresa's situation and her fiancé would best reassure their mother. Carmen's role of intermediary continued when Teresa returned home for a visit several months after the wedding. The three women were talking together when their mother elbowed Carmen, gave her a meaningful look, and said, "Ask her! Go ahead, ask her." With their mother standing right there, Carmen asked, "Now that you're a married woman, do you know about having regular Pap smears?" Teresa turned to her mother and assured her that Pap tests are available and routine in the United States too. Even when she was standing right there, her mother felt more comfortable having her older daughter mediate between herself and her youngest daughter.

Several oldest sisters, in telling me what frustrates them in their younger sisters, described occasions when the younger ones had slighted not them but their parents. In one case, the younger sisters didn't make enough effort to get home for a major holiday. They didn't appreciate how much it meant to their mother to have the whole family together at those times. In another, the oldest daughter tried to get her siblings to agree on a weekend to celebrate their parents' fiftieth wedding anniversary at the family's summer home. She herself was ready to cancel almost any commitment to make this happen, but her siblings didn't seem to want to cancel anything. One had tickets to a show, another had an office party, a third had a child's Little League game. She was incredulous that their small concerns counted more than such a big occasion in their parents' lives. She herself saw their mother's perspective automatically. In the end she gave up. Trying to herd her adult siblings to do the right thing by their parents, she felt as she had when they were kids and she was left in charge—and they didn't want to listen to her. Now that she was middle-aged, she was tired of being their parents' ambassador to her younger siblings' court.

If older sisters can blame younger siblings for being insufficiently attentive to their parents, they themselves can be blamed for getting along with parents too well! For example, one oldest sister said, "It has been a point of contention with my younger siblings my entire life, that I visited our mother, called her, spent time with her, and wasn't bothered by things she said, while they struggled with being around her." How could the same parent spark such different responses from her children? A mother may behave differently with different children—and this could happen in part because they behave differently with her. One oldest sister told me that her younger siblings avoid their mother because they find her hard to deal with; she's stubborn and has a temper. But the older one finds her easy to tame. When her mother yells, she yells right back, and Mom backs off. The others never see that side of their mother because they never yell back.

How one person responds to another is partly a matter of temperament, but position in the array of age plays a role too. The older of two sisters told me that when they were children and their parents had violent arguments, she and her sister responded differently. "When I heard them fighting," she said, "I'd run down and get in the middle and try to break up the fight. My sister would hide in the closet." In this heartbreaking scenario, the older sister felt it was her job to protect her parents from each other. In trying to do that, she physically joined her parents and focused on them, while her younger sister got as far away from them as she could for self-protection.

Follow the Leader

A woman recalls that throughout her childhood, when she rode in a car with her mother and older sister, her sister always sat in the front while she rode in the back. This seating arrangement positioned the older sister beside their mother, so of course they'd be talking to each other. Anyone sitting in the backseat would feel excluded in this situation, but the woman who told me this is Deaf, so her exclusion was even more profound. From the perspective of a younger sister in the backseat, sitting in front is one more way that the oldest has a special relationship with their mother—an alliance that can't be penetrated. The scene is symbolic in another way too. Those sitting in the front seat are looking ahead to where they're going. Most of the time, they're not looking at the ones in the back at all. But anyone sitting in the back always has the front-seat sitters in her sight—even if only the backs of their heads. The parent and older sister together seem permanently to be leading the way.

Girls often choose to follow the lead of their older sisters. It's not by chance that Cheryl's handwriting resembles her older sister Roxane's. As a child, Cheryl spent hours tracing her sister's cursive writing, because she thought it was beautiful. Cheryl wanted to be just like her older sister, and this was a concrete way she could try to make that happen. The resemblance between their handwriting is a charming small reminder of how Cheryl looked up to Roxane when they were kids.

Sometimes an older sister's influence is more significant, extending to life choices such as what work to do and when (and consequently whom) to marry.

Heather, the middle of three sisters, owns her own real estate agency, and her younger sister, Flory, works for her. It's a decent job, and Flory is glad to have it. She's saving to open her own agency one day. But Flory didn't choose real estate because it appealed to her. She had studied journalism in college; her dream was a career in broadcasting. She went to work with her sister to tide her over while she sent applications to radio and television stations across the country. When her inquiries went unanswered, Flory simply stayed on at Heather's agency, and it eventually turned into a career. But Heather didn't choose real estate either. It was their oldest sister, Clara, who'd done that. Clara loved real estate; she loved everything about it—the houses, the ability to set her own hours, the chance to meet many different people but also to escape those who got on her nerves. It was Clara who had encouraged Heather to get her real estate license, just in case nothing else came through. All three sisters ended up in the business that the oldest had chosen.

Sometimes whatever your older sister does just seems like the norm. One woman, for example, married the first young man who proposed to her after she finished college because her older sister had married right out of college. Since her older sister did it, she figured it was the thing to do.

Because You Didn't

Though many girls (and later women) may try to be like their older sisters, others try to be anything but. A woman asked her older sister when they were both long since grown, "Did you ever wonder why I played the bagpipes?" "No," her sister answered. "Why did you?" The younger replied, "Because you didn't." Another woman remarked of her younger sister, "She made it a point of pride to do everything different from me." These younger sisters, too, were being guided by their older sisters' behavior, though they chose to be guided in a different direction.

There are many reasons a younger sister might want to do things differently. One is to feel she's her own person. Another might be to avoid what looks like an unappealing fate. Many older sisters are amazed and a little (or more than a little) resentful to see younger ones get far better treatment than they themselves got. That can happen in part *because* the older was treated harshly—motivating younger ones to find ways to avoid the same fate. A woman explained that she was punished far less than her two older sisters because she saw what they did to bring down their father's wrath—and made sure never to do those things.

There's another way that the leniency enjoyed by younger sisters can be attributed to the older ones' less enviable experience. A lightning rod absorbs the force of lightning by being the first thing a bolt of lightning strikes. Just so, an oldest child sometimes absorbs the first strike and full force of parents' fears, concerns, and confusions, which are weakened by the time younger ones come around. It's one of the liabilities of being the oldest.

There are privileges that come with the position too. An African-American woman recalls that in Arkansas, where her family lived before moving up north, older siblings were treated with deference and given preference if resources were limited. If there was money to buy one dress, the oldest sister got it. On guard against this injustice, she herself, a second sister, insisted on receiving her birthday present the same day as the oldest. She wasn't taking any chances on getting slighted. Privileging the oldest is customary in many cultures of the world. A woman who grew up in the South Pacific kingdom of Tonga resented her older sister when they were growing up because of the many privileges that went to the oldest. For example, her sister got pretty ribbons for her hair while she herself never did. One day she decided to do something about the inequity. She grabbed the ribbons right out of her sister's hair and climbed a palm tree with them.

Sometimes liabilities and advantages are intertwined and inseparable. Oldest sisters benefit from being given independence, but one reason for that independence is also a loss: When a baby arrives, parents have less time and attention for them. And the privileges that accrue to the oldest can also mean being left out of the camaraderie that her siblings enjoy, especially in large families or when there are extra years between her and the ones that came later.

What Elephant?

Not all older or oldest sisters have taken or been assigned stances toward younger ones like those I've described here. "Oldest" can be a state of mind—or a state of alignment toward others—as much as a function of a child's position in the array of age. A sister who is second rather than oldest sometimes gets the role I've described as typical of the oldest—for example, when the first child is a brother, or a girl who is always buried in a book, or a child with disabilities. In her memoir *Audition,* Barbara Walters explains that she felt responsible for her older sister Jackie, and eventually for her entire family, because Jackie's mild mental retardation rendered her unable to take that role. Although Barbara was younger in years, she was, in effect, the older sister in her family. But Jackie was a typical oldest sister in another way. Walters notes that her sister was "the strongest influence in my life." The power of an older sister to shape the life of a younger is something I heard often—and often it was to an extent of which the older was unaware.

I received an e-mail from a woman, Marcy, who was baffled and hurt. She had just spent three glorious days with her sister, full of magic sister moments. Marcy was still basking in the glow of the wonderful visit when an e-mail arrived from her sister saying how awful the visit had been and how many terrible things Marcy had said and done. How could her impression and her sister's be so different? I asked Marcy if she was the older sister. She was. I had suspected this because I'd heard so many similar experiences from older sisters. The reason, I surmise, is that her sister saw her as far more powerful than she saw herself, so small comments she made or little things she did took on more meaning than she suspected. And her sister may have refrained from saying anything at the time for the same reason: An older sister often seems too powerful to confront.

Amanda, whose brother blamed her for not organizing a dinner the night before his wedding, had a similar experience. She learned of her brother's resentment in an e-mail he sent with the subject line, "just to acknowledge the elephant." He regarded his displeasure as an elephant in the room—so obvious that he assumed she was as aware of it as he was. But Amanda hadn't been aware of it at all; his anger came as a complete surprise. Amanda was surprised by many things her younger siblings told her when they were adults. For example, her younger sister said that she had envied Amanda the new clothes she wore to school. This amazed her because Amanda had paid no attention to what her sister wore to school.

Again and again, I heard from older sisters that they couldn't believe how much attention their younger sisters had paid them, since the reverse wasn't true at all. Like the sister sitting in the front seat of the car—*as* the sister sitting in the front seat—an older one can easily lose sight of the younger, who is far less likely to lose sight of her. A woman I spoke to summed up what I heard from many others about their older sisters: "She was my gateway to the world, the interpreter of my parents. She was a much bigger figure in my childhood than they were in terms of how I should act and the way things work." What a privilege to hold so huge a role—gateway to the world—but also what a responsibility.

Oldest Sister: A Role Like No Other

Oldest sisters are often looked up to and even idolized, but they can be resented or demonized too, all the more as the responsibilities they assume increase.

An archetypal example of a demonized older sister is Katherina, the title character in Shakespeare's *Taming of the Shrew.* According to literary critic Barbara Hodgdon, there are many similar tales in folklore, fiction, and drama dating to Shakespeare's time and earlier. In all of them, the shrew character is the older of two sisters. Early in the play, Shakespeare implicitly motivates Katherina's behavior by portraying her as an older sister. She bullies her sister, Bianca, ties her up, and accuses their father of favoring her— for which she threatens revenge. Bianca, for her part, promises her older sister that "what you will command me will I do." By showing Katherina mistreating Bianca, Shakespeare prepares the audience to accept, perhaps even to cheer, Petruchio's "taming" Katherina—that is, mistreating her—later in the play. From this perspective, Katherina is punished for being a typical older sister. Put another way, Petruchio cuts the older sister down to size.

A scene from childhood that a woman recounted captures the outsized expectations and disproportionate anger to which an older sister can be heir. I heard it from the younger sister:

> I was six and my sister was sixteen when our mother passed away. Shortly after she died, my sister was trying to smear butter on a piece of bread as a snack for me. The bread was the soft white squishy kind; the butter was straight from the refrigerator, cold and hard. As she tried to spread the butter, the bread tore apart into pieces. I was angry and cried because a *real* mother would have done it right. She was angry because a *real* mother would not have died.

How easy it is to understand the disappointment of a six-year-old who has lost her mother—a mother who can't be replaced by a sixteen-year-old. And how moving it is to see a teenager trying to take the mother's place by caring for a vulnerable child, even as she herself is an orphaned child with no one replacing her mother by caring for her.

As a youngest sister, I understood in a gut way the perspectives of other youngest and younger sisters. Talking to older and oldest sisters helped me see the world from their point of view. I'd always been aware of the special rights that older sisters have. But I came to better understand the special responsibilities that also fall on their shoulders, and the special challenges of being a child placed in a motherlike role. My research gave me enormous sympathy and admiration for oldest sisters.

CHAPTER SEVEN

It's All Talk
Sisterspeak and Genderlect

In my quest to understand sister relationships, conversation is the lens through which I peer. It makes sense for talk to be my starting point, since my field is linguistics, the academic discipline devoted to the study of language. But there are also other reasons that it makes sense to focus on talk. For one, sisters do a lot of it. Another, related reason is that talk has a special place in girls' and women's close relationships.

As I put it in *You Just Don't Understand: Women and Men in Conversation,* for girls and women, talk is the glue that holds a relationship together. In that book I traced styles of speaking common among women to the way little girls learn to use language at play. (I also stressed that not all girls and women use language in the ways I described there and will very briefly recap here.) From the time they're nursery-school age, girls tend to spend a lot of time talking, often in twos. For girls, a best friend is the one you tell everything to—especially secrets. (In contrast, for boys, a best friend is the one you do everything with, or the one who will stick up for you in a fight.) If girls don't like another girl, they refuse to play with her. That's why girls are said to be clique-y. It's true, they are. But they have to be, because of the role talk plays in their social world. Only friends can know your secrets, so you can't include someone you're not friends with, or don't want to be friends with. As a result, a girl who is disliked is socially stranded—and girls learn to fear, above all, being left out.

These dynamics from childhood stay with us when we become adults. When women told me how their sisters had hurt or frustrated them, the experiences they described often had to do with feeling left out—because they weren't included in activities or weren't told personal information. Much of what is treasured and what is troubling among sisters can be traced to these aspects of talk.

Why Didn't You Tell Me?

For many women, telling what's going on in your life, exchanging personal information, is what makes people close. If you find out that you weren't told something important—or something mundane—you feel you've been pushed away: You're not as close as you thought you were; you were left out. For example, Pearl told me that her sister frustrates her by not keeping her informed about what's going on with their mother, who lives with her in a different state from the one where Pearl lives. When Pearl expresses concern about their mother and says she wants to be more involved, her sister says, "If you want to help out, you could send some money. That would be a help." Pearl is happy to send money, but she wants information too. Living in a different state in itself makes Pearl feel left out; not being told what's going on intensifies that feeling.

The desire to know what's going on can be even stronger if you live not only in a different state but in a different country. Natalia makes her home in the United States, while her sister Olena lives with their parents in their native Ukraine. Natalia talks often to her parents and her sister, as a way of keeping in touch. And she depends on her sister to keep her informed of what's going on with their parents. During one conversation Olena mentioned that she was taking their mother to a doctor to see about her eye problem. "What eye problem?" Natalia asked.

"Oh, didn't I tell you?" Olena said. "There's something wrong with Mama's eye. It doesn't close quite right."

"No, you didn't tell me," Natalia said. "How long has this been going on?"

"Gee," Olena replied. "I guess about four months."

"Four months!" Natalia gasped. Learning that her mother had been having a problem she knew nothing about for four whole months zapped

Natalia with a flash of pain. It reminded her with a jolt that she is no longer a part of her parents' daily life, as her sister is.

The assumption that closeness requires knowing what's going on in someone's life can create conflict when a spouse wants personal information kept inside the family—his immediate family. Many husbands believe that loyalty requires not telling anyone anything that might reflect badly on them. Catha tried hard to walk this fine line. She was close to her sister Trudy and told her nearly everything. But when her husband Neil lost his job, he didn't want anyone to know; it was too humiliating. Respecting how strongly Neil felt about this, Catha didn't tell Trudy until Neil found a new job and said it was okay to tell. Trudy was deeply hurt. "All those months you were going through that and I didn't know," Trudy said. "It makes me feel like an idiot to think I was prattling on about small stuff while you had this big thing on your mind. It makes me feel like an outsider." Catha felt she'd had no choice. In a matter that was so important to him, she had to honor her husband's wish. But she understood and regretted her sister's reaction; she knew that feeling like an outsider in her family is one of the worst feelings a woman can have. It's a throwback to being a little girl who is left out.

Left Out

When Marian was a child, she and her older sister often ate dinner at their aunt's home because their mother worked late. At dinner everyone sat around the aunt's kitchen table—aunt and uncle, their children, and Marian's sister. Not Marian. She had her own little table apart from the others, where she ate alone. She wasn't being punished, though it felt that way. The main table could only accommodate one extra person, so her aunt decided to seat the youngest child somewhere else. Her aunt probably wasn't thinking of this practical solution from the child's point of view: a family gathered around a big table while one small child sits at another, all by herself—left out.

The feeling of being left out sometimes results not from anything anyone did but just from the number of siblings or their relative ages. A frequent culprit is the number three. A woman who is one of five very close sisters told me that she and her sisters enjoy vacationing together, in different combinations. She added that they've learned to avoid any combination of three. When three sisters travel, she said, one always ends up feeling left out. Right! I thought when I heard this, remembering trips I'd taken with my two sisters—or just time spent with them. I was relieved to be reassured that I'm not crazy because when I'm with them I often feel . . . left out. I can feel that way when I'm not with them too. Once when my sisters were together without me, they called and left a message on my answering machine, so I'd know they were thinking of me. I appreciated their thoughtfulness, but the effect was the opposite of what they intended: Rather than making me feel included, hearing them laugh together gave me that familiar twinge of feeling left out.

There's a special place in legend and literature for three sisters, as in the Grimms' fairy tale "Cinderella" and Shakespeare's *King Lear*. But the constellation of three is often two against one. Cinderella's stepsisters both treat her cruelly; she stands apart as they team up against her. In *King Lear*, Cordelia's behavior toward her father is different from her sisters' behavior; they both treat him in the same way. Goneril and Regan both profess extravagant love for their father when they can gain by it, then turn against him once he has given them his land and his power. Cordelia modestly declines to echo her sisters' hypocritical declarations of love but stands by her father when they cast him out. In both stories, the heroine represents the good path, her two sisters the bad. By contrast with two sisters rather than just one, the stand-alone heroine's virtue is highlighted even more. Both Cinderella and Cordelia are odd one out.

Many sibling constellations have a built-in risk of making one or another feel left out. Picture this scene: Five girls are jumping on beds and running around the house amid peals of laughter as their oldest sister is trying to get them to settle down and go to bed. Evading her, the five younger ones are having the time of their lives—and establishing a sense of camaraderie that will remain with them when they grow into adults. The oldest sister won't be able to share that camaraderie, any more than she could run around the house with them when they were kids and she was responsible for getting them into bed. Having been given a motherlike role to supervise her younger sisters results in her being left out of their adult sisterly circle. (A mother too can feel that way. One woman told me that she and her sisters sometimes sense that their mother wants to be one of the sisters, so as not to feel left out.)

A sibling can find herself stranded in the family if the others' ages create natural pairs or groups or if there are extra years between them and her. Facets of character, talent, or interests can also make a sister feel like an outsider: She doesn't have the musical or artistic ability that the others share; she's the only sports fanatic among a family of readers or the only reader among a family of jocks; she's Deaf in a hearing family or hearing in a family whose other members are Deaf; she's gay; or, for any of a myriad possible reasons, she's a child who got overlooked. A sister might also feel left out for reasons that arise from adult circumstances. The others live in the same town, have kids the same age, travel together, talk more often. It's hurtful when everyone's together for Thanksgiving, and one sister has to keep asking, "Who was that?" "When was that?" because the others are talking about people and events she doesn't know.

Feeling left out can be at the heart of complaints that don't seem on the surface to have anything to do with that. For example, Thelma told me she dislikes her sister's habit of talking to anyone within range of her voice. She'll get into lengthy exchanges with waiters in restaurants and with the people sitting next to her on buses or trains. Thelma regards talking to strangers as a bit much, but the worst is that it makes her feel left out. She's sitting right there, yet she's not included in her sister's conversations.

The circumstances that can create a sense of exclusion are vast and diverse; the hurt caused by being left out is the same. When you feel it among sisters—the family members who should make up your team—it hurts all the more.

My Sister, My Sister's Kids

All the dynamics discussed in earlier chapters recur, replay, and take on new dimensions when sisters have children of their own. Just as with sisters themselves, relationships with sisters' children can bring deep satisfaction to all concerned, but they also present opportunities for new kinds of pain and variations on old familiar ones.

Arlene was delighted when her sister invited her daughter to dinner. Arlene thought this was a great idea. Then she thought of how it could be even better: She'd join them. The restaurant her sister had chosen was one she'd been wanting to try. And it was close to where Arlene worked, so she could get there easily and give her daughter a ride home. She called her sister, enthusiastically proposed this great idea, and was hurt when her sister rejected it. For her part, the sister resented being put in the position of having to reject Arlene. She was annoyed that Arlene wanted to horn in; even worse, it felt like her sister was trying prevent her from establishing an independent relationship with her niece. Arlene might have been doing that, or she might simply have been responding to the impulse to not be left out.

There's another, more positive way to think of this impulse: The circle of family is expanding, and Arlene wants to be a part of it. That may also be the impulse that motivated Annette. She was excited to have a new grandchild and wanted to share that excitement with her sister Juliana. Annette suggested that Juliana come to see the new baby at a time when Annette would be there as well. But Juliana preferred to visit after Annette left. Both preferences make perfect sense. To Annette, sharing the excitement of her new grandchild included the pleasure of seeing her sister see the baby, like wanting to be there when someone opens a gift you bought them: Witnessing their pleasure adds to yours. To Juliana it made sense to go when Annette wasn't there so she'd have more time to focus on the baby and the baby's parents. The specter of feeling left out explains both sisters' preferences. Annette felt left out to think of her sister enjoying her daughter's new baby without her. But if Annette were there, Juliana would feel left out, an aunt outside the inner circle of mother, daughter, and granddaughter.

Sometimes it's the aunt who includes her sister's child in an inner circle, excluding her sister. Veronica was thrilled to receive a package from her sister on her birthday; how nice that Ann had remembered! But it didn't seem nice at all when Veronica opened the package and discovered it contained a gift not for her but for her son, Ann's godson. The gift had arrived on Veronica's birthday by chance, but the timing reminded her that much of the attention and affection Ann used to express toward her was now being showered on her son. Veronica wanted her sister to love her son, but she didn't want her son to eclipse her in Ann's affections. In other words, she had expected that her sister would join her in her love for the boy. Instead, her sister was forming an alignment with her son that left her out.

They're My Kids, Not Yours

In Hindi, as I mentioned in Chapter Three, the word for a mother's sister is *masi,* which comes from *ma jaisi,* meaning "like a mother." An aunt can be like a mother to her sister's children, helping to care for them, taking them places, giving them gifts. This can be deeply rewarding for both sisters, and the children benefit from the extra helpings of motherly attention and love. It can be a joy to see your children spending time with your sister, knowing they have another adult to love and care for them. But as with everything in close relationships, the source of comfort can also chafe. Some mothers feel that their sisters fall short: They forget your child's birthday, show insufficient interest, express inadequate love. Other women believe that their sisters carry aunting behavior too far, acting too much like mothers instead of like aunts. It can feel as though your sister is trying to steal your children, just as she stole your dolls or sweaters when you were kids.

This can happen in seemingly insignificant conversations, and it can be difficult to pinpoint the source of discomfort. Alice Mattison depicts a subtle example in her novel *Nothing Is Quite Forgotten in Brooklyn.* Constance's mother has died, and her sister, Barbara, who lives in London, flies home and joins Constance in their mother's apartment. So does Con's daughter, Joanna. Constance had been staying at the apartment while their mother was away, and she has befriended a neighbor named Peggy. When Barbara arrives, Constance and Joanna go out to greet her. On the staircase they meet Barbara and also Peggy. Mattison describes the encounter: "After she and Barbara embraced, Con tried to introduce both Barbara and Joanna to Peggy, but Barbara was exclaiming over her niece, whom *she* then introduced to Peggy." It's a subtle encroachment, a tiny usurpation of her sister's prerogative. From Barbara's point of view, it was natural to introduce her niece to the stranger she had just met. Or would have been natural, except that Joanna was Constance's daughter, not hers, and Peggy was Con's friend. So the privilege of introductions rightly belonged to Constance. In this fleeting scene, Mattison captures the way an aunt can seem to render her sister invisible—and lay claim to her daughter.

This scene is a minor one in Mattison's novel. It isn't followed up; it doesn't lead to an argument. But subtle encroachment on parental prerogative explains why minor comments can lead to arguments among sisters. Cara appreciated that her sister Alicia was a generous aunt to Cara's children. She took them to movies, bought them generous gifts, and was effusive in showing them affection. Yet it bothered Cara when Alicia talked to Cara's children as if they were hers. On one visit, her frustration heated to the point that it boiled over. Alicia told Cara's son, "You can't drink cola with dinner. If you want something sweet, drink juice." Cara exploded: "Don't tell my children what they can and can't do!" Alicia was hurt and also baffled. "But you told him that the other day!" she protested. As is so often the case, the problem wasn't the message—the pros and cons of drinking cola—but the metamessage: When Alicia monitored what Cara's children ate and drank she was usurping the role of mother. For the loving aunt, her sister's resentment was baffling because it was obvious to her that she wasn't the mother. But it's easy to overreact to a sister's incursions, especially if they remind you of when you were little and your sister took what was yours, acted as if you didn't exist, or was favored.

The flare-up between Cara and her sister was sparked by a small incursion, though it was bigger than the very subtle one Mattison portrayed in her novel. A sister's closeness to your children can be a source of significant tension, even if you generally are glad that she's close to them. For example, you may feel hurt if your daughter goes to spend a holiday with her aunt instead of with you, even if you understand her motivation. Maybe your sister lives closer; maybe your daughter hasn't seen her for a while; maybe her cousins are home and she wants to see them. All these reasons are rational, but emotions are not. On an emotional level it can feel like your sister is taking your place, not only in your daughter's travel itinerary but in her affections. And then there's the discomfort of thinking of them together, laughing and talking, when you're not there, leaving you out.

The emotions associated with being displaced by a sister increase in intensity in proportion to the significance of the occasion. Few events in a mother's life are more momentous than her own daughter becoming a mother. Imagine Ginny's feelings when she learned that her daughter wanted her aunt—Ginny's sister—to be present when she gave birth to her first child but did not want her mother there. Ginny understood the reason; her sister is an obstetric nurse. But reason rarely trumps emotions. Ginny would not have assumed she should be in the delivery room, so she wouldn't have felt excluded if her sister hadn't been included. Anything a sister has can make what you have gain or lose significance, by comparison: Her gain sets in relief your loss.

When your daughter is friends with your sister, the thing your sister has and you don't can be that precious commodity of women's closeness: secrets. Rita was devastated to learn that her daughter was getting a divorce—and had told Rita's sister before she told Rita. There are many reasons why a daughter might prefer to confide in her aunt. It may be not that she feels closer to her aunt—though it feels that way to her mother— but that she feels more distant. The distance means an aunt can hear what's happening without reacting as emotionally as a mother would— and as Rita did when she learned of her daughter's divorce. Rita's daughter might not have been ready to deal with what she knew would be her mother's extreme distress on hearing the news. Telling an aunt first may have been like dipping a toe in the water of family reaction before plunging in.

That children might say things to their aunts that they wouldn't say to their mothers isn't always a problem; it can be a boon. For example, May's sister has an easy, comfortable relationship with May's teenage son; she can ask him questions that May can't. If May asks her son about his private life he clams up. She has to wait for him to volunteer, doling out tidbits at his discretion. May was against her son getting a tattoo, but he got one anyway. So she knew better than to ask why he chose the design he did: a snake. One day her sister was visiting when May's son walked in. Noticing the tattoo, she casually asked why he had a snake on his arm. He answered that among ancient Celts the snake represents rebirth and renewal because it sheds its skin. He wanted this symbol to remind himself that nothing is irrevocable and that a new start is always possible. Listening in, May was impressed by her son's knowledge of Celtic lore and moved by the spirit behind his choice. She was grateful that her sister had given her this glimpse of a side of her son he would not so easily have shown to her.

Pass It On

The arrival of a new generation offers fresh possibilities to heal old wounds—or reopen them.

The death of a sister or brother is among the most painful losses a person can endure. So is the loss of a sibling who is still alive. If there are wounds beyond healing, fractures beyond repair, a close and loving relationship with a sister's child can be especially precious. Several women I spoke to told me that they have close relationships with the adult son or daughter of a sister with whom they have little or no contact, by their own choice or hers. They have come to love their nieces or nephews as individuals. But they also treasure the extra level of comfort in knowing they have this link to a lost sister.

At the same time, a new generation can also provide fertile new ground for old seeds to take root and sprout. Seeing childhood hurts replicated toward your children brings those hurts back with added intensity. This can take many forms. For example, if a sister is playing favorites with your children, and as a child you felt a sibling was favored over you, the two offenses merge to form a single bigger one. Your childhood hurt comes hurtling back, magnified. And it's magnified even more if the person causing your child pain is the very sibling who was favored over you.

Whenever more than one sister has children, there's a risk that one sister's children will be—or seem to be—favored over those of another. It's as inevitable as the "You got what I wanted" competition that you played when you were kids. For example, a woman who has three sisters took a trip with her family and decided to take along one of her nieces to keep her daughter company. She could only take one. But all her sisters have children around the same age as hers, so she was bound to offend the two sisters whose children she didn't invite. The same thing would have happened if she'd wanted to take a sister along, but her sisters' resentment was greater when it was their children who were being slighted rather than themselves.

Sisters can replay their own competition through their children or ask for things for their children that they wouldn't ask for themselves. When grandparents or other relatives pass away, sisters who graciously say to each other, "Take anything you want," might object to a sister taking things for her children. A woman who would never say, "I want that," might hear herself saying, "My son wants that." On one level they're just expressing a mother's desire to look out for her children. It's also possible that they're reviving resentments that began, and that they thought had ended, when they themselves were children. In a way, they re-inhabit their own childhoods when they see the world—and their families—through their children's eyes.

If it was hurtful to see your sister get more attention from your parents, it can send you into a tailspin to see her kids get more attention than yours. That's what happened to Sandy, whose mother exclaimed, when Sandy's sister had a baby, "I'm so happy to finally have a grandchild." Her mother was discounting Sandy's own two children, because they were adopted. Hearing her mother talk as if her children didn't count hurt in the same way as seeing her parents act as if *she* didn't count. It was worse, in a way, because of Sandy's fierce desire to protect her children from the pain she had felt growing up. Sandy actually decided to stop seeing her mother, to avoid exposing her children to that pain. It was a relief to be able to do that, since she had not been able, as a child, to protect herself from the favoritism her mother had shown to her sister.

Don't Tell

Because of the place of talk in many women's relationships, and the expectation that closeness requires exchanging personal information and secrets, sisters can get caught up in complicated scenarios of who-knows-what. For example, a woman confides in her sister that she thinks her daughter is angry at her. Her sister repeats this to her own daughter, who repeats it to her cousin—that is, to the daughter in question—who then *becomes* angry at her mother for talking about her behind her back. Perhaps the woman should have warned her sister not to repeat what she said. But that in itself creates complications.

If you say "Don't tell" to a family member—especially a sibling—you are giving her a time bomb. The bomb is sure to go off when the information comes out, and the person holding it has to decide whose lap to throw it in. If you tell something to one sister and ask her not to tell another, she has to betray one of you. Honoring your request not to tell means betraying the sister kept in the dark. Violating the request and telling that sister means betraying your confidence.

Yet for many reasons sisters do put each other in this position. For example, Allie has two sisters as well as a son. One of the biggest challenges she faces in her life is that her son has problems with drugs, so he gets into all kinds of trouble. She struggles with how to respond when situations arise, and it helps to talk out her options with those she's close to. She often does this with one of her sisters, but not with the other, because that sister is critical of her son and she doesn't want to provide more fodder for the sister's disapproval. What are her choices? Talk to neither sister? That's not fair to her. Why lose her friendship with both when only one is a problem? Talk to both? That's not appealing; she has good reason to avoid telling the one who will be critical. So she does what most sisters in this situation would do: She talks to the sister she finds sympathetic and asks her not to tell the other. It usually comes out eventually, and the third sister is hurt or angry or both. No one can really be faulted (though a sister who feels critical can try not to let her disapproval show). It's a liability of sisters, given the importance of talking about personal problems among women.

Beth Henley's play *Crimes of the Heart,* set in Mississippi in 1974, portrays a scenario where one sister learns that a second sister has revealed her secret to a third. Lenny, the oldest at thirty, has confided to Babe, her youngest sister, that a man she met through a Lonely Hearts club but is no longer seeing became her first-ever lover. She has not told her middle sister, Meg, who has only recently returned from Hollywood, where she had gone to pursue a singing career. At this point in the play, Meg becomes angry when Lenny makes a reference to Meg's past:

Lenny: Why I've long since given up on worrying about you and all your men.

Meg: (*Turning in anger.*) Look, I know I've had too many men.
         Believe me, I've had way too many men. But it's not my
         fault you haven't had any—or maybe just that one from
         Memphis.
Lenny: (*Stopping.*) What one from Memphis?
Meg: (*Slowly.*) The one Babe told me about. From the—club.
Lenny: Babe!!!
Babe: Meg!!!

At the same moment, Lenny turns in anger against Babe for revealing her
secret and Babe turns in anger against Meg for letting Lenny know that
Babe told her.

You can see why Lenny would not want Meg to know; Meg uses the
knowledge against her. The scene continues:

Lenny: How could you?!! I asked you not to tell anyone! I'm so
         ashamed! How could you?! Who else have you told? Did
         you tell anyone else?
Babe: (*Overlapping, to Meg.*) Why'd you have to open your big
         mouth?!
Meg: (*Overlapping.*) How am I supposed to know? You never
         said not to tell!
Babe: Can't you use your head just for once?!! (*Then to Lenny.*)
         No, I never told anyone else. Somehow it just slipped out
         to Meg. Really, it just flew out of my mouth—
Lenny: What do you two have—wings on your tongues?

Words flying out of their own accord, "wings on your tongues"—Lenny's
accusation and Babe's excuse are apt descriptions of how often and how
inevitably secrets are told and repeated in families, especially among
women for whom secrets are the currency of connection—both establishing and disrupting it.

Henley's play is ultimately about the sisters' love for one another, and
that comes out in this scene too. Babe is truly sorry to have hurt her
sister—and Meg truly regrets having hurt them both:

Babe: I'm sorry, Lenny. Really sorry.

Lenny: I'll just never, never, never be able to trust you again.

Meg: (*Furiously, coming to Babe's defense.*) Oh, for heaven's sake, Lenny, we were just worried about you! We wanted to find a way to make you happy!

Lenny soon runs upstairs in tears, and Babe runs after her, yelling at Meg, "Why do you have to make Lenny cry? I just hate it when you make Lenny cry!" We then see that Meg hates it too. An old friend arrives, and Meg confesses that she hurt her sister: "I'm upset about it," she says. "Why can't I keep my mouth shut?" But it turns out to be a boon that Babe told Lenny's secret to Meg. When Meg learns that Lenny told her beau she no longer wanted to see him only because she feared rejection, she urges Lenny to call him and "untell him." With her sister's encouragement, she does, and the relationship resumes.

The play ends with the three sisters united in laughter. Yet the metaphor of winged tongues is fitting to reflect the way words can fly around, hitting people and sometimes hurting them, when women talk about personal information and tell secrets, their own and others'.

Phyllis was dating a young man, and she was falling in love. She had not told her family about the relationship because the man was of a different race, and she knew they would disapprove. She hated the secrecy, though, and was filled with the joy of first love. In a moment of intimacy, she confided in her older sister, who promptly told their mother. The family was plunged into turmoil. Her mother "went ballistic" and accused Phyllis of endangering the life of her father, who had suffered a heart attack some years earlier. Unable to withstand the maelstrom, Phyllis broke up the relationship. Soon after, she met and married a man of the same race and faith as her family—and divorced him three years later. Phyllis has no way of knowing how that first relationship would have turned out, had it run its natural course. She did know that marrying the first man she met that her parents approved of was a reaction to the uproar that her previous relationship had caused. Yet it wasn't the relationship that had sparked the conflagration; it was her sister's revelation of it—her sister's telling her secret.

I'm the Same Way

There is another aspect to girls' and women's friendships that establishes connection through talk. Saying "I know, I'm the same way" is almost a requirement of women's conversations. My student Sharon Stirling taped a conversation between sisters that includes a simple example of how "the same thing happened to me" can establish connection. Twenty-six-year-old Maureen was home for Thanksgiving, sitting on the bed and talking to her twenty-one-year-old sister Kendall. While telling Maureen about her new boyfriend, Kendall said her boyfriend thought she shouldn't have told her older sister that they'd met at a bar, because he feared she'd disapprove. Maureen assured Kendall that she didn't disapprove: "It's fine," she said. And then, to assure her younger sister how really fine it was, she added, "Bob and I went home from a bar." Maureen's situation had actually been different: "I mean we knew each other from beforehand too," she said. To connect with her sister, Maureen emphasized what was similar (the bar), not what was different (she knew him already).

For many women, the claim "we're different" comes across as creating distance—or as a put-down. It's true that "She's different from me" can be a way of saying "There are things about her I don't like." Ostensibly telling me merely that she and her sister are different, one woman said, "She's a couch potato and I'm not." There isn't much doubt that being "a couch potato" is not admirable. Another woman said of her sister, "She's flashy, likes a lot of rings and sparkly things; I don't like to be showing off." Liking rings and sparkly things is a matter of style, but showing off is a character flaw. Yet another woman said of her sister, "She's a perfectionist, never a hair out of place." This could be good or bad, but what she said next could only be bad: "She's narcissistic." And when a woman told me, "My sister wears all these expensive clothes," she was implying that their lives and their values differ—and her sister's are superficial.

These are extreme examples of how "We're different" can be a put-down, creating distance, while connection is reinforced when someone says, "I'm the same." But saying "The same thing happened to me" doesn't always contribute to a satisfying sense of connection either. These words can be an annoying shift of attention from speaker to listener. It's especially annoying coming from a sister, whose concern for you is supposed to be guaranteed. Here too, Alice Mattison's *Nothing Is Quite Forgotten in Brooklyn* provides an example, a glimpse of how a sister can seem self-centered when you want her to care about you.

Constance was distraught because her teenage daughter, Joanna, had disappeared. To make matters worse, her husband, Jerry, was away on a trip. In desperation, Constance called the police, then set about trying to locate Jerry, who hadn't told her where he'd be staying. She finally located him at a motel and learned from the desk clerk that Jerry had a young woman staying with him—Joanna. He had taken their daughter along on the trip without telling his wife. Constance had called her sister Barbara when she thought Joanna was missing, so she called again now to tell her that Joanna was safe. After delivering this news, Constance added, "I'm leaving Jerry." Her sister asked, "Just over this?" Here's how the conversation proceeded:

> "No, of course not." It was hard to explain. "It's because this was so clearly Jerry. It's his defining act, taking Joanna and not telling me."
>
> "What's *my* defining act?" said Barbara. "Does everyone have a defining act?"
>
> "I don't know but Jerry does."
>
> "Quitting that job," said Barbara, "was my defining act. Anybody wants to know anything about me, they could see a two-minute clip of me walking out of that office."
>
> "Well, I guess so." Con couldn't recall when they'd begun discussing Barbara's personality instead of Con's marriage.

Ruminating on a philosophical point, "Does everyone have a defining act?" would be appropriate in another conversation. So would applying another's question to yourself: "What's *my* defining act?" But in response to the announcement that her sister's marriage is ending, philosophical rumination and self-analysis are not what the reader, or a sister, would expect. In the novel, this conversation is Barbara's defining act. It defines her as oblivious to her sister and overly focused on herself. Barbara's self-absorption is a failure of connection, a failure that is particularly stark in a sister. If your sister can't—or won't—focus her attention on you at a time of crisis, you feel more abandoned than you would if you had no sister in the first place. Barbara's failure to come through for her sister comes through in her conversation.

Don't Start a Fight

I recognized a pattern in many of the anecdotes I heard. One sister (often the oldest) was shocked to learn that another sister had been angry at her, while she herself had no idea there was anything wrong. For example, an older sister, Libby, told me she was astonished when her younger sister accused her, weeks after a visit, of having attacked and insulted her. I asked what attacks and insults her sister was referring to, and she said she had no idea. Then she said, "Why doesn't she call me on it instead of making a check mark in her notebook?" When she pressed her sister, she learned that one offending remark had been made while they were cleaning up after dinner. Libby felt that her sister had misinterpreted the remark. And Libby, in turn, blamed her sister for not saying anything. "Had she called me on it, I would have told her what I was thinking," she told me. "Instead she says nothing, the moment passes, and we go on with something else. She's upset, hateful, vengeful, and I'm thinking I need a different cleaner for the sink. Now there's a huge problem. We've been robbed of the opportunity to deal with it right then."

Libby's take on this is eminently sensible. It seems obviously better to say something and work it out rather than harbor resentment that festers and swells. Then why is Libby's experience so common? At least part of the explanation is many women's inclination to avoid open conflict. Researchers have observed this tendency in little girls at play. (Of course girls also engage in open conflict at times, and boys at times avoid it.)

Linguist Amy Sheldon videotaped preschool girls and boys playing in groups of three. In one example she analyzed, two girls, Eva and Kelly, establish a role-play scenario in which they are a married couple. When the third girl, Tulla, tries to join their play, Sheldon notes, "Eva doesn't refuse Tulla outright but postpones her participation." She assigns Tulla a role, but it's one that precludes her taking an active part: "You can be the baby brother, but you aren't born yet." At one point Tulla tries to join the play by making her toy figure relevant as the baby brother: "I'm sleeping. You know who's sleeping? Your brother's— Lookit, he's sleeping!" Eva holds Tulla at bay without disputing her claim to be a baby brother and without rejecting her from play; she says, "He's still in the *tummy.*" In this and many other examples, Sheldon shows that the girls are "highly assertive" in a way that "has the effect of softening rather than escalating discord." They pursue their own goals while at least appearing to allow others to get what they want too.

In a paper she wrote for my class, Ellen Herman recalls a similar pattern in a game that she and her two sisters played as children. Ellen is the oldest; Kate is two and a half years younger; and Anne is five and a half years younger than Kate. Here's how Ellen describes the game, which they called "Castle": "Anne would be the Queen, Kate would be the Princess, and I would be the Servant. Although this hierarchy is an inversion of our ages, we were all satisfied with our roles and harmony was maintained." Ellen explained how this could be:

> As the oldest, I normally would have protested having to be the low-status character in our game. However, I knew that as the Servant I could direct the game and order my sisters around with statements like "Your highness has a ball to get ready for!" I got to run the game, so I felt as though I was maintaining my control over my sisters. Kate also enjoyed the game because she knew that princesses in fairy tales were the main characters. By getting to be the princess, she felt as though she had "won" over me. This made her happy. Anne was too young to understand that princesses were the main characters, and it was very easy for Kate and me to tell her that as Queen, she was the "mom" of us and was therefore in control.

As Ellen Herman explains, she and Kate found a way to get what they wanted without conflict by arranging for the others to get—or believe they got—what they wanted too.

My grandniece Tovah, at two and a half, had mastered this approach. Up late because she was sick, Tovah was enjoying the company of four adults: She and her parents were saying an extended good night to her visiting grandparents, who were staying in the guest room. When her mother told her it was time for them to leave the guest room and let the grandparents go to bed, Tovah didn't want to break up the party. She protested by arguing for her grandparents' interests rather than her own. "If we leave," she said, "Grandma and Grandpa will be lonely."

What does all this have to do with Libby's frustration that her sister didn't confront her on the spot when Libby said something her sister found offensive? Part of the reason could be a habitual inclination to avoid open confrontation, especially with an older sister who appears particularly powerful.

Brothers: A Different Way of Talking

It would be misleading to claim that girls and women always avoid confrontation, or that boys and men never do. Research comparing children at play consistently finds that the difference is of degree: Boys also mitigate conflict and cloak their requests in ways that appeal to connection, but girls do it more. The same can be said of other patterns that distinguish boys' and men's styles from girls' and women's—and often make conversations with brothers different from talking to sisters.

When I spoke to women who had brothers as well as sisters, I asked them about their brothers too. There were patterns to their answers. I'll mention some of them here, not to make claims about brothers in general—I didn't talk to brothers directly, so I can't do that—but because the women themselves contrasted their brothers with their sisters.

A student in my class, Leigh Hunt, wrote a paper about conversations she had with her two sisters and her brother. When the family dog died, the sisters all spoke on the phone, telling each other how terrible they felt and how much they missed the dog. Her brother called too, but the conversation Leigh had with him was a little different. He expressed his concern for everyone in the family but said nothing about what he himself was feeling. Leigh didn't doubt that inside he felt the same as the others; he just wasn't talking about it. I would bet that making the call served exactly the same purpose for him as her sisters' calls did for them: connecting with others who cared about the dog as much as he did and were feeling the same loss.

The relationships women described with their brothers spanned a vast range, just as there was a vast range in relationships women had with sisters, from seeing each other daily to not being in touch at all. But many of the comments I heard reflected a pattern much like the contrasting conversations Leigh Hunt described. Many women told me they are close to their brothers, but even so there is a difference. For example, a woman who said she's close to both her sister and her brother added, "I can talk to my brother about almost anything. I can talk to my sister about absolutely anything." The difference between "almost" and "absolutely" is talk about intimate personal matters and how she feels about them.

This contrast, like the contrast in Leigh Hunt's conversations with her sisters and her brother, highlights the special role that talking about their personal lives and emotions typically plays among girls and women, and the contrasting tendency that is common among brothers. In a study of conversations between college students ranging in age from eighteen to twenty-five and their siblings, Cindy Mathieu found that the young men talked to their brothers about sports more often than the women did, and the young women talked to their sisters about relationships and family more often than the men did. Part of this pattern no doubt reflected expectations about what their siblings wanted to hear. Students of both sexes were more likely to express emotion to their sisters. In another study of brothers and sisters between seventeen and twenty-five, British psychologists Liz Wright and Tony Cassidy found that brothers who had no sisters seemed to observe "a conspiracy of silence not to talk."

This doesn't mean that every individual woman likes to talk about personal problems and emotions. Recall Jeanne and Colleen, the elderly sisters holding hands in bed; it's hard to imagine an image of greater intimacy between sisters. Yet Colleen and her sister did not discuss personal problems (though they did "just talk"). And they are not unique. More than one woman told me that her sister frustrates her by refusing to talk about feelings. This is evidence that not all women follow the "typical" pattern—but also that many women expect this kind of talk from those they're close to and are disappointed when a sister doesn't fulfill that expectation. It's also possible that the offending sister talks to others about her feelings; she may not want that kind of closeness to the sister who made the complaint.

Tell Me How You Feel

A woman who has two sisters and two brothers told me that she's close to them all. But it's a different closeness. She talks to her sisters on the phone for hours, mostly about personal topics. She talks to her brothers for hours too—about history, geography, and books. And one brother sometimes calls her at 5 A.M. as a prank.

A woman who has three sisters and two brothers was more typical. She said she talks to her sisters on the phone but with her brothers she exchanges e-mails—and her brothers don't communicate with each other at all. A woman who has three sisters and one brother, after telling me at length about her interactions with her sisters, told me (when I asked) that she calls her brother from time to time to check in, and from time to time he e-mails her funny videos.

Here are a few comments I heard about brothers that were typical:

"My brother's a loner."

"He's very closed, he's very quiet, he's very introspective, he's pretty introverted. And he doesn't share a lot of information."

"He doesn't have in-depth conversations."

"He doesn't get too bothered by things. He just wants to act. There's less tension."

"He generally does not offer up too many details about things going on in his life."

"He's hard to read."

Remarks like "He's closed" and "He doesn't have in-depth conversations" reflect the kinds of conversation that the sisters value. "Closed" implies not being "open" about personal information, not saying what's going on in his life and his heart. "In-depth" would be exploring personal experiences and emotions as well. I suspect that not getting "too bothered by things" also comes down to different ways of talking. A brother might be bothered, but a sister might not know it because he doesn't talk about it. If "he just wants to act" then he is bothered; only he is handling it in a different way, and that way is not talk.

The comment "There's less tension" is particularly revealing. Many psychologists, like many women, have concluded that talking about emotions is good. British researchers Liz Wright and Tony Cassidy discovered that young people who had grown up with at least one sister tended to be happier and more optimistic, especially if their families had been split by divorce. The researchers attribute this pattern to girls' tendency to talk about emotions. In a study of adults in middle and old age, Victor Cicirelli found that both men and women who felt they had a close bond to a sister showed fewer signs of depression. Another researcher, Judy Dunn, reports a similar pattern among older adults, for whom "relationships with sisters appear to be particularly important"—a finding "generally attributed to women's emotional expressiveness." But all that talk can also complicate relationships, contributing to greater "tension," as well as greater intimacy, among sisters.

Communication Is Women's Work

A pattern I noticed immediately when women compared their sisters to their brothers was that most talked to their sisters more often. For example, a woman who has two sisters and five brothers said she calls her brothers when she has a specific reason; she calls her sisters just to chat. She added that her sisters talk longer—and worry more.

In many families, communication itself is the domain of women. Two sisters who also have a brother commented that they keep up with their brother's life through his daughter—even though he lives in the same house as one of the sisters! (She moved back to the family home when their mother needed help, he moved back when his marriage broke up, and they both stayed on after their mother passed away.) Another woman told me she is in continual touch with her sister but not her three brothers, though she keeps in touch with one brother through his wife. Her conversations with her sister are long and rambling; when she does talk to her brothers, their conversations are "a bit more straightforward." I heard similar comments from women who told me they are close to their brothers. For example, a woman who told me she and her brother are very close gave him the highest praise: "He gets me." But she went on to say that she's not in communication with him that much. They e-mail once or twice a month. If he calls, as he did to ask if she'd be coming for Thanksgiving, the conversation is practical and short.

Even though these patterns frequently distinguish brothers from sisters, many brothers speak frequently to their sisters and to each other. Ari Emanuel described his older brother Rahm, President Obama's Chief of Staff, as his best friend. Before Rahm assumed his current position, Ari said, "we would talk four, five times a day. Now we just talk on Saturdays." Nonetheless, in many families, keeping everyone in touch is women's work. Psychologists Lynn White and Agnes Riedmann found that sisters had more contact with their siblings than brothers, and that brothers had more contact with their siblings if at least one sibling was a sister. Indeed, the British researchers who found that young men with at least one sister are happier believe that this is because a sister will "break down" her brother's "conspiracy of silence." The women I interviewed who had brothers as well as sisters uniformly characterized their relationships with their sisters as based more on talk, especially personal talk about what's going on in their lives and how they feel about it.

There is another way that women tend to be in charge of communication within families, one that causes no frustration, as far as I can tell, and enriches family life. A woman who has a sister and two brothers commented that she and her sister are the ones in their family who are charged with "legacy and remembrance"—to listen to, recall, and pass on family stories. There are many men who tell stories of their forebears. In my own family, it was my father, not my mother, who often spoke about the past and from whom I learned details of his mother's relatives in Poland. But passing on family stories is more common among women.

Elizabeth Stone discovered this while writing her book *Black Sheep and Kissing Cousins: How Our Family Stories Shape Us*. When she began her research, she expected to hear stories of women's families from women and of men's families from men. She found instead that often she heard the men's family stories from women. It wasn't unusual for a wife to tell her a story of her husband's family that the husband didn't even know. Family stories were typically passed among women: Wives heard them from their husbands' mothers or sisters. "Legacy and remembrance"—

preserving and passing on family history through stories—is yet another way that women typically use language to create connections.

Not all women speak in the ways I've characterized here as common among women, and those who do may manifest these styles to a greater or lesser degree. Being female or male is only one of many influences on the ways we speak. Other influences on conversational style include ethnicity, class, regional or cultural background, age, sexual orientation, profession, and so on, all overlaid on temperament and personality. I'll discuss some elements of conversational style, how they can differ, and how those differences can affect sisters, in the final chapter.

CHAPTER EIGHT

Sisterness

The Good, the Bad, and
How to Get More of the Lovely

My father's cousins Gertrude and Anna lived together nearly their entire lives. When her husband died tragically after less than a year of marriage, Gertrude went to live with her sister, Anna, and Anna's husband and son, and continued to live with her after Anna was widowed and her son married. Their names, in my mind, were fused: GertrudenAnna. I never saw one without the other. When they were old and their footing unsure, they walked with arms linked and bodies pressed close, supporting each other so neither would fall. The image of these sisters, well into their eighties, arm in arm as they cautiously stepped off a curb, remains with me as a model of sisters in lifelong mutual support.

Many fortunate women (I count myself among them) have sisters who support each other in innumerable ways, even if they fought as children or grew apart at earlier times in their lives. As a woman said of her sister, "We're completely for each other." And many women told me, when I asked if they have sisters, that they have found sisterhood in friends. One who said this, Kitty Bayh, called them "heart-sisters—women who have been my Sacagawea, and me theirs, on our life and spiritual journeys." I asked her how a friend can be her Sacagawea. She replied (in an e-mail):

Just as Sacagawea was a pathfinder for Lewis & Clark's expedition westward, my heart-sisters have been my guide on life's journeys. Just as Sacagawea was an interpreter for the Indian and white man, my heart-sisters help me render into language what I'm feeling. As Sacagawea dug for roots and collected plants for medicine, my heart-sisters plumb their own experiences and offer them as a healing balm to my own.

This description comes pretty close to the ideal reflected in the word "sisterhood." But the reality of sister relationships—real-life sisterness—can vary a bit or a lot from this ideal. I say "sisterness" because "sisterhood" brings to mind only the support side of this relationship. Real sisters can experience less gratifying sides as well.

In the popular imagination, sisters represent not only mutual support but also the conflict epitomized by the stereotypical metaphor for female animosity, the cat fight. Novelist Philippa Gregory draws on this cultural icon in her novel *The Other Boleyn Girl*. Inspired by the historical fact that, before he married Anne Boleyn, King Henry VIII had an affair with her older sister, Mary, Gregory portrays the Boleyn sisters as locked in competition for the king's favors. "I was born to be your rival," Anne says to Mary. "And you mine. We're sisters, aren't we?"

One evening, Anne and Mary are together in Mary's chambers when their brother joins them and tells Anne that the king was asking about her. On hearing this, Mary spreads her "fingers like claws on the red silk sheet of the bed." "Like claws" brings to mind a cat fight, while the red color of the sheet suggests the blood that a cat's claws can draw. In another scene Mary accuses, "You want anything that's mine. You've always wanted anything that was mine." In retaliation, Anne orders her sister from the room. Mary reminds her, "This is *my* room." Then, Gregory writes, the sisters "glared at each other, stubborn as cats on the stable wall, full of mutual resentment and something darker, the old sense between sisters that there is only really room in the world for one girl. The sense that every fight could be to the death." (That Anne Boleyn married King Henry and was later beheaded by him lends resonance and weight to the phrase "to the death.")

Seeking Understanding

These are two sides of sisterness: GertrudenAnna's mutual support and the Boleyn sisters' rivalry. Support and rivalry, connection and competition, combine in varying ways in all relationships and therefore in all conversations. These two dynamics come together in particularly intense forms in sisterness. Sisters seeking to maximize the support and minimize or benefit from the rivalry may wonder whether there is a secret to such success.

"The reason my siblings and I are close and we're all good friends," one woman said, "is that our mother always told us, 'You have to stick together. Whatever the differences are, deal with them and support each other.'" This is excellent and wise advice, but I doubt that it alone explains these siblings' closeness. Another woman, Terri, has never gotten along with her sister despite receiving similar advice. Their mother even hung a poster in the sisters' shared bedroom that read, CHANCE MADE US SISTERS, HEARTS MADE US FRIENDS. Terri didn't take this advice to heart; the poster made her cringe. She didn't want her sister as a friend. Having her mother pressure her to feel otherwise only increased her resistance.

There is no single secret that explains why some sisters have better relationships than others. I'm sure a lot has to do with individual personalities and with how those personalities mesh or clash. But it's always possible to change the way others behave or talk by changing the way you behave with or talk to them. And if nothing changes, it can still be helpful to understand what led to your or your sister's reactions. In this chapter I'll explore some of the ways that sister conversations balance the connection of mutual support with the competition of mutual rivalry. I'll also consider how differences in conversational style play a role. Understanding these processes makes it easier to find ways of enhancing the support and managing the rivalry among sisters and in other sisterlike relationships.

Joined at the Head

"Remember?" is the abracadabra of sister conversation. "Remember the time . . . ?" we ask, then laugh together at an incident pulled from our shared past like a rabbit from a hat. Lori Lansen's novel *The Girls* about twin sisters conjoined at the head can be read as a metaphor for sisterness. Sisters are joined at the head in the sense of sharing memories and a past.

In Lansen's novel, one twin says of the other, "I bear Ruby's weight, as I tote Ruby on my hip." We all tote our sisters on our hips metaphorically, because almost any move made by one affects the other. Among the most obvious and significant examples are literal moves. When sisters move to different towns, states, or countries, the sisters who remain may get more responsibility for taking care of aging or ill relatives. A sister who moves away might regret that her children will grow up without seeing their cousins as often as she saw hers—but so will her sister's children. When I asked women what frustrates them about their sisters, a frequent answer was, "She lives too far away." This was frustrating because the sisters didn't see each other enough, didn't spend time in each other's homes, and weren't part of each other's daily lives. Celebrating holidays together figured in many accounts I heard from sisters—both the happy outcome when everyone attends, and the disappointment when one or more either can't or won't. A sister's decision to stay away makes the holiday celebration incomplete for the others.

Here's another way that sisters are metaphorically joined at the head: Their heads are filled with the same people—their parents. When I talked to women about their mothers and their daughters for my book *You're Wearing THAT?* I sometimes heard about siblings. A daughter might say that her mother favored another sibling, often a brother. A mother might comment that one daughter was easy and another tricky; she had to watch what she said with one, not the other. But when I talked to women about their sisters, every single one spent time talking about her parents. More often than not, they described their own or their sisters' personalities by referring to their parents' personalities. Many explained their sisters' relationships with loved ones by reference to their parents as well. For example, a woman commented that her sister has bad luck in relationships with men because her relationship with their father was not good. Ideas about who was favored could be mentioned as explanations for just about anything.

Over and over I heard women say, She is (or I am) like our mother, like our father, or determined to be different from one or the other. One woman said, "I have my father's discipline and drive, but I have my mother's drive for enjoyment." Personalities were often illustrated by the differing ways sisters responded to the same parents. "My father had a wicked temper," a youngest sister said. "But I sweet-talked him into letting me off, so I got punished very little. I kind of knew when you could push his buttons and when not." Another, an oldest, said of her mother, "I can say things to her the others can't. Like 'You really shouldn't talk like that, Ma.' " She added, "I can talk to her. The others are just going *aargh!* I can match her. And we can have fun together." The *aargh* represented the frustration her sisters experience when dealing with their mother. They don't respond to her in ways that stop her from saying things they don't like or would bring out the side they could have fun with.

Ways of speaking were often explained as recapitulating relationships with parents too. A woman wrote in an e-mail that she treasured her sister, but their relationship was fraught: "power struggles, small and large misunderstandings, hurt feelings, each trying to take care of ourselves while taking into account the other. In trying to be firm, we cross the line and sound mean and intractable." She explained that neither returns the other's calls immediately because each feels she has to prepare by bracing herself and making sure she finds a moment when she feels strong. She attributed these strains to having grown up with a mother who had frequent screaming rages and severely beat them. She summed up communication with her sister by saying, "What is most sad is that we are applying the same strategy to each other that we used to use toward our mother." Their mother, long since deceased, lives on in their heads, hovering over their relationship, her voice echoing in their conversations.

Parents are the founders and CEOs of the family life that constitutes a child's world. As Louise Glück put it in her poem "Rain in Summer," describing a scene from her childhood, "In my mind, my parents / were the circle; my sister and I / were trapped inside." And parents remain shadow figures in their children's lives and relationships—especially the children's relationships with one another—long after they are children no more. This can be comforting or frightening, depending on the aspects of parents that are kept alive.

Older sisters who came from families where a parent was abusive or alcoholic uniformly expressed regret and guilt for not sufficiently protecting younger ones or for abandoning them by leaving home for college or work. This guilt is a shadow cast by their parents' abuse. But keeping parents alive in shared experience and memory can be a precious gift of sisterness, if it preserves the warmth given off by parents' love.

Coming Through—or Not

Among the most moving stories I heard were of sisters coming through in times of crisis. More than one woman told me that when her husband died, her sister was on a plane within hours—or that her sister came and stayed for days, weeks, or even months when she was ill. A woman who was stricken with cancer said that one of her sisters left her home across the country and moved in for several months to help care for her through the surgery, chemotherapy, and long recuperation. Another sister, a physician, supervised her medical care from afar, speaking on the phone with her every day. In addition to deeply appreciating the help these sisters provided, she said, the best thing was the renewed connection their care and contact established and the chance to get to know better sisters who lived in distant parts of the country. On the other hand, a third sister who lived nearby failed to come through at all: She rarely called and visited only twice during the whole ordeal. Describing these contrasting responses to her medical crisis encapsulated this woman's diverse experiences with her sisters through the years.

In a parallel way, some women illustrated their sisters' failings by telling me something they had said in a moment of crisis. For example, when a woman told her sister she had been diagnosed with Parkinson's, her sister said, "Aren't you worried about me? Parkinson's can run in the family!" The most extreme example I heard was the phone call a woman received four hours after her husband's death. It was her sister, who began, "Dad told me that Greg died," then continued, "Is this a good time to tell you what's going on with me?" In these examples, the offending sisters shift focus to themselves at times when it's stunningly obvious that they should be offering support. Their responses are the opposite of coming through.

Your Way or Mine?

Most complaints I heard were of far less serious, more mundane frustrations. Jamie loved her sister Stacey and was thrilled when Stacey came to visit. Yet she always found herself getting irritated after a few days. She wanted Stacey to feel at home in her house, but it rubbed her the wrong way when Stacey seemed literally to think Jamie's home was hers. Her back was up when Stacey opened cabinets, looking for a glass, and opened the refrigerator, looking for a drink to put in the glass. Jamie thought Stacey's offense was obvious: Everyone knows it's intrusive to open cabinet or refrigerator doors in someone else's home. But as obvious as this was to Jamie, it was equally obvious to Stacey that she was doing what any sister would do—and be welcome to do. Stacey could see from the look on her face that Jamie did not like what she was doing. The only thing she could imagine Jamie disapproving of was her choice of drink. She had taken out a bottle of wine. Did Jamie think she was drinking too much wine?

Some readers will think that Jamie was right to bristle because Stacey behaved inappropriately; anyone is a guest in another's home, sister or not. Others will feel that opening a sister's cabinets without asking is a heartwarming sign of connection—only natural, because sisters are family. Jamie will probably never feel that way, but she might feel better about her sister's behavior if she kept in mind that Stacey's differing expectation about proper behavior in a sister's home is also reasonable. You don't have to like it, but it helps to respect it. Your sister's habits can drive you crazy. That's real. But it doesn't mean there's something inherently wrong with those habits. Maybe you can't stand it that, when you go out to a restaurant together, she never accepts the first table offered and half the time she sends back her food. But you may drive her crazy by being too passive, always accepting what you're given whether or not it's what you want.

Jamie's and Stacey's assumptions about sisterly behavior correspond roughly to differing conversational styles that I have studied and written about at length, inspired by the work of linguist Robin Lakoff. Stacey's style corresponds to what I've called "high-involvement," a style guided by a maxim Lakoff calls "Maintain camaraderie." It's a style that places the highest value on connection: You show caring by emphasizing the ways you're close. Jamie's differing assumption corresponds to a conversational style I have called "high-considerateness," following the maxim Lakoff identifies as "Don't impose." This style places the highest value on respecting another's independence: You show caring by making sure not to encroach. We all have ideas about when and how to maintain camaraderie as well as when and how to refrain from imposing. But we have personal as well as cultural styles by which we tend toward one or the other in given ways and given situations. Frustrations result when two people have different conversational styles.

Conversational styles are developed and become habitual as children hear talk around them growing up. The styles heard are influenced by many factors, including ethnicity, class, regional background, age, sexual orientation, and personality. Though many of these are shared by sisters, others may not be, and even if they are, individuals can react differently to the same influences, so sisters' conversational styles can differ. To sort out frustrations, it's important for sisters, as for spouses, acquaintances, and even strangers, to understand the dynamics of conversational style.

It's How You Say It

One element of conversational style entails habits about pacing, pausing, and rights to the floor. Speakers may have different assumptions regarding how quickly or slowly it is normal to speak; how long a pause to leave between turns at talk, and whether and when it's acceptable or even preferable to talk while another is talking.

Some people think it's great to talk along when someone else is speaking, in order to show enthusiasm, interest, and understanding. There is a payoff in connection. Others think only one voice should be heard at a time, so anyone who begins speaking while another voice is heard is interrupting—an encroachment on the other's right to the floor. A related difference is how long a pause feels natural, either between turns or while you're speaking. Whoever expects a longer pause between turns has trouble getting the floor, because the shorter pause comes first, and the shorter-pauser will fill the uncomfortable silence before the longer pause ever comes. The result is mutual accusation: "You interrupt; you don't give me a chance to talk"; "You don't hold up your end of the conversation." We saw this in Chapter Three, where a college student accused her older sister, "You totally just talked over me like fifty times!" Meanwhile, the sister and her boyfriend had talked over each other too, yet neither had felt interrupted.

Another element of conversational style is relative directness and indirectness. Some people think it's best to state preferences outright and express opinions in the strongest possible terms. Others find this rude, believing that preferences and opinions should be communicated gently—or not at all, if they will lead to disagreement. One person might ask, "Would you like to visit Harry?" to begin a discussion in the course of which she will let you know what she would like to do. If you don't operate that way, you may reply "No," and never suspect that you have come across as selfish to someone who never suspected you did not intend your reply to be the last word. In Chapter One, we saw sisters who frustrated each other because of different habits regarding directness where one was hurt that the other didn't offer to lend her an evening gown, and the other felt unjustly accused because her sister hadn't asked for it.

A particularly interesting element of conversational style is what I call "agonism": ritual fighting. You insult each other but it's friendly teasing. You punch each other but it's playful roughhousing. You have a passionate argument about politics and enjoy the verbal sparring. Agonism is tricky, because those who don't share enjoyment of playful fighting can take offense and point to the literal meaning—insults, punches, verbal attacks—as self-evidently offensive and unacceptable. Claire Bonin, in a paper she wrote for my class, describes how she and her sister enjoyed agonism when she was twenty and her sister sixteen. They were riding in the family car when Claire spotted a dog of a breed their mother had as a child. "Look, a Schnauze!" Claire called out, using the family's shorthand for the breed. Her sister retorted, "Your *face* is a schnauze!" This is an example of "you had to have been there" humor. You also had to have shared habits regarding agonism. Claire reports that she couldn't come up with a retort because she was laughing too hard; she found the insult to be not insulting but funny. It was funny because it was silly—they were acting like kids—and because her sister had surprised Claire with an insult, reminding her of their shared agonistic style of humor.

Fights between sisters can be real and still be signs of closeness. Another student, Kaley Ervin, also reported that she enjoys agonism with her younger sister. They fight, Kaley says, about trivial things like who gets to sit on the comfortable couch, who gets to choose which TV show to watch, and which music to play in the car. For example, one evening they went to a concert together, with Kaley driving and her sister navigating.

Her sister kept telling her about turns at the very last minute, so Kaley had to cut across lanes of traffic in dangerously short time. Her anger mounted and then focused on something else: the music. She wanted to change the station her sister had chosen, and she felt righteous in her demand: It was late, and she needed peppier music to keep her awake at the wheel. The argument that erupted was so rancorous that they drove much of the way home in angry silence. They never made up; they just forgot it. The next morning they got up, and it was as if nothing untoward had happened. Kaley says that her sister "is one of the only people with whom I can fight and not fear negative repercussions on our relationship."

Learning Styles, Learning Differences

Claire Bonin and Kaley Ervin experienced and illustrated a joy of sister-hood: the pleasure of shared conversational style. They both love to argue and tease, so outsiders might think they're having a fight, but the sisters know it's in fun. Any shared style can yield that pleasure. It doesn't matter what the style is; what matters is that it's shared. You have the same sense of rhythm, so you both interrupt and talk over each other, or each gives the other plenty of room to finish a thought. You both like to talk for hours about people in your life, or you both prefer impersonal topics such as books you've read, TV shows you watch, movies you've seen, or music you like. We expect this of sisters: They grew up in the same home, so they should have similar conversational styles.

But wait. The conversational styles you learned at home come from your parents' styles, and your parents' styles may not be the same. They grew up in different homes, and possibly in different parts of the country; perhaps they came from different ethnic, class, or cultural backgrounds— not to mention that they are usually different genders. These and many other influences can result in different conversational styles. Parents' con-versational styles can be passed down to children, but so can parents' style *differences*. If this happens, the stage may be set for parents' mutual frus-tration to be replicated in sisters.

That's the result described by another student in my class, Tara Healey. Tara adopted her mother's conversational style. They like to talk— about people or whatever else is on their minds—and their talk is explicit.

Her sister Alexa adopted their father's style. She doesn't like to talk—at least not to other family members—and especially not about feelings or problems. The result is that the sisters frustrate each other, more or less the way their parents frustrate each other. Maybe more, because their parents know that they came from different backgrounds. Their mother is Jewish and grew up in New York City; their father is Irish and from New England. But Alexa and Tara are the same sex and grew up in the same family, so they expect to be able to talk to each other easily. Having different conversational styles is not only frustrating but also surprising and disappointing, because it's not what they expect of sisterhood.

One Talks About Feelings, the Other Doesn't

The aspect of Alexa's style that frustrates Tara the most is that she keeps so much of her life secret. Many women regard it as self-evident that people who are close confide in each other, talking about their emotions and personal problems. But not all women share this view. A sister who finds it obvious that people who are close confide in each other will be frustrated by a sister who doesn't like to talk about feelings or explore motives. And the reverse is also true. What could be more annoying than having a sister who keeps asking about feelings and problems, when you find such talk pointless and unpleasant and such questions intrusive? Moreover, you're being pushed to do something you're not good at, because you don't do it often, by someone who likes such talk and is good at it because she does it a lot. It feels like she's trying to get you to play a game she knows she can win. I have talked to many pairs of sisters whose styles apportion this way. In some cases, the pro-talker prevails by insisting, "We have to get this out and clear the air." They do, and the air is cleared. At other times, the no-talker prevails, and the problem recedes or is even forgotten. Either style can work well and often does, especially if the style is shared but even if one or the other accommodates to a style different from her own.

The words we use to refer to these habits reveal value judgments. The word "gossip" is a good example. It renders a negative value judgment of talk about people. Reflecting the other style is the word "honest." A woman told me she wishes her sister were honest about her feelings, by which she meant that she wishes her sister would talk about them. The opposite of talk is silence, but the opposite of honest is lying. Someone who takes for granted that emotions should be aired and explored in conversation does, in a way, regard silence as a lie—you're not telling the truth. But sometimes not telling isn't a lie. It's just not telling.

Laughing Matters

Those who don't like to talk about problems or emotions may handle them by joking, another element of conversational style. To someone who assumes problems should be talked about, joking about them is avoidance. You're doing something inappropriate to avoid doing what you should: talk. But for some, joking is a way of dealing with emotionally loaded topics— a different way. It allows you to bring the issue up, show that you're aware of it, and even show your perspective on it. What you're avoiding, in this style, is not the difficult subject but the difficult conversation. Talking directly and joking can both be effective ways to deal with difficult issues, and both can be maddening to someone who assumes the other approach is the right one. You can't change other people's styles, but you can change your assumption that your way is right and the other way is wrong.

There's another benefit to joking rather than talking about a difficult issue: You get to laugh, and laughing together reminds you of the connection that the problem may threaten. Laughter can be a means of tapping into a reservoir of past connection.

I'm going to describe a scene that will make me look ridiculous, but that's the point. With sisters you can be ridiculous, just like you were when you were kids—even more, because you're acting like kids when you're adults. Picture three women in their fifties and sixties standing before their gathered families and singing—replete with the usual arm gestures—the children's song "I'm a Little Teapot." This is one of the things my sisters and I have been known to do when our extended families get together. We don't often get through the whole thing because we're guaranteed to collapse in laughter before reaching the end. My sisters' (grown) children often egg us on, maybe because kids like to see their parents look like fools.

I drew courage to tell this story from having heard many similar recollections from other women—women who looked perfectly mature and responsible when we talked. Dolores, at sixty-two the oldest of four, told of a hilarious time she'd recently had with her son and her siblings, a brother and sister, when they all returned to a hotel after a family wedding. They stayed up most of the night, got "stinking drunk," and engaged in a boys-against-girls singing contest, where each team would start a song and the other team had to complete it. When the sing-off was over, she and her sister were jumping on the bed, thinking up and singing songs they should have used in the contest; her son came into the room and said, laughing, "You guys are idiots!" But they just told him, "No, listen to this one! Listen to us!" and carried on carrying on. When they were singing and laughing together, Dolores explained, hierarchy dissolved in connection: "The oldest didn't know more or feel responsible, the youngest wasn't the baby, the brother wasn't special, and her son wasn't of another generation."

A history of laughing together is a bank account from which you can draw goodwill when it's needed. Something that could annoy can be reframed as funny. Here's an example: While visiting her sister Dana, Erin remarked, "Your house is dusty." "Hey," Dana replied, "you said that last time. I made a point to clean before you came. I even went out and bought this." She retrieved from the closet a feather duster on a short stick. "But look," Erin said, running her finger over the slat of a venetian blind. Then she grabbed the duster and began dusting the venetian blinds.

This conversation sounds very much like anecdotes I heard to illustrate the offense of a critical sister. But that wasn't the spirit of this scene. Everything was said with a smile, and when Erin snatched the duster and ran it over the blinds, their smiles turned to laughter. Maybe it was because Dana was older, and criticism from a younger sister rarely has the same bite as criticism from an older one. Maybe it was because Dana was known in the family for having the neatest and best-kept house, so Erin's comment implied, You're not as perfect as I thought you were! which is very different from implying, You've messed up like you always do. And maybe it was just that they both knew the exchange they were having came straight from a stereotype of mothers and daughters, and they were making fun of themselves by mouthing these predictable lines and performing stereotypical gestures, like running a finger over a surface to call attention to a layer of dust.

Behind Her Back

Many people expect me to advise that one sister should never talk about another sister to other family members. But I don't. Once again, we are dealing with different styles, each of which can work poorly or well, depending on the situation and how they are used. There are different and equally valid ways of accomplishing the same goal.

Some families adhere to a strict policy: Never talk to one family member about another who is not there, the proverbial and stigmatized "talking behind her back." If you're angry at a sister, you do not talk about it to anyone else. Conflicts and disagreements must be settled between the people involved. That can work well. In other families, talking behind each other's backs is a cottage industry. That can work well too. One woman, for example, was describing how close she and her two sisters are: They e-mail one another daily, regularly take vacations together, and feel blessed to be sisters and friends. She also said, "If I get angry with one of them I vent to the other." The result is that "it just blows over."

With some conflicts, trying to talk things out just starts them up all over again, whereas talking to another family member can help in a number of ways. In addition to being a safety valve, it can be reassuring just to hear "I know, she does the same thing to me." Sometimes the offense can be transformed into a foible if you laugh at it together. A third party can also shed light, helping you understand the offender's point of view. What's crucial is keeping the discussion between you, so the third party doesn't take your words back to the person you were talking about—nor do you repeat what the third party said. That's where mischief comes in.

This is not to say that it is never mischievous to talk about others behind their backs. If the information is untrue or otherwise destructive, it can be damaging. There's a big difference between talking *about* and talking *against* someone. Amber recalls the damage done by talking *against*. When they were in high school, her stepsister told everyone that Amber was wild, partying and drinking till all hours—but it wasn't true. Amber believes her stepsister was motivated by competition: Amber's mother was married to the stepsister's father, so Amber lived with him. Talking against is almost always mischievous. In this case, the friends who reported to Amber what her stepsister said were looking out for her. But telling someone what a family member said about them isn't always constructive, regardless of the repeater's intentions.

A woman told me of something hurtful her father had said about her: "I don't know why she's working on a PhD. She'll never finish." I asked how she knew he'd said this. Her sister had told her. Hmmm, I thought. Why did her sister tell her? Was it loyalty, giving her information she needed to know? Or was her sister intentionally fomenting discord, telling her something that was sure to hurt her feelings or make her angry? Maybe the woman should have been angry at her sister in addition—or instead. This would be true regardless of what her sister's intentions were. Good intentions don't ensure benign effects. I often quote an Arab proverb that says, "The one who repeats an insult is the one who is insulting you."

Repeating to a sister what your mother said about her can be hurtful even if it's not critical. A woman told her sister Toby that their mother was worried because Toby gets off work late and walks alone to her car. "I told her to stop bugging me about that!" Toby said in exasperation. "I can take care of myself!" Her sister reassured Toby that she'd explained that to their mother. That's why she brought it up: to let Toby know she stood up for her. Toby's sister's intentions were good, but the effect was not. Toby felt bad about being the cause of her mother's distress, so being reminded of it was distressing to her.

When we tell one person what another said we may sincerely think that we are simply conveying another's words, expressing someone else's opinion. But we're not. There is a proverb in Wolof, an African language, that says, "Everything can be taken from one place to another except words." The same words have different meanings if they're spoken in different contexts. Something said about a person who is absent is fundamentally different from the same idea expressed in the person's presence. For one thing, the words are rarely the same. We put things differently when speaking *to* someone rather than *about* them. And the very fact of being talked about is hurtful, because it gives you a glimpse of yourself as not a person but a subject of conversation. It's one more way to feel invisible. Furthermore, people say different things to different people—on purpose. Saying something behind your back that they would not say to your face may be not hypocrisy but considerateness. For all these reasons, sometimes what's destructive is not the talking behind a person's back but repeating to that person what was said about her.

What Did You Expect?

We all have expectations about how others should behave in particular roles and circumstances. Expectations can be useful guidelines about how to behave and how to evaluate others' behavior. But expectations can set you up for disappointment if your sister's expectations differ from yours. This can easily happen, because the range of normal sister behavior is vast. Take something simple, like how frequently sisters should talk to each other. "We talk often" could mean "twice a day" or "once a month." Some sisters who are happy with their relationship speak on the phone or exchange e-mails many times a day. Others who are happy with theirs speak every few months. Any frequency is fine so long as both share the expectation that that's how often they should be in touch. Trouble arises when expectations differ: One thinks a good sister relationship means talking daily, and the other finds that way too often. One likes to send frequent e-mails, while the other is overwhelmed by e-mail at work and wants none at home—or doesn't use e-mail at all.

Differing expectations about whether or not to spend holidays together can also lead to disappointment. When Maura's family moved to the town where her sister Kaitlyn's family lives, she assumed they would spend Thanksgiving together. "Whose home will we have Thanksgiving at?" she asked Kaitlyn. She was shocked and hurt by Kaitlyn's response: "What do you mean 'we'? Your family is yours and mine is mine." They both felt discomfort: one for being excluded, the other for being encroached upon. Since refusal overrides longing, Maura had to change her expectation. But it should help to know that many loving sisters do not celebrate holidays together, just as loving sisters vary greatly in how frequently they communicate.

Another way to think about Maura and Kaitlyn's mutual frustration is their differing definitions of family. For Maura, family always includes the family you're born into. Kaitlyn's idea of family begins and ends with her husband and children; her sister may be invited to join them, but she is not a charter member. Family is comforting, if you're included in it—and you want to be. But the claim "we're family" can be off-putting if you don't want to be merged with the person who's speaking. These differences can arise when both sisters have families of their own: spouses or children or both. But they can be especially noticeable—and problematic—if one sister has and the other hasn't.

There's no way to avoid disappointment when expectations differ or just can't be fulfilled. Tracing the disappointment to differing expectations can reduce it; so can understanding that there are many ways to be loving sisters. The way that seems obvious to you is not the only one.

New Opportunities, New Risks

Emerging technologies for communication provide new opportunities to amplify comfort and new risks to aggravate tensions between sisters.

Not so long ago, most young people stayed where they were born and raised. Sisters lived near each other and were part of one another's daily lives. In our more mobile society, it's common for siblings to live in different states or even different countries. Luckily, communication technology has evolved as well, enabling more and varied contact among people who are physically separated. When my grandmother emigrated to America in 1920, the only way she could communicate with her family in Europe was to write letters that took weeks to travel over the sea or, in rare urgent cases, to send telegrams. Sisters today have access to a blizzard of electronic communication pathways—cell phones, text messaging, e-mail, instant messaging, MySpace, Facebook, Twitter, webcams, Skype, personal blogs—and continually emerging new technologies. Each medium has unique advantages and liabilities, and each affects relationships in different ways.

Electronic pathways make possible more frequent communication and allow sisters to stay in touch far more than was possible before. Cell phones allow for conversations in contexts where they previously would have been impossible: while running an errand, waiting in line, traveling to—or while at—work or school. Aubrey, a college student, had a great conversation with her fourteen-year-old sister Marni. They talked about Marni's plans for the next week, how things were going at school, her friend's birthday party. There's nothing surprising about this, except that they had this conversation in the middle of the day, while Marni was at school. She had spoken to her sister on her cell phone during a break.

Even cell phone conversations can't take place in all situations and may take more time than you have. Making a phone call stops what you're doing and initiates a new activity. Texting is parenthetical to your activity, not a full stop. With texting, you can send a message while you're engaged in something else.

Meghan had offered Olivia mints, which her sister turned down, saying, "They look like old people's mints." The following week Olivia received a text message from Meghan saying that she was sitting on a couch facing a bowl of those mints—in her friend's grandmother's house. Her text message was an indirect way to say, "I'm thinking of you" and "You were right!" It would have been rude for Meghan to make a cell phone call in that setting, and unthinkable to call someone and comment on the mints in the bowl before her. If she made a mental note to tell her sister later, she probably would forget, and if she remembered, it might no longer seem important enough to tell. Texting made it possible for Meghan to tell her older sister, "You were right," when she thought of it. Even more, by texting she brought Olivia into the room and metaphorically invited her to join her on the couch.

Facebook is ubiquitous in many young people's lives (and, increasingly, in older people's too). It's a way to keep in touch with far more people than you could e-mail individually. A "wall" is a Facebook feature whereby a user can post messages on another's page, or profile, which other users can see and comment on. A college student, Jody, visiting home for a holiday, was picked up at the airport by her high-school-age sister. Smelling the unmistakable odor of cigarette smoke, Jody admonished her sister that she shouldn't smoke. Her sister responded, "You smoke too!" "How do you know?" Jody asked. Her sister explained: "Someone wrote on your wall that you left a pack of cigarettes somewhere." Facebook had opened a door for Jody's sister to peek through.

E-mail: Handle with Care

E-mail is great because it's easy and quick, a terrific way to keep in touch when you're pressed for time. It's especially good to let a sister know you're thinking of her or to set a time and place to meet. Sending jokes by e-mail is popular, I think, because it's an easy way to do what is most fun about being together: making each other laugh.

My sisters and I were planning a trip. We exchanged e-mails about where we might stay. Should we go for a B and B that would be charming or a hotel that would have more amenities? Then came an e-mail from Mimi saying she had checked out the B and B; it couldn't accommodate three people in one room, so she made us hotel reservations that were cancelable up to 6 P.M. on the day of arrival. Then Mimi and I had this e-mail exchange:

Me: Mim, you're amazing—a woman of action. Thank you.
Mimi: You are too easy to impress! Like when we were kids.
Me: You made me laugh out loud. Like when we were kids.

Mimi's e-mail did make me laugh out loud. But our e-mails did something else too, something especially sisterly: We reminded each other of laughter from our shared past. The humor resulted from the brief, quick nature of e-mail.

A feature of e-mail that can be particularly dangerous is the cc line. It's easy to enter multiple names and have more than one sister get the same message at the same time. When there are many sisters, writing each one individually might take an awful lot of time. Sending group e-mails allows everyone to keep in touch and feel part of the group. But it's also easy to forget that others are cc'd and mention information you wouldn't have chosen to tell them. Or it can raise the specter of being left out. I know my sisters sometimes get together when I can't join them, but I don't like to listen in when they make plans to meet. They wouldn't cc me on an e-mail that was exclusively making arrangements for an event I wasn't included in, but sometimes they make references to arrangements in e-mails that began on other topics for which I was cc'd.

E-mail is rarely the best way to handle problems or anger. It can easily make things worse. There are many liabilities inherent in e-mail. You don't have tone of voice or facial expression to clarify how you mean something, so it's easy to take offense at a quip meant as a joke. If you're angry, it's too easy to press SEND before your emotions cool off. Also, e-mail, like voice mail, is one-way and absentee. With no one in front of you or on the phone, you have no way of knowing your recipient's reaction, or if you're coming across in a negative way. You may dig yourself in deeper with each word, whereas you'd have changed course if you'd known how the person was reacting. And if you do intend your words in a negative spirit, you can get carried away with how articulate and reasonable you think you're being, certain that the person reading it will see the light, when in reality what she sees is red as she gets angrier by the minute.

Several people told me they had sent conciliatory e-mails to their sisters following an argument and were surprised to receive belligerent responses. In several cases, they sent me the e-mails. Their attempts to repair the damage were clearly sincere, but I could see how the e-mails would come across as provocative. If you feel you've been wronged, "I'm willing to forgive you" is a major concession. But it implies, You are at fault and I'm blameless. Since the sister receiving the e-mail no doubt feels wronged too, that implication denies her experience and is likely to anger her. An apparent apology can also aggravate rather than soothe. On the surface "Whatever I did to offend you, I'm sorry," looks like an apology because it includes the words "I'm sorry." But an apology needs several elements: It has to admit fault, express remorse, acknowledge the damage done, and promise to make amends or at least to not repeat the offense. A general apology (like the one frequently heard from public figures: "I'm sorry if anyone was offended") really isn't an apology at all; it lacks all four parts. Finally, in coming to terms with a perceived offense, it's helpful, maybe even crucial, to see the vulnerability of the person who hurt you, even to feel sorry for her. That's compassion. But telling someone "I feel sorry for you" is something else entirely. It's provocation.

These problems aren't exclusive to e-mail; they could have arisen in face-to-face or phone conversation. But in two-way conversation, you see the other's response and adjust your talk accordingly. With e-mail, you can think you're heading for reconciliation, while the path you're confidently treading is leading to increasing dissension.

To Each Her Own

When my father talked of his cousins GertrudenAnna, he often remarked on how different they were. Anna was practical, a businesswoman who owned a store and knew the ways of the world. Gertrude was a dreamer, an intellectual, a linguist—not as a profession (she worked in a library) but in the sense that she spoke many languages. In his view, they were close not despite their differences but, at least in part, because of them. Anna's practicality made possible Gertrude's life of the mind. Gertrude's intellectual interests enriched Anna's life. In this way, too, these sisters provide a model of lifelong sisterness. Each respected and benefited from the ways the other was different.

My sisters and I used to laugh at how different our visits to our parents were. Naomi would take our mother to nature preserves, Mimi would take her shopping, and I'd sit with her for hours, talking. Our mother loved being out in nature, shopping for clothes, and talking about people; each of us gave her something she enjoyed, according to our own predilections. We found it funny that our ways of entertaining our parents were so different and so consistent. Sometimes, though, a sister behaves in ways she usually doesn't, and that can result in the other sister taking up the role left vacant.

Victoria was shy, her sister Kirsten outgoing. When someone had to step forward and speak for them both or stand up for their rights, Kirsten was the one who did it, even though she was younger. But if Kirsten's nerve gave way, Victoria stepped in. When Kirsten was fourteen and Victoria sixteen, they were traveling together to attend a family wedding abroad and had to change planes in London. The flight from London, due to depart at 11 P.M., was overbooked, and they were bumped. The agents offered no further assistance. The girls were on their own, just as Heathrow Airport was shutting down for the night. Shops were closing; the maintenance crew was locking things up and shutting off lights.

Kirsten, normally the assertive one, was scared: Where would they spend the night? How would they get to the wedding? She started to cry. Seeing her younger sister in distress was all Victoria needed to find her courage and take charge. She located the airline office, where a few employees had not yet left, and insisted they be given lodging for the night and seats on the first flight out the next morning. It worked. The next day, however, they were back in their customary roles; Kirsten took the lead in communicating with the driver who returned them to the airport. This story can be a model for flourishing sister relationships: Each one came into her own when her strengths were required.

Here's another example of sisters reversing roles in a frightening situation. It comes from Sue William Silverman's *Because I Remember Terror, Father, I Remember You*, her wrenching account of being sexually abused by her father throughout her childhood. Silverman's older sister protected herself from the destructive family by finding ways to escape: "My sister will wander off to a nearby stream, or she will climb a tree." Sue envies her sister's fearlessness; she has fear for them both. But the one time her sister admits to being frightened, Sue becomes unafraid.

The family has moved to St. Thomas, Virgin Islands, where their father opened a bank. A riot has broken out, because some islanders suspect the bank will exploit them. The sisters, nine and eleven at the time, have been locked in a warehouse for safety. Silverman writes:

> "Do you think they'll be okay?" my sister asks—meaning our parents. I stare at her, stunned, confused. I didn't know my sister felt fear. I nod, suddenly transformed into the older sister. "Of course," I say, nodding to reassure her, then not even afraid of the warehouse.

Sue rubs her sister's back to calm her, and keeps rubbing even when her own leg falls asleep and her arm aches with the effort, because when she stops her sister will once again move away. Fear is apportioned between the sisters: If one experiences it, the other is free of it. Sue needs to be fearless for this brief time, to balance the scale.

If you're not comfortable with the alignments you have experienced or the roles you have occupied in your family, you can try to change them. April, the oldest of five, was the one her three sisters called when they needed advice or someone to listen to their problems. (Her brother didn't call for advice or to talk about what was bothering him.) She didn't tell them about her problems; it didn't occur to her that she might. But the older she got, the less comfortable April felt about this. She wished her sisters could be more like friends. So she made a decision: She would talk to them the way she talked to her friends; she'd tell them about her own problems. At first it felt odd to talk this way to a younger sister, but she did it anyway, and soon it felt right. It was a relief, too, not to have to find solutions and fixes for all her sisters' problems. Now she could just listen, as she would with her friends, and they could just listen to her.

Come Closer, Call Now

Elaine and Nicole grew up in a family where politics was a frequent topic of talk. As adults, they loved continuing this tradition. But they don't do it anymore because Nicole married a man whose politics differ. In the past, if the subject of politics came up when their families were together, Elaine ended up having huge fights with her brother-in-law. Because they never socialize without their families, the sisters can no longer engage in a kind of talk they really enjoyed, and an aspect of their sisterness is lost.

Even if there are no obvious differences in philosophy or interests, it's often less relaxed to be together with spouses than it is when spouses aren't there. They did not grow up with you and may not share your sense of humor or conversational habits such as rhythm, timing, directness, and so on. They certainly don't share your memories. And if your spouse or partner is with you, you might worry about him or her. For these reasons, many sisters told me that they take time together without partners or spouses. Some plan trips together at regular intervals. If that's not possible, they take a day to go somewhere, just them, when the extended families are together. Taking a vacation—even just spending a day—with sisters and no spouses or partners can be a relief, a pleasure, and a way to reconnect.

My student Samantha Demetriou organized and recorded a discussion among three of her friends, twenty-one-year-old college students who exchanged stories about their sisters. As the discussion drew to a close, one of them said she was afraid that once her younger sister had also left home for college, they'd never again be as close as when they both lived in the same house. Another said she hoped her younger sister would choose a college nearby so they could grow close and "share a part of our futures together." The third young woman, Lauren Treadaway, ended the group's discussion with a sentiment I'd like to borrow, to end this chapter.

How close geographically you are doesn't really dictate how close emotionally and how close your friendship will be. But it definitely makes it harder. You definitely want to think, in the future, that you're going to be able to call your sister over for Thanksgiving dinner when it's at your house. When you're younger it seems to me that family is annoying and they're the people that you want to try to impress the least because you feel like, "You guys will always be here." But once you get older you have to actually put some effort into it, and so it's scary to think that after being invested in it for however many years, twenty-one years, however long, you guys can still fade away. Down the drain, your most valuable resource. I'm definitely calling my sister after this.

Epilogue

Last year my sisters and I visited the neighborhood where we grew up in Brooklyn. It was a magical two days, beginning when I met Naomi at Pennsylvania Station, in Manhattan, and we took the subway to the hotel in Brooklyn (how many years had it been since we'd ridden the subway to Brooklyn?) where we eagerly awaited Mimi's arrival.

Together the three of us walked the blocks to P.S. 217, where we all had gone to elementary school. How special to see that building from my childhood, and to see it with sisters who had experienced it too, so were seeing it with the same emotions. But our pasts were different. The most nostalgic blocks for me were along Cortelyou Road, my route to the subway every day on my way to high school in Manhattan. My sisters didn't go to that high school, so those blocks meant less to them. When we came upon a boarded-up synagogue, Mimi recalled the time she and her friend had hidden behind it to smoke. Naomi and I didn't hide behind the synagogue because we weren't mischievous and we never smoked. Then we walked to Macdonald Avenue, where Naomi was reminded of the bus trip she took daily to the distant junior high school she had attended, but neither Mimi nor I had. I hadn't even known she'd gone to that junior high. When I turned thirteen, a new one had just been built around the corner from our house; that building, deeply resonant for me, meant nothing to my sisters.

The trip to Brooklyn reminded us of the past we shared, and how lucky we are to have shared it. But it also reminded us of how different our young lives had been—and how little each of us knew about whole chunks of the others' lives.

When I had a complete first draft of my last book, I sent a copy to each of my sisters. Naomi read it and sent me detailed and helpful comments. Mimi kept it awhile and then told me she'd begun reading it but hadn't gotten very far. She realized that she'd rather make beads than read my manuscript, so how about if instead she gave me a necklace of lampwork beads she made herself? I couldn't have been more thrilled. The necklace is beautiful, and wearing it reminds me of Mimi's loving support, as well as her talents, so different from mine. I see her putting on goggles, firing up a torch, and melting colored rods of glass into beautiful beads— something I could no more do than walk to the moon. Each sister honored my work in a way that was comfortable for her; both ways were precious to me.

I have another reminder of Mimi's support. Posted over my desk is a sheet of paper folded to reveal an e-mail message dated 1996. It's a short message, and its last line is highlighted in yellow: "Stop reading this and go back to writing. Love, Mim." Mimi had sent it in response to an e-mail in which I'd complained of demands that were distracting me from the book I was writing at the time. I've kept Mimi's note posted over my desk like a cheerleading squad, urging me to get back to work when I'm distracted. Having it there makes me feel my sister is keeping me company in the solitary pursuit that writing is.

When each of my books was published, I appeared on television to talk about it. One of the most gratifying things about this was that my parents would be watching. I always knew that when I arrived home, the light on my answering machine would be blinking, and when I pressed PLAY I'd hear my mother's voice saying something like: "I loved watching you, you were wonderful, you looked great, I'm so proud of you!" My mother died while I was writing my last book. The tour for that book would include my first television appearances she wouldn't be watching. More than once it crossed my mind: Why bother being on television if my mother won't see it? The first time I arrived home after a TV interview about that book, I dreaded walking by the dark, silent answering machine. But I did walk past it, and the message light was flashing. I pushed PLAY—and heard my sister Naomi's voice: "I loved watching you, you were great, I'm so proud of you."

One of the joys of writing this book has been remembering the many parts my sisters have played in my life and continue to play. Writing it has been like taking one more journey with them.

Acknowledgments

This book draws life and breath from the stories of sisters entrusted to me by the more than a hundred women I interviewed and countless others with whom I had casual conversations or chance encounters. I offer first thanks to them. I am especially grateful to those who invited friends for group discussions: Caleen Sinnette Jennings, Addie Macovski, and Sheila Meyer. Samantha Demetriou helped enormously by providing a window on her college-age peers in several ways: interviewing her friends, recording their discussions, and serving as a consultant on their use of Facebook. I am also very grateful to Bea Lewis for publishing a notice in her *Palm Beach Post* column inviting volunteers with sisters to contact me.

Whether or not I used specific examples or quotations from their conversations, everyone I spoke to enhanced my understanding of the vast and complex range of sister relationships. In addition to those who are named in the book and those who preferred not to be named, I want to thank Lilia A. Abron, Malaika Adero, Kate Addison, Mmelika Akanegbu, Ebele Akanegbu-Brown, Caren Anton, Goldey Auster, Romaine Bailey, Naomi Baron, Lori Brigham, Barbara Eskew Cannon, Cecilia Castillo-Ayometzi, Emma Cheuse, Joyce Chung, Elizabeth Clouatre, Cordelia Coleman, Jamilla Coleman, JoEllen Collins, Theresa Bilotta Colombo, Marcia Gere Connelly, Deanna Cooke, Anne Dauer, Angela Davis, Susan Dodson, Danielle Dray, Nicole Dray, Chrysoula Economopoulos, Maria Economopoulos, Rona Eisner, Rachel Ellis, Zhaleh Feizollahi, Diane

Fuchs, Victoria Garner, Elizabeth Sarah Gere, Margaret Gere-Planer, Ronni Ginott, Dora Goldstein, Pat Gurne, Jo Ann Hairston, Millie Hallow, Sarah Harman, Judy Harris, Naomi Henderson, Laura Jacobson, Naomi Julia Jacobson, Roberta Jacobson, the Jennrich girls, Elaine Jost, Christina Kakava, Karen S. Kalish, Jean Kaufman, Jan Kern, Elizabeth Kissling, Elizabeth LaFarge, Ashley LaRiccia, Joanne Leedom-Ackerman, Willee Eskew Lewis, Shura Lipovsky, Trinh Luong, Eleanor E. Maccoby, Alan Marx, Beth Marx, Sue Mather, Mary Alice McDowd, Leah McLaren, Tamara Meyer, Ursula Meyer, Gwendolyn Mikell, Marie Eskew Miller, Emily Millett, Hillary Millett, Judith Mueller, Amanda Murphy, Kathleen Murphy, Rahel Musleah, Irene Natividad, Jennifer Nelson, Laura Oliff-Maxey, Sally McNagny, Jenny McPhee, Patricia O'Brien, Mary Alice O'Dowd, Geneva Overholser, Gail Paster, Micah Perks, Rebekah Perks, Marica Perlstein, Leonilla G. Perry, Susan Philips, Carol Phipps, Susan Resneck Pierce, Terri Pilkerton, Jenny Poole, Mary Poole, Tina Poole, Marcia Pord, Melissa Pritchard, Christina Radomsky, Judy Rapoport, Jillian Raymond, Janice (Ginny) Redish, Erika Rose, Rina Rosenberg, Barbara Ross, Cecily Ross, Cynthia Roy, Victoria Roy, Maria Schlafly, Theresa Schlafly, Erin Seaboyer, Barbara Seeger, Peggy Seeger, Kate Shreve, Amy Tan, Kathryn Temple, Carolyn Jacobson Tilove, Alla Tovares, Veena Trehan, Martha Keller Tuohey, Polly Ulichny, Fay Vaughn-Cooke, Anita Cooke Wells, and Joan Zofnass.

I am extraordinarily fortunate to have taught at Georgetown University for the past three decades, where so many members of the university community have been supportive over the years. As always, students, colleagues, administrators, and staff all contributed. The graduate students who took part in a seminar I taught on family interaction helped by locating and summarizing related academic research; they are Leslie Cochrane, Rebecca Rubin Damari, Aubrey Logan-Terry, Anastasia Nylund, Theresa Schlafly, and Kathleen Williams. Many undergraduate students in my Cross-Cultural Communication classes provided helpful perspectives on sister relationships in class discussion and written assignments. My colleagues in the sociolinguistics program—Heidi Hamilton, Rob Podesva, Deborah Schiffrin, and Natalie Schilling-Estes—have been extremely magnanimous in accommodating my scheduling requests. My assistant Laura Myers has helped in many ways, including tracking down references and citations on short notice with acuity and aplomb.

The book was immeasurably improved by the comments of readers of early drafts—Sally Arteseros, Harriet Grant, Phyllis Richman, and Naomi Tannen—and by those of Jennifer Hershey, my editor extraordinaire, to whom I am also grateful for her enthusiastic support. As ever, I offer boundless thanks to Suzanne Gluck, who has been my agent for over two decades and five books. I can't imagine a more dedicated, inspired, or wise advocate.

My family is my foundation. My adored sisters, Mimi and Naomi, have a special place this time. If I didn't have them as sisters, I would not have been able to write this book, nor would I have wanted to. They have been generous, patient, and insightful in answering my questions and in allowing me to turn their lives into material along with my own. And my debt to them has been set in relief by another circumstance: This is the first book I have completed, and therefore the first acknowledgments I have composed, for which my mother and father are no longer alive. My parents' absence from this space, as from my life, is yet another reminder of how precious is my sisters' presence in it.

My husband, Michael Macovski, partner in life and in love, has helped in more ways than I can list—and "help" is too wan a word, "thanks" too pallid a sentiment, to convey the depth of gratitude I feel to and for him.

Author's Note

A word is in order about the sources of the quotations and examples I present and discuss.

Most of the examples come from interviews I conducted with more than a hundred women. In most cases I spoke to one woman alone. On four occasions I spoke to women in small groups; two of those groups included pairs of sisters as well as unrelated women. In a number of cases, I spoke to two or three sisters together, or separately to two, three, or four sisters from the same family. In a few cases I spoke separately to mothers and daughters.

Perhaps "focused conversations" would be more accurate than "interviews." I did not ask a set list of questions, because I didn't want to impose my assumptions and expectations. I wanted to see what came to each woman's mind about her sisters. In order to maintain an informal tone, I interjected comments about my own sisters, just as I would in any conversation. At some point I always asked, "What do you particularly appreciate about your sisters, and what frustrates you?"

I did not want to slow the conversations down or distract the people I was talking to by taking notes while they were speaking, so I recorded the conversations (with permission, of course) that took place face-to-face. I later had the recordings transcribed, or I listened to them and took notes. When I interviewed someone by phone, I wore a headset and typed notes as we spoke. If an exchange occurred over e-mail, I printed the messages.

If I heard something in a casual conversation that I thought important or interesting, I'd jot down the comments along with the name and e-mail address of the person I was talking to.

From a given interview I might use a single example or quote, or several, or none, but all contributed in their entirety to my understanding. I often recast examples as narratives, providing specific settings and dialogue. Sometimes I crafted a single example by merging details from stories I'd heard from two or even three different women, and sometimes I changed details to ensure anonymity.

I checked every example and quotation with the person who inspired it by showing her exactly what I had written. I asked, first, if she felt comfortable with my using the material. If the answer was no, it was out. If the answer was yes, I asked whether I had gotten it right and if there was.anything I should change, for reasons of privacy or accuracy. If someone suggested changes, I cleared my revised wording with her as well. I usually use pseudonyms, first names only. If I identify the source of an example by her real name (in accordance with her preference), then I use both first and last names.

My basic method of linguistic analysis consists of recording and transcribing naturally occurring conversation and then analyzing the transcripts. Many of the examples I include here were recorded and transcribed by students in my classes at Georgetown University, as I note when I present them. I also note when the analyses I include were made by the student in her paper. I cleared my use of these examples in the same way as I did the others. The names of the students who wrote the papers are clearly identified. The names of speakers in their examples are either real names or pseudonyms, as they preferred. I checked the stories from my own life with my sisters, and they have approved my accounts of incidents involving them. I interviewed them too and frequently called or e-mailed with questions that came to mind while I was writing.

In choosing women to interview, I began with people I knew—some well, some slightly—who have sisters and were interested in talking to me about them. Some of them suggested others whom they knew and I did not. Sometimes women I interviewed put me in touch with their sisters, whom I interviewed either in person or by phone. A number of women contacted me after reading a notice calling for volunteers that Bea Lewis generously published in her column, "This Day and Age," in the *Palm Beach Post*. Because I sought a range of ages, I talked to my friends' daughters and mothers and to my mother-in-law's friends. In some cases, examples I give of sisters were stepsisters or half sisters. If the speaker referred to her as "my sister," so do I.

Throughout the book, I present examples not as proof but as illustrations of patterns I observed. Though I made an effort to include women from a range of backgrounds, I did not attempt to generalize about any group; I was interested in patterns that emerged from all the women's accounts. When I give an example, I don't identify the age or ethnicity of the source unless it seemed important in order to fully understand the context, or if the woman herself talked about her experience in terms of her ethnicity.

I undertook this study in hopes of understanding "sisters in conversation throughout their lives." I know that many readers will wonder whether what I write about sisters is equally true of brothers. I have no doubt that some of my observations are and some aren't, just as any pattern I describe may or may not apply to a particular sister, or may apply to a greater or lesser degree. It would be interesting to undertake a direct comparison and to look at the various possible combinations: brothers in families with no sisters, sisters and brothers in the various positions (oldest or youngest brothers compared to oldest or youngest sisters), as well as the common constellation of one brother and one sister. But these would be different studies, so describing their findings will have to wait for those studies to be done.

Notes

PREFACE

4 Delany and Delany, *Having Our Say.* The quotations are on pp. 9 and 5.

ONE: SISTERS IN LIFELONG CONVERSATION

11 *woman who was with Anne Frank* Brandes-Brilleslijper, p. 73.
13 *in trying to recall the film title* Deliverance Reason and Lucas, "Using Cognitive Diaries to Investigate Naturally Occurring Memory Blocks," p. 66.
13 *"beautiful faces and fair skin"* Tatar, pp. 116, 119.
14 *"beautiful and well favoured"* The story of Rachel and Leah, Genesis 29:17, KJV.
14 *There is also a folk song* Seeger recorded four versions of this song, also called "The Twa Sisters," with Ewan MacColl, as part of a series entitled *The Long Harvest.* My source of information on this song is her Web site: pegseeger.com.
15 *nonhuman species* Bird species in which older chicks kill younger ones by pushing them from the nest include masked boobies (see "Seabirds Give New Meaning to Sibling Rivalry," the National Science Foundation Web site, June 1997) and Nazca boobies (see www.v-liz.com/galapagos/murder.htm). For the other species men-

tioned, see Chang, "Savage Siblings." Research on spadefoot tadpoles is attributed to biologist David Pfennig, on sand tiger sharks to marine biologist John Wourms, and on spotted hyenas to biologist Laurence Frank.

TWO: "WE'RE CLOSE BUT WE'RE DIFFERENT"

33 *an article in the* Washington Post "At Sisters' Reunion in Bowie, Memories of Lipstick and Love," June 18, 2007, pp. B1–2. The quotation is on p. B2.

36 *"the cline of person"* A. L. Becker introduces and discusses this concept in his essay "Person in Kawi," a chapter in his book *Beyond Translation.*

45 *"I didn't join the Girl Scouts"* Barbara Walters, *Audition,* p. 4.

46 Handler, "I Won't Roll the Biological Dice." *Newsweek,* April 27, 2009, p. 16.

50 *When actor Ashley Judd broke her ankle* Shelley Levitt, Kate Klise, and John Griffiths, "Eternal Triangle," *People Weekly,* May 22, 1995. The six-page article begins on p. 64.

53 *The Olsen twins, Mary-Kate and Ashley* Cindy Clark, "A Second Act for the Olsens," *USA Today,* October 31, 2007, p. D1.

THREE: LOOKING UP AND TALKING DOWN

62 *In Korea, for example, women address friends* My source on the use of *"enni"* by Korean women is Professor Minju Kim of Claremont McKenna College. She presents her analysis of Korean women's use of *enni* in her paper "Women's Talk, Mothers' Work: Power and Solidarity in Korean Women's Conversation."

62 *In Indian families* Shilpa Alimchandani first called to my attention these Hindi terms for "aunt." I later discussed these and other Hindi kinship terms with Manil Suri as well. He directed me to the following Web site that has more detailed information on Indian kin terms: http://www.brighthub.com/education/languages/articles/18030.aspx.

65 *According to biographer Sheila Weller* Weller, *Girls Like Us,* p. 350.

66 *When tennis champion Serena Williams beat her sister* Lynn Zinser, "A Dazzling Display by Williams Sisters," *New York Times,* September 4, 2008, p. D1.

71 *In one conversation I taped* The conversation is analyzed in my book *Conversational Style.*

72 Glass, *I See You Everywhere,* p. 24.

74 Cohen, "The Ethicist," *New York Times Magazine,* November 11, 2007, p. 32.

79 *One gardening Web site assigns birth order roles* iVillage GardenWeb. The URL is http://faq.gardenweb.com/faq/lists/teach/2003045238014436.html.

79 *"the spiny squash plants also help"* Renee's Garden Web site; the URL is http://www.reneesgarden.com/articles/3sisters.html.

FOUR: WHOSE SIDE ARE YOU ON?

80 *Luci Baines Johnson and Lynda Johnson Robb* "First Moving Day: Relations," *The New Yorker,* November 24, 2008, pp. 41–42. The quotation is on p. 42.

81 Atwood, "White Horse," pp. 154–55.

88 Joyce Maynard, "A Tale of Two Sisters," p. 250.

93 Darrah, Freeman, and English-Lueck, *Busier Than Ever,* p. 185.

104 *"Ashley is the part of my mom"* Shelley Levitt, Kate Klise, and John Griffiths, "Eternal Triangle," *People Weekly,* May 22, 1995. The six-page article begins on p. 64.

FIVE: "I'LL BE THE PRINCESS, YOU BE THE FROG"

107 Rona Maynard, "A Tale of Two Sisters," p. 249.

108 *A scene in Patricia O'Brien's historical novel* O'Brien, *Harriet and Isabella,* pp. 108–109.

112 *I wrote a play based on my family* The play, *Acts of Devotion,* was produced by Horizons Theater in Washington, D.C. The first act is included in *The Best American Short Plays, 1993–1994* (New York and London: Applause Books, 1995, pp. 217–30).

113 *"The first child is pure poetry"* O'Brien, *Harriet and Isabella,* p. 233.

113   Grinker, *Unstrange Minds,* p. 26.

114   Olsen, "I Stand Here Ironing," pp. 12 and 9.

121   The statistic that half of all pregnancies in 2001 were unintended is on the Web site of the Guttmacher Institute, in a report titled "Poorest U.S. Women Increasingly Likely to Face Unintended Pregnancies." The statistic is attributed to the National Survey of Family Growth. According to the report itself, on the Web site of the Department of Health and Human Services Centers for Disease Control and Prevention, 14 percent are unwanted and 21 percent mistimed.

SIX: GATEWAY TO THE WORLD

129   Obama, *Dreams from My Father,* p. 447. After I wrote this, the resulting photo appeared in *Newsweek,* January 19, 2009, p. 3.

131   Mapes wrote her paper for a class she took with Professor Christina Kakava at the University of Mary Washington. I am grateful to Professor Kakava for suggesting she send it to me.

133   Alvarez, *In the Time of the Butterflies,* p. 44.

134   *"I'm like an excited puppy"* Anastasia Nylund found this comment posted by London182 on a Web site entitled "Experience Project" at www.experienceproject.com.

134   *"Corn provides a natural pole"* iVillage GardenWeb.

136   Glass, *I See You Everywhere,* p. 7.

153   *"the strongest influence in my life"* Barbara Walters, *Audition,* p. 3.

155   Hodgdon, "Shrew-Histories," p. 3.

155   *"what you will command me will I do"* *The Taming of the Shrew,* 2.1.6.

SEVEN: IT'S ALL TALK

162   Mattison, *Nothing Is Quite Forgotten in Brooklyn,* p. 257.

167   Henley, *Crimes of the Heart,* pp. 47, 48, and 50.

171   Mattison, *Nothing Is Quite Forgotten in Brooklyn,* p. 88.

172   Sheldon, "You Can Be the Baby Brother, but You Aren't Born Yet."

The quotations appear on pp. 63 and 69. Sheldon calls the girls' strategy "double-voice discourse."

175 *"conspiracy of silence"* Tony Cassidy, quoted in Kate Devlin, "Having a Sister Makes You Happier and More Optimistic, Say Psychologists," Telegraph.co.uk, April 3, 2009.

177 Liz Wright and Tony Cassidy, "Family Structure and Environment in Psychological Adjustment." Paper presented at the annual meeting of the British Psychological Society, Brighton, England, April 2, 2009. The findings were reported in all the major British newspapers, in stories dated April 2 or 3, 2009, including "Sisters 'Make People Happy,'" BBC World News American Web site, April 2, 2009; Gerry Moriarty, "Sisters Are Doing It for Your Health," *Irish Times,* April 2, 2009; "Having a Sister Makes You Happier and More Optimistic, Say Psychologists," Telegraph.co.uk.

177 Dunn, "Sibling Relationships," p. 225.

178 *Ari Emanual described his older brother Rahm* "School Days: Hug It Out," *The New Yorker,* May 25, 2009, pp. 28, 31. The quotation is on p. 31.

EIGHT: SISTERNESS

181 Gregory, *The Other Boleyn Girl.* The quotations are on pp. 196, 197, and 232–33.

182 Lansen, *The Girls,* p. 4.

184 Glück, *The Seven Ages,* p. 35.

186 Lakoff introduced her "rules of politeness" in a 1973 paper entitled "The logic of politeness, or minding your p's and q's." She presented this system in the context of gender differences in communicative style in *Language and Woman's Place,* the book that launched the field of language and gender. It is reprinted in *Language and Woman's Place: Text and Commentaries,* edited by Mary Bucholtz.

188 *Conversational styles are developed and become habitual* For a fuller discussion of conversational styles, see my book *That's Not What I Meant!: How Conversational Style Makes or Breaks Relationships,*

written for a general audience, as well as *Conversational Style: Analyzing Talk Among Friends,* written for a scholarly audience.

188   *what I call "agonism"* Agonism is the topic of my book *The Argument Culture.*

201   Silverman, *Because I Remember Terror, Father, I Remember You.* The quotations are on pp. 9 and 38.

References

Alvarez, Julia. 1995. *In the Time of the Butterflies*. New York: Penguin.

Atwood, Margaret. 2006. "White Horse." *Moral Disorder and Other Stories*, 142–66. New York: Doubleday.

Becker, A. L. (with I Gusti Ngurah Oka). 1995. "Person in Kawi: Exploration of an Elementary Semantic Dimension." *Beyond Translation: Essays Toward a Modern Philology*, 109–36. Ann Arbor: University of Michigan Press.

Brandes-Brilleslijper, Janny. 1991. In Willy Lindwer, *The Last Seven Months of Anne Frank*, translated by Alison Meersschaert, 37–85. New York: Anchor Books.

Brashares, Ann. 2001. *The Sisterhood of the Traveling Pants*. New York: Delacorte Press.

Chang, Maria L. 1997. "Savage Siblings," *Science World*, January 10, 1997.

Cicirelli, Victor G. 1996. "Sibling Relationships in Middle and Old Age." In Gene H. Brody, ed., *Sibling Relationships: Their Causes and Consequences*, 47–73. Norwood, N.J.: Ablex.

Darrah, Charles N., James M. Freeman, and J. A. English-Lueck. 2007. *Busier Than Ever: Why American Families Can't Slow Down*. Stanford, Calif.: Stanford University Press.

Davies, Catherine. 2008. " 'We Had a Wonderful Time': Individual Sibling Voices in the Joint Construction of a Family Ethos Through

Narrative Performance." Paper presented at the Georgetown University Round Table on Languages and Linguistics, Washington, D.C., March 2008.

Delany, Sarah, and A. Elizabeth Delany with Amy Hill Hearth. 1993. *Having Our Say: The Delany Sisters' First 100 Years.* New York: Kodansha.

Dunn, Judy. 2002. "Sibling Relationships." In Peter K. Smith and Craig H. Hart, eds., *Blackwell Handbook of Childhood Social Development,* 223–37. Malden, Mass.: Blackwell.

Esquivel, Laura. 1992. *Like Water for Chocolate,* translated by Carol Christensen and Thomas Christensen. New York: Doubleday.

Glass, Julia. 2008. *I See You Everywhere.* New York: Pantheon.

Glück, Louise. 2001. *The Seven Ages.* New York: HarperCollins.

Gregory, Philippa. 2001. *The Other Boleyn Girl.* New York: Simon & Schuster.

Grinker, Roy Richard. 2007. *Unstrange Minds: Remapping the World of Autism.* New York: Basic Books.

Henley, Beth. 1981. *Crimes of the Heart.* New York: Dramatists Play Service.

Higley, James Dee, and Stephen J. Suomi. 1986. "Parental Behavior in Primates." In Wladyslaw Sluckin and Martin Herbert, eds., *Parental Behavior,* 152–207. Oxford: Blackwell.

Hodgdon, Barbara. 2007. "Shrew-Histories," *Asides* (newsletter of the Shakespeare Theatre Company, Washington, D.C.), September, pp. 3–4.

Kim, Minju. 2008. "Women's Talk, Mothers' Work: Power and Solidarity in Korean Women's Conversation." Unpublished manuscript.

Lakoff, Robin. 1973. "The Logic of Politeness, or Minding Your p's and q's." In Claudia Corum, T. Cedric Smith-Stark, and Ann Weiser, eds., *Papers from the Ninth Regional Meeting of the Chicago Linguistics Society,* 292–305. Chicago: Chicago Linguistic Society.

———. 1975. *Language and Woman's Place.* New York: Harper & Row.

Lakoff, Robin Tolmach. 2004. *Language and Woman's Place: Text and Commentaries,* edited by Mary Bucholtz. New York and Oxford: Oxford University Press.

Lansen, Lori. 2005. *The Girls.* Boston: Little, Brown.

Mathieu, Cindy K. 2000. "Verbal Communication Between College Students and Their Siblings." PhD dissertation, Texas A & M University.

Mattison, Alice. 2008. *Nothing Is Quite Forgotten in Brooklyn.* New York: HarperCollins.

Maynard, Joyce. 2007. "A Tale of Two Sisters: Joyce's Tale," *More* magazine, September 2007, pp. 175–76, 178, 250, 251.

Maynard, Rona. 2007. "A Tale of Two Sisters: Rona's Tale," *More* magazine, September 2007, pp. 175, 177, 179, 249.

Obama, Barack. 1995. *Dreams from My Father: A Story of Race and Inheritance.* New York: Crown.

O'Brien, Patricia. 2008. *Harriet and Isabella.* New York: Simon & Schuster.

Olsen, Tillie. 1989 [1956]. "I Stand Here Ironing." In *Tell Me a Riddle,* 1–12. New York: Dell.

Reason, James, and Deborah Lucas. 1984. "Using Cognitive Diaries to Investigate Naturally Occurring Memory Blocks." In J. E. Harris and P. E. Morris, eds., *Everyday Memory: Actions and Absent-Mindedness,* 53–70. London and New York: Academic Press.

Sheldon, Amy. 1996. "You Can Be the Baby Brother, but You Aren't Born Yet: Preschool Girls' Negotiation for Power and Access in Pretend Play." *Research on Language and Social Interaction* 29(1) 57–80.

Silverman, Sue William. 1996. *Because I Remember Terror, Father, I Remember You.* Athens and London: University of Georgia Press.

Stone, Elizabeth. 1989. *Black Sheep and Kissing Cousins: How Our Family Stories Shape Us.* New York: Penguin.

Suomi, Stephen J. 1982. "Sibling Relationships in Nonhuman Primates." In Michael E. Lamb and Brian Sutton-Smith, eds., *Sibling Relationships: Their Nature and Significance Across the Lifespan,* 329–56. Hillsdale, N.J.: Erlbaum.

Tannen, Deborah. 1986. *That's Not What I Meant!: How Conversational Style Makes or Breaks Relationships.* New York: Ballantine.

———. 1990. *You Just Don't Understand: Women and Men in Conversation.* New York: HarperCollins.

———. 1998. *The Argument Culture: Stopping America's War of Words.* New York: Ballantine.

———. 2005 [1984]. *Conversational Style: Analyzing Talk Among Friends.* New edition: New York and Oxford: Oxford University Press.

Tatar, Maria. 2004. *The Annotated Brothers Grimm.* New York: Norton.

Walters, Barbara. 2008. *Audition: A Memoir.* New York: Knopf.

Watanabe, Suwako. 1993. "Cultural Differences in Framing: American and Japanese Group Discussions." In Deborah Tannen, ed., *Framing in Discourse,* 176–208. New York: Oxford University Press.

Weller, Sheila. 2008. *Girls Like Us: Carole King, Joni Mitchell, Carly Simon, and the Journey of a Generation.* New York: Simon & Schuster.

Wells, Rebecca. 1996. *Divine Secrets of the Ya-Ya Sisterhood.* New York: HarperCollins.

White, Barbara A. 2003. *The Beecher Sisters.* New Haven, Conn.: Yale University Press.

White, Lynn K., and Agnes Riedmann. 1992. "Ties Among Adult Siblings," *Social Forces* 71(1) 85–102.

Wright, Liz, and Tony Cassidy. 2009. "Family Structure and Environment in Psychological Adjustment." Paper presented at the annual meeting of the British Psychological Society, Brighton, England, April 2, 2009.

Index

About the Author

DEBORAH TANNEN is University Professor and professor of linguistics at Georgetown University. Among her many books, *You're Wearing THAT?: Understanding Mothers and Daughters in Conversation* was on *The New York Times* bestseller list for ten weeks, and *You Just Don't Understand: Women and Men in Conversation* was on *The New York Times* bestseller list for nearly four years, including eight months as #1, and has been translated into thirty languages. Her book *Talking from 9 to 5: Women and Men at Work* was a *New York Times* business bestseller; *The Argument Culture: Stopping America's War of Words* won the Common Ground book award; and *I Only Say This Because I Love You: Talking to Your Parents, Partner, Sibs, and Kids When You're All Adults* won the Books for a Better Life award. She has written for and been featured in most major magazines and newspapers, including *The New York Times, The Washington Post, USA Today, Time, Newsweek,* and *The Harvard Business Review.* She is a frequent guest on television and radio news and information shows, including *The Colbert Report, 20/20,* the *Today* show, *Good Morning America, The Oprah Winfrey Show,* and NPR's Morning Edition, All Things Considered, and The Diane Rehm Show. She has also been McGraw Distinguished Lecturer at Princeton University and was a fellow at the Center for Advanced Study in the Behavioral Sciences, following a term in residence at the Institute for Advanced Study in Princeton, New Jersey. In addition to her books and articles about language in personal and public life, she also has published poems, short stories, and essays. Her play *An Act of Devotion* is included in *The Best American Short Plays: 1993–1994.* It was produced, together with her play *Sisters,* by Horizons Theater. Her website is www.deborahtannen.com.

About the Type

This book was set in Fairfield, the first typeface from the hand of the distinguished American artist and engraver Rudolph Ruzicka (1883–1978). Ruzicka was born in Bohemia and came to America in 1894. He set up his own shop, devoted to wood engraving and printing, in New York in 1913 after a varied career working as a wood engraver, in photoengraving and banknote printing plants, and as an art director and freelance artist. He designed and illustrated many books, and was the creator of a considerable list of individual prints—wood engraving, line engravings on copper, and aquatints.

Deborah Tannen on Video and Audio

TRAINING VIDEO

TALKING 9 TO 5: WOMEN AND MEN IN THE WORKPLACE

ChartHouse International Learning Corporation
www.charthouse.com   800-328-3789

Educational Lectures on Video

THAT'S NOT WHAT I MEANT!: LANGUAGE, CULTURE, AND MEANING
DEBORAH TANNEN: 1 ON 1 COMPANION VIDEO

HE SAID, SHE SAID: GENDER, LANGUAGE, AND COMMUNICATION
DEBORAH TANNEN: IN DEPTH companion video

Into the Classroom Media
800-732-7946
fax 914-273-7567

Educational Lectures on Audio

THAT'S NOT WHAT I MEANT!: THE SOCIOLINGUISTICS OF CONVERSATION

WOMEN, MEN AND LANGUAGE

EACH IS A SERIES OF 14 LECTURES AND ACCOMPANYING STUDY GUIDE
Recorded Books
Modern Scholar series
www.modernscholar.com   800-636-3399
Also available at Barnes & Noble bookstores